Being Comanche

BEING COMANCHE

A Social History of an American Indian Community

Morris W. Foster

The University of Arizona Press   Tucson

The University of Arizona Press

Copyright © 1991
The Arizona Board of Regents
All rights reserved

♾ This book is printed on acid-free, archival-quality paper.
Manufactured in the United States of America

96 95 94 93 92 91   6 5 4 3 2 1

LIBRARY OF CONGRESS CATALOGING-IN-PUBLICATION DATA

Foster, Morris W. (Morris Wade), 1960–
    Being Comanche : a social history of an American Indian community
  / Morris W. Foster.
       p.   cm.
    Includes bibliographical references and index.
    ISBN 0-8165-1246-9 (acid-free)
    1. Comanche Indians—History—Sources.   2. Comanche Indians—
  Social conditions.   3. Comanche Indians—Ethnic identity.
  4. Social structure—Oklahoma.   I. Title.
  E99.C85F67   1991
  976.6′004974—dc20   91-12781
                                              CIP

British Library Cataloguing in Publication data are available.

For Lance (1965–1989)

Contents

Preface

I first became acquainted with Comanches in August 1984. I was interested in the shift they had made from using the Comanche language to using the English language for everyday social interaction. While this was a topic that I pursued enthusiastically in our conversations, it was not one which Comanches found terribly intriguing. Instead, they spoke of the kinds of situations in which they used language, both Comanche and English, to interact with one another. They recalled dances, church services, peyote meetings, holiday encampments, and other occasions—the ways in which these gatherings had begun and how they had changed—and always they spoke of the uniquely Comanche nature of the events.

Gradually I caught on to the idea that it was not the specific means that Comanches have used to interact and communicate with one another that have allowed them to maintain their distinctive identity. Rather, they have continued to "be Comanche" because they have continued to risk their faces, their images of moral worth, in one another's presence and thereby have engendered cooperation in the social organization of a moral community.

I began, then, to collect an oral history of changing forms of public gathering in the Comanche community. Later, as I worked through this information and received comments back from my readers at Yale, it became clear that there was an important connection between those changing forms of gathering and changes in Comanches' relations with Euro-Americans. I turned to the archival evidence and published interpretations of these relations to substantiate the linkage. In the present study I have tried to bring together Comanches' comments about the history of their community with Anglo records and representations of that same historical community.

I have called this a social history because it examines the ways in which Comanches have used social units and situations to organize their relations with one another. Thus, in interpreting their history I have focused on accounts of their social arrangements. What I present in the following pages is an interpretation that explicates the continuity of being Comanche in the course of three hundred years. It goes without saying that there are other ways of looking at the Comanche community, both historically and ethnographically. The archival material available could encompass a number of research projects, and the community itself remains a vital, constantly changing sociocultural entity. Each of the discussions of historical periods that follow could easily be expanded into a book and, at least so long as being Comanche remains a viable interactive option, the last word on Comanches will be their own.

In telling their story, I have relied on six types of information: my interviews with Comanches who either experienced the events in which I was interested or who knew relevant community traditions; my own experience of Comanche gatherings from 1984 to 1990; the unedited transcripts of two previous oral history projects, one conducted in the late 1930s and the other in the late 1960s; the published reports of various ethnographic and ethnohistorical studies carried out among Comanches between 1912 and 1986; archives of the various Indian agencies responsible for administering Comanche-Anglo relations; and finally, published histories based on those documents. Each of these sources requires some further discussion here.

CONSULTANT INTERVIEWS

Over the two-year period from August 1984 to August 1986, I was in southwestern Oklahoma almost every week, and I spoke with a number of Comanches, particularly at community gatherings. As most anthropologists do, however, I established close relationships with a small circle of consultants whom I believed to be knowledgeable and representative of the community and with whom I hit it off. These are the people whom I most often quote in the following chapters.

Haddon Nauni was in his mid sixties when I knew him and lived between Cache and Indiahoma. He had been a member of the Comanche Business Committee and was an active gourd dancer. Mr. Nauni also had participated in peyote gatherings and was a member of a predominantly Comanche church outside Cache. Mr. Nauni attended Fort Sill Indian School, served in World War II, worked as a bookkeeper in the Lawton area, and then moved to Wichita to work in an aircraft factory as part of the federal Indian Relocation Program. When he returned to Oklahoma, Mr. Nauni worked at the Indian hospital in Lawton until his retirement in 1987. Mr. Nauni passed away shortly after he retired.

Leonard Riddles is in his early seventies and lives in the Walters area. He also has been a member of the Comanche Business Committee. Mr. Riddles attended Fort Sill Indian School, served in World War II, and since that time has farmed his allotment south of Walters. Under the name Black Moon, taken from his maternal grandfather, Mr. Riddles has become a leading Comanche artist, painting in the traditional style of flat figures on a solid background. As a traditional artist, Mr. Riddles has made an effort to collect oral history from older Comanches since 1946.

Robert Coffey is in his eighties and lives in Lawton. Mr. Coffey is the pastor of the Deyo Baptist Church, located between Lawton and Cache. Prior to becoming pastor in the early 1960s, Mr. Coffey was a farmer and then a civilian employee of the Fort Sill Military Reservation. Mr. Coffey served on the Kiowa, Comanche, and Apache and Comanche business committees from the 1930s through the 1960s.

Edward Wermy is also in his eighties and lives outside Fletcher. Mr. Wermy has been a peyote participant and leader since the late 1920s.

Tennyson Echawaudah is in his seventies and lives in Cyril. He also has been a peyote participant and leader since the early 1930s. In addition, Mr. Echawaudah is known as a leading Comanche artist whose work focuses on themes associated with peyote beliefs and ritual.

George "Woogee" Watchetaker is in his early seventies and lives outside Elgin in the rural area known as Pleasant Valley. At the time I knew him, Mr. Watchetaker was a member of the Comanche Business Committee. He is known in the Comanche community as a champion war dancer and has been actively involved in the organization of powwows. Mr. Watchetaker is also a participant in peyote gatherings and is a member of the Methodist church.

Haddon "Red" Codynah was in his mid seventies and was living in Cyril when I knew him. Mr. Codynah was the official chaplain of the Comanche Tribe, and a well-known peyote leader. Mr. Codynah served in the Comanche Code Talkers unit during World War II, a group formed by the Signal Corps to baffle German listeners by communicating radio messages in Comanche. Mr. Codynah passed away in 1988.

Other Comanches with whom I have spoken in some detail include Eva Riddles, Anna Coffey, Delores Summers, Tony Martinez (who was ninety-three at the time I interviewed him), Ned Timbo, Carney Saupitty, Lucy McClung, Charles Kurchee, Jr., Hammond Motah, Ray Neido, George Wallace, Baldwin Parker, Kenneth Saupitty, William Poafybitty and various family members of the gentlemen I have listed above. Finally, I benefited from the insights into their community of three of my students at the University of Oklahoma: Sarah Shield, Phyllis Attocknie, and Daren Paddyaker.

COMANCHE GATHERINGS

My study also has benefited from more informal, sometimes anonymous conversations with Comanches at powwows, church meetings, political gatherings, and other social occasions, and from my observations of those events. While the thrust of this study is historical, my experience of these contemporary public gatherings has helped me in understanding the dimensions of gatherings recounted from memory or recorded in archives.

A gap in my personal experience is peyote gatherings. While I have been present in the evening when a meeting was being set up and in the morning when a meeting was concluding, I did not attend an all-night gathering. The Comanches I know who participate in peyote meetings are sincere believers who emphasize the importance of belief in being present in the tipi. Because I respect their beliefs, I chose not to attend meetings simply for the purpose of observation.

I also visited and stayed overnight in Comanche homes and observed private, informal interactions among family and friends. While I have, in places, referred to my observations of private interaction, I have tried to do so in as general a manner as possible so as not to take advantage of the hospitality and kindness I always encountered in Comanche homes.

ORAL HISTORY INTERVIEWS

Two oral history projects include interviews with Comanches. I have made use of both. The Indian-Pioneer Papers was a WPA project of the mid-1930s in which interviews were conducted with both Indians and Anglos who had experienced life in Oklahoma before statehood in 1907. These interviews are particularly useful for understanding Anglo attitudes toward Indians before World War II.

The Doris Duke Oral History Collection was compiled during the 1960s. Interviews with Comanches were conducted mostly by David Jones, who was at the time working on his study of the Comanche medicine doctor, Sanapia (Jones 1968, 1972). Consequently, many of the interviews reflect Jones's special interests. This material is most useful when the interviewee digresses from a question to reflect on some aspect of the Comanche community.

The Comanches whom I quote from both oral history projects were known to my own consultants and were considered by them to be knowledgeable persons. Sarah Pohocsucat, whose interviews are among the more interesting, passed away in 1988 at the age of ninety-four.

ETHNOGRAPHIC STUDIES

Compared to other Plains peoples, Comanches have received relatively little attention from anthropologists. While James Mooney mentions Comanches in his studies of the Ghost Dance and peyote use, his primary focus was on Kiowas. Robert Lowie (1915) spent a few weeks interviewing Comanches in 1912 but found them less than ideal informants. It was not until 1933, when Ralph Linton led a Santa Fe Laboratory of Anthropology party that included E. Adamson Hoebel, that Comanches became the subject of focused anthropological interest. Subsequently, Linton published a few articles based on his Comanche material (e.g., Linton 1935, 1949), and included Comanches as case studies in several of his book-length, comparative studies of human cultures (Linton 1936, 1940, 1955). It was, however, Hoebel who made the greater use of the Santa Fe group's information—in his 1940 study of Comanche law and in a more general 1952 account written with Ernest Wallace.

The latter work has become the primary source about Comanches' pre-reservation culture and society for anthropologists and others. It is based on Wallace's historical research (which leans heavily on the previously published work of Rupert Richardson) and the oral history collected by the Santa Fe party. By the time the Santa Fe anthropologists interviewed older Comanches about prereservation practices, the Comanche community had already undergone nearly sixty years of change. Working within the prevailing Boasian model, however, Linton and Hoebel took little account of happenings after 1875, when Comanches were finally confined to a reservation, and none of happenings after 1901, when that reservation was broken up into scattered allotments and the remaining land opened to Anglo homesteaders.

For better or worse, the accounts of Linton, Hoebel, and Wallace will remain our best sources about prereservation Comanche life from a Comanche perspective. It should be kept in mind, though, that the information these scholars used was separated by a considerable passage of time, and by a number of changes in the community, from Comanches' experience of nomadic Plains life.

In 1940 a Columbia University party led by George Herzog visited the Comanche community. While Thomas Gladwin (1948) attempted to reconstruct prereservation kin behavior, Joseph Casagrande (1955) and David McAllester (1949) studied contemporary aspects of Comanche linguistic acculturation and peyote music, respectively. Later, in the late 1960s, David Jones (1968, 1972) studied the life history of a Comanche medicine doctor, Sanapia, but his general comments on the Comanche community are derived mainly from Wallace and Hoebel (1952). Elliot Canonge (1958) worked with the Comanche language for a number of years. James Armagost, Jean Charney and Lila Wistrand Robinson currently are engaged in the study of the Comanche language. Wistrand Robinson and Armagost (1990) have cooperated on a forthcoming dictionary of Comanche based on Canonge's field notes. Most recently, Daniel Gelo (1986) and Thomas Kavanagh (1980, 1986) have undertaken ethnographic fieldwork in the Comanche community. While I disagree with some of their interpretations, I am indebted to both for their comments and insights.

ARCHIVAL INFORMATION

Fortunately, the raw files of the Kiowa Agency, which administered Comanche-Anglo relations beginning in 1872, have been preserved in the Oklahoma Historical Society. I am indebted to Robert Nespor and Kay Zahrai of the Archives Division of the Oklahoma Historical Society for their assistance in using this material. These files, and those of earlier agencies having jurisdiction over territories occupied by prereservation Comanche bands, provide insights into Comanche-Anglo relations and occasionally into the Comanche community itself. When I began this research, I worked with the original documents, identified only by the agency filing system. Since then, the bulk of the agency materials have been microfilmed and are now identifiable by roll and frame numbers (which begin with the prefix KA).

The annual reports of the various agents responsible for Comanche relations also are useful. These were published each year in the *Annual Report of the Commissioner of Indian Affairs* until 1906. Narrative and statistical reports written from 1907 to 1938 were obtained from the National Archives (microfilm M1011).

The bulk of Kiowa Agency documents from the twentieth century have ended up at the Fort Worth Branch of the National Archives. I am indebted to Meg Hacker for assistance in obtaining copies of this material, which is identified by file name.

Other microfilmed documents used from the federal Indian Record Group (75) are: Letters Received, Office of Indian Affairs (M234); Records of the Central Superintendency of Indian Affairs (M856); and Records of the Southern Superintendency of Indian Affairs (M640).

The Western History Collection of the University of Oklahoma holds various manuscript accounts, oral history collections, rare documents and published books and journals that have been of use in my study. I am indebted to Don DeWitt, Nathan Bender and Ray Miles for their assistance in using this material.

The Museum of the Great Plains in Lawton continues to build an important research collection on native peoples of southwestern Oklahoma. Some of the information used here come from the archive, and I am indebted to Joe Hays for his assistance and advice in exploring it. The archival collection at Fort Sill also is a valuable repository of Comanche materials, providing some of the other information in this book. I am indebted to Towana Spivey for his assistance and hospitality there.

HISTORICAL STUDIES

Three studies of Comanche history, all based on archival materials, have been invaluable. Elizabeth John (1975) has written a very useful account of Comanche-European relations to 1795, working mainly from Spanish colonial archives. Rupert Richardson (1933, 1963) remains the primary authority on Comanche–United States relations from 1803 to 1875, though Thomas Kavanagh (1986) may soon provide the standard reference for this period when his dissertation is revised as a book. Finally, William Hagan (1976) has written the definitive account of Comanche–U.S. relations from 1875 to 1901.

Michael Tate's annotated research bibliography (1986) has also been an extremely useful tool in studying Comanche history.

ACKNOWLEDGMENTS

Many people have read versions of this work and provided helpful comments. Foremost among these were my dissertation readers at Yale—Keith Basso, Harold Conklin, John Middleton, and Harold Scheffler—who kept me to the straight and narrow and taught me much about anthropology and scholarship in the process. The work that has evolved from that thesis is still very much my own, which is what I imagine they had in mind. I am especially indebted to John Middleton, who did much to develop my sensibilities as an anthropologist, and Keith Basso, who made me aware of the ways in which anthropologists' works are surrounded by words: both their own and those of the people whom they study.

My colleagues at the University of Oklahoma have also helped in the shaping of this work. William Bittle first interested me in anthropology and American Indians. Troy Abell, Stephen Thompson, Susan Vehik and Joseph Whitecotton were helpful in suggesting references and commenting on some of my ideas. Susan Vehik, Nicholas Howe, and William Hagan were kind enough to read earlier drafts and advise on the organization and structure of the present version. Hagan has been most generous in sharing his research materials on Comanches. I look forward to the publication of his biography of Quanah Parker. John Moore was always available to talk about our shared interest in American Indians and to contrast my experiences with Comanches with his own extensive experiences with Cheyennes. Pam Innes, Martha McCullough, Bill Meadows and Jack Schultz, all graduate students in anthropology, have been helpful as well in talking about their work with Indian peoples in Oklahoma. I look forward to their future scholarly contributions.

I am particularly indebted to Loretta Fowler and Raymond DeMallie for their careful critiques of previous versions of this study. Greg McNamee and Stephen Cox, of the University of Arizona Press, have been helpful and supportive throughout the editorial process. Alan Schroder has been a patient and thorough editor.

It goes without saying that I am indebted to the Comanche people whose homes I visited, whose time I took, whose gatherings I attended, and who have always been open, hospitable and kind to me. While I have already named those whose words I have quoted, I want to acknowledge again my special debt to the late Haddon Nauni and to Leonard Riddles and Robert Coffey.

Finally, I want to thank my parents, Wade and Mary Alice Foster, whose support and confidence made my fieldwork possible, and Joan Cuccio. Without Joan's love and patience, this work would not have been completed.

1

Comanches
and Indians

*This buffalo. Just a young calf. Don't know
where it come from, up there. Must've got
separated from its momma and daddy up in
those mountains. Just came down across the
creek over here [Cache Creek to the west of
the present town of Cache, Oklahoma]
where some Comanches were camped. Men
and boys, some been on the warpath and
some hadn't, rode out and killed it with
spears, arrows, old way. Last buffalo Comanches killed.* Haddon Nauni

*They can tell the sad story of the last run-
ning, about the ragged band of Comanches
who came all the way from their reservation
in Oklahoma to Goodnight's ranch on the
Quitaque, to beg a buffalo of him. At first
he refused, but in time he relented and gave
them a scrawny young bull, thinking they
would drive it back to the reservation and
eat it. Instead, whipping their thin, miserable ponies, they ran it before him and
killed it with lances and arrows, then sat
looking at it for a time, remembering glories
and centuries gone.*

*Such a story catches a whole people's loss,
but only a few old [Anglo] men and writers
tell it today, and the old men, for that matter, usually tell it as a story about the crazi-
ness of Indians.* Larry McMurtry

These two stories, ostensibly told about events of the same outward significance in the history of an Indian people, illustrate an important difference
between the way in which Anglos look at Comanches and the way in which
Comanches look at themselves. Though they agree in many of the details—a
young bison, reservation days, and the last hunt with spears and arrows—
each story represents a perspective that is peculiar to the cultural background
of the storyteller.

The story that McMurtry (1968:18–19) tells is set in a context of Anglo-Indian interaction and is heavy with nostalgia and sadness. It speaks, first, of the irrevocable end of a fiercely independent Comanche way of life, full of glory but now only a memory. Then, when the story speaks of Comanches after confinement to the reservation, they are referred to as Indians, a more general category that is a denial of any connection with a unique preservation culture and history. These reservation Indians are ragged, "crazy" in the Anglos' eyes, and since their native identity is slipping away, almost lost. In these contrasting images we can see the ways in which Anglos have used the category "Indian" to characterize the native peoples of North America as the subject of a romanticized myth about the time before their encapsulation by Anglo society and as a devalued stereotype thereafter.

In telling the story of Comanche peoples, it is easy to play on the romantic image of the last bison and of defeated Comanche warriors riding across the plain to kill it. The coincidence of that image with the reservation period can be made to symbolize neatly the end of a way of life, a transitional time of alienation and eventual absorption into Euro-American society. The Anglo image of the last bison hunt, however, tells us more about Euro-American conceptions of Indian peoples and their histories than it does about Comanche conceptions of themselves.

Anglo writers, artists, museum curators, movie directors, and even scholars have, like McMurtry, used images like the last bison hunt to punctuate their representations of the histories and identities of American Indian peoples at the beginning of the reservation period. In the hundred years since Plains peoples were forced onto reservations, Anglos have looked diligently for that last bison (and its evocative equivalents) in myths, archives, oral histories, and statistics as they have tried to bring to a close the accounts of the societies and cultures constructed by Native Americans, and to begin the story of their social and cultural incorporation into the Anglo world.[1]

In contrast to McMurtry's tale, though, the story that Haddon Nauni tells is set in a context of Comanche-Comanche interaction. It is not embellished with regret or with a sense of finality. Instead, it speaks with curiosity about how a bison might have survived in the mountains and come down to the plain for some Comanches to kill it. The story simply tells something that happened in the Comanche community at some time in the past.

In Anglo representations of Indian peoples, too often the activity is emphasized over the people who participated in it. Comanches like Haddon Nauni, however, have not forgotten that the maintenance of a traditional community depends on people, not on a fixed set of behaviors, syntactic structures, or food sources. We have largely overlooked the Comanches who surrounded and killed that last, disoriented bison and then went on with their lives. Those lives continued, bison or no, as did the Comanche community they shared. At the time of the last bison hunt (perhaps sometime in the early 1880s) Comanches already were participating in public gatherings of their community different from those of five or ten years before. They were getting on with the business of what they still talk about as "being Comanche."

EURO-AMERICAN IMAGES OF "INDIANS"

In the last twenty-five years, a considerable literature has developed around the study of Euro-American conceptions of native North Americans (e.g., Pearce 1965; Jennings 1975; Berkhofer 1978; Drinnon 1980; Vaughan 1982; Rawls 1984; Trigger 1985, 1986; Simmons 1986, 1988; Martin 1987). As Berkhofer (1978:27) summarizes the conclusions of this approach to American Indian historiography: "Many commentators on the history of White Indian imagery see Europeans and Americans as using counterimages of themselves to describe Indians and the counterimages of Indians to describe themselves." This practice may be seen on the southern Plains in one of the earliest descriptions of Comanche peoples, by a Spanish observer in 1750: "As there is no organization or authority among these Indians [Comanches], they give full rein to their barbarity, the deity of their adoration being atrocity and the effusion of blood, and their first law being an abundance of women to increase their progeny."[2] Later, in 1820, another Spanish official described the "barbarous" Comanches as "treacherous, revengeful, sly, untrustworthy, ferocious, and cruel . . . cowardly and low. . . . They are inconstant in their friendships and break their contracts for any cause. They are perfidious and disloyal. They are not clean."[3] An Anglo-American observer writing in 1838 perpetuated a similar image of Comanches as the counterimage of Euro-Americans: "As for honesty and integrity they [Comanches] know not the meaning of the word—they are a nation of robbers, and would at any time murder a man for the value of one farthing, provided they could do it without running any risk of danger themselves."[4] Each of these descriptions portrays Comanches as possessing qualities opposite to those that Euro-Americans idealized in themselves.

Only when Comanches were perceived as becoming more like Euro-Americans was the image reversed. Thus, a description of Comanches from their Indian agent in 1885: "[Comanches] from being the most cunning, bloodthirsty, and warlike of all the Plains Indians, have become the most tractable and are making greater strides toward civilization than any tribe of blanket Indians to my knowledge. They are obedient, truthful, and honest."[5]

One consequence of treating native peoples as the opposite of Euro-Americans was the construction of a singular category of "Indian" to include all Native American peoples without regard for differences in language, culture, and social organization (Berkhofer 1978:25). Euro-Americans assumed that all Indians possessed the same fundamental characteristics, at least until Euro-American self-interest dictated a more discriminating interpretation (Jennings 1975; Trigger 1986:254). Even then, however, there was a strong tendency to merge Indian peoples into as general and uniform a range of subcategories as possible. Thus the Comanches were first categorized by the Spanish as among the "Indios Bárbaros," the nomadic peoples of the south central Plains. Anglo-Americans, who succeeded the Spanish in Texas and the Louisiana Purchase in the early nineteenth century, categorized Comanche peoples as among the "wild Indians," those who had not been brought onto a federal reservation. Once on a reservation, the Comanches were categorized as "blanket Indians," meaning that their origin was west of the Mississippi, in contrast to the "civilized" tribes who had been removed to Indian Territory from east of the Mississippi. Beginning with the Treaty of Medicine Lodge in 1867 and continuing until 1966, the Comanches were administratively lumped together by the federal Indian Office (later the Bureau of Indian Affairs) with the Kiowas and Kiowa-Apaches (now referred to as the Apache Tribe of Oklahoma or Plains Apaches), with little statistical or legal identity of their own.

Uses of Eurocentric Indian imagery continue. Most Anglo citizens of the present state of Oklahoma have only a sketchy knowledge of cultural distinctions among the native population of the state and refer to native peoples almost exclusively as Indians, meaning a single cultural category. When a more specific cultural identity is mentioned, such as Comanche, it is more often cited in reference to the historic period of nomadic Plains life than in reference to the contemporary community.

Evidences of the continued romanticization and stereotyping of American Indians may be seen throughout contemporary Oklahoma on highway billboards, in the names of motels and other businesses, in the postcards and other items for sale in souvenir shops, and as curated in the western art displayed in museums. The Anglo population of the state uses images of Indians to define the historical identity of Oklahoma (the very name of the state is derived from a Choctaw word meaning, loosely, Red People) both as a means of reinforcing internal solidarity and self-identity (hearty settlers struggling across the open Plains and battling fierce Indians to carve out a productive economy) and as a way of representing the state to outsiders (visiting dignitaries and businessmen—lately mostly Japanese—are invariably presented with an Indian headdress by some Anglo state official). In contrast, where living Indian people are concerned, the most persistent stereotypes held by Anglos are those of laziness, drunkenness, ignorance, and willful poverty at the expense of Anglo taxpayers. While Anglos in Oklahoma have found extensive uses for their retrospective images of Indians, they often have little use for Indians themselves.

ANTHROPOLOGICAL IMAGES OF INDIANS

As Berkhofer (1978), Trigger (1985, 1986), and Simmons (1988) point out, anthropological representations of Indians and Indian peoples in the late nineteenth and early twentieth centuries were products of the same preconceptions and self-interest that informed popular images of Indians: "Most social scientists, as well as their White countrymen, continued to speak and write as if a specific tribe and all Indians were interchangeable for the purposes of description and understanding of fundamental cultural dynamics and social organization" (Berkhofer 1978:26).

Certainly this was true of the social evolutionists associated with the Bureau of American Ethnology in the nineteenth century. In their attempts to show that American Indian societies prefigured Euro-American societies, Morgan (1877) and Powell (1888) described the Indian societies in terms that would have been familiar to any nineteenth-century soldier, politician, or lawyer (Simmons 1988:3). Indian societies were interpreted as either primitive precursors of European societies or the embodiment of what European societies were not (reversed as matriarchies or negated as promiscuous hordes). Where formal systems of social organization were not evident, the notion of anarchy was invoked. While Boas and his students argued against these general, evolutionary frameworks, the notion of cultural relativism they substituted simply relocated the generalizing tendency to the next level down, treating tribes as isolated, static, homogeneous collectives (Trigger 1985:114–115; Trigger 1986:257). The concept of the "culture area" was used to merge these smaller units into a reductionary set of Indian types keyed to common geographical features of the home ranges on which native peoples lived. These, along with the highly inclusive Amerindian language families constructed by Sapir and others, may be interpreted as refractions of the Euro-American tendency to construct a singular category of "Indian."

Early anthropological conceptions of American Indian societies had at bottom the idea that social systems are embodied in the conceptual structures that order memberships, relationships, roles, and identities (e.g., Lowie 1920, 1927, 1948; Hoebel 1954). The primary objects of study were what native peoples shared, not their situated acts of sharing. Thus we see Kroeber studying Arapaho cradleboards, Dorsey studying Cheyenne body-painting patterns for the Sun Dance, and Mooney studying Kiowa tipi configurations but no one asking why these different peoples found it useful to share the various conventions at specific points in their histories.

The research problem for that first generation of academic anthropologists was to record what could be remembered of precontact (or at least prereservation) Indian cultures before the Indians disappeared altogether. Thus anthropologists have tended to speak of American Indian societies and cultures as precontact, contact, and postcontact phenomena, with the implication that Indians' contacts with Euro-Americans were of a qualitatively different nature and consequence from their contacts with each other.

When the societies and cultures of those native peoples whom anthropologists categorized as Plains Indians changed in the late nineteenth century as many of their conceptual systems were altered or abandoned, the logical conclusion of Anglo-American anthropologists was that the societies and cultures themselves were being abandoned within the context of the plural matrix of Anglo-American society. If one defines a society as a particular bundle of culture traits or self-reproducing structures and functions rather than as a historical community of social actors, such a conclusion is inescapable.

In the view of Boasian ethnographers, native social systems already had been broken apart by the temptations of European trade goods, the demographic catastrophes of epidemics and genocide inflicted on Indian peoples by Euro-Americans, and the forced relocations that resulted from federal reservation and allotment policies (Trigger 1986:256). We find anthropologists such as Elsie Clews Parsons (1941:5) explicitly referring to American Indian communities in the twentieth century as "broken cultures."

With these assumptions and models, academic anthropologists did their best to avoid the issue of Indian–Euro-American interaction, attempting to reconstruct precontact Indian life from oral traditions and the memories of elderly informants, then representing the reconstructions as if they were contemporaneous. In practice, however, this meant that anthropologists dated the end of Indian life to the external creation of reservations and defined what remained of "Indianness" according to the way it contrasted with Euro-American society and culture.

THEORIES OF ACCULTURATION

The anthropological ideal of a pristine prereservation Indian life endured into the 1930s. At that time, some anthropologists were surprised to discover that, fifty years after the last reservations were established in the 1880s, Indian peoples continued to constitute distinct social and cultural communities. While anthropologists had visited some of these communities over a period of several generations, primarily for ethnohistorical purposes (e.g., Dorsey 1884, Fletcher and La Flesche 1911, and Fortune 1932 on the Omahas), it soon became evident that those communities constituted ongoing manifestations of "Indianness" in the midst of twentieth-century America (e.g., Mead 1932 on the Omahas).

The persistence of Indians well after the time when they were expected to have become assimilated into Anglo-American society became a primary research problem for the second generation of academic anthropologists. This was labeled as the study of acculturation, with a growing body of theory focused primarily on American Indian peoples (Redfield, Linton, and Herskovits 1936; Linton 1940; Bruner 1957; Herskovits 1958; Spicer 1961). As defined by Linton (1940:463–464) acculturation "comprehends those phenomena which result when groups of individuals having different cultures come into continuous first-hand contact, with subsequent changes in the original culture patterns of either or both groups." While such general statements of acculturation theory were careful to express the possibility of two-way influence, studies of acculturation in twentieth-century American Indian communities focused almost exclusively on changes within native communities as a result of their contacts with Euro-Americans (e.g., Linton 1940; Spicer 1961). Indeed, Trigger (1985:165) has characterized acculturation as the study of ways in which native peoples have responded to different forms of European domination.

"Traditional" American Indian cultures were defined as elements and patterns that are relatively static, while culture change was associated almost exclusively with the forcible impact of one culture (usually the dominant one) on another (Spicer 1971:795). Thus Euro-American contact was seen as a transforming and generalizing process that relocated native cultures within the controlling context of an emerging Anglo-American culture. Whereas with Boasian culture areas the relationship of culture to environment was the basis for generating general Indian types for the prereservation period, acculturation studies used the relationship of Indian peoples to Anglos to construct general Indian types for the period after the establishment of reservations. "One senses," wrote Spicer, "that the varied surfaces of life, while real enough in their uniqueness for each group, obscure the fact that there are fewer than a half dozen, perhaps no more than three or four, ways of life, or that is to say distinctive cultures, in all the reservations of the United States and Canada" (Spicer 1961:2).

The picture anthropologists have painted of precontact native North America is of gradually evolving sociocultural entities that experienced change but that also went through stable long-term relationships with particular environments and with one another (e.g., Steward 1938). This depiction often is tied to an evolutionary framework and an ecological approach for explaining cultural features, suggesting a sui generis concept of culture that is adaptive, organic, and largely self-sufficient.

The postcontact picture, however, is, as Trigger (1986:256) has observed, of externally provoked rapid and catastrophic change transforming Indian life. This suggests a situation in which changes in economic and social circumstances outstrip the ability of the traditional culture unit to respond to them. Indian peoples, employing a pastiche of cultural frameworks, form a series of transitional social entities. Culture ceases to be portrayed as an integrating whole and is increasingly depicted as a passive set of available categories from which different symbols, forms, and meanings are selected according to the prevailing social situation.

The acculturation approach has had a continuing impact on the ways in which anthropologists and others portray Indian peoples in the twentieth century. Thus Castile (1981b:176–179), the editor of a festschrift for Spicer, pointedly refers to "reservation Indians." He uses this term to distinguish contemporary native peoples, whose ways of life are determined materially by federal Indian policies, from their ancestors, whose ways of life were determined by their ecological adaptations to specific habitats. Castile even goes so far as to suggest that the former is a spurious Indianness, implying that the real Indians were those untouched by Euro-American contamination. A similar, though more extreme, perspective on Indianness may be found in Clifton 1990. These are, of course, examples of the familiar phenomenon of defining Indian peoples according to their contacts with Euro-Americans. As Berkhofer noted, "If the Indian changed through the adoption of civilization as defined by Whites, then he was no longer truly Indian according to the image, because the Indian was judged by what Whites were not" (Berkhofer 1978:29).

The work of Scollon and Scollon (1979, 1981) in a multilingual community in which Cree, Chipewayan, French, and English are spoken is a good example of the continuing legacy of the acculturation approach. In explaining the differences between native and Euro-American segments of the community, the Scollons propose a distinction between what they label a "bush consciousness," associated with the native community, and a "modern consciousness," associated with the European community, based on what they take to be fundamental differences between "oral" and "literate" societies. Although portrayed as a universal distinction, this is in effect a contrast between a generalized native cultural conception of appropriate interaction and a generalized Euro-American cultural conception. Not surprisingly, the former is characterized, in most respects, as the opposite of the latter. Whereas the bush consciousness is said to be individualistic and integrative, the modern consciousness is described as normative and abstracting (Scollon and Scollon 1979:206).

What the Scollons have done is to reify Anglo perceptions of the ways in which Indians violate their expectations in interaction as a distinctive, generalized native style and model for interaction. Indians are defined as what Anglos are not in a paired contrast of Anglo and native communicative means (Scollon and Scollon 1979:249; Scollon and Scollon 1981:36).[6] The native worldview is described as "holistic" and the Euro-American view as "decontextualized" or "plural" (Scollon and Scollon 1981:48–50, 100–102). This is a reification of the distinction between a traditional Boasian concept of culture and the more situational concept used in the "new ethnicity." Thus Anglo-American society is said to contain within it a number of small worlds, while native society is focused on a single, unified social world (Scollon and Scollon 1981:50). Like most theories of acculturation, the Scollons' approach plays on the contrast between similar and dissimilar social and cultural forms, with various shadings in between. Not surprisingly, when the problem is set up in this way the analysis of the native order invariably falls somewhere along that spectrum.

THEORIES OF ETHNICITY

Like theories of acculturation, theories of ethnicity are focused on how people respond to rapid, externally induced social and cultural change. But ethnicity theory differs from acculturation theory in the degree of instrumental choice allowed social actors. Acculturation theory is more concerned with social groups as determined by shared cultural background, while ethnicity theory is more concerned with how individuals, motivated by changing economic and political circumstances, form social groups and then use cultural symbols to represent and legitimate those social groups.

Ethnicity theory assumes that people mobilize as interest groups according to relationships of domination and dependency. Most scholars of eth-

nicity view ethnic groups as the unique consequence of an increasingly urbanized, global world system in which dominance-dependence relationships
are the primary social facts of everyday life (e.g., Barth 1969; Gumperz
1982a, 1982b; Bentley 1987).[7] Ethnic identities are interpreted as strategic
means for subordinate or minority populations to interact successfully
within more inclusive economic and political structures.

The assumption of an emerging world system and of dependent populations within it fits in quite well with the notion that American Indians'
contacts with Euro-Americans have been of a qualitatively different order
from their contacts with one another. This is also a view compatible with
those definitions of "Indian" which are based on the ways in which Native
Americans differ from Anglo-Americans. Describing native peoples as "ethnic" or "dependent" populations implies that their unique identities are
calculated primarily in reference to the boundaries and symbols that mark
them as separate from members of the dominant society. Thus Cohen
(1978:384) has made the claim that "the study of contemporary peoples in a
complex world has now clearly shifted from ethnic isolates, 'tribes' if you
will, to one in which the interrelations between such groups . . . is a key,
possibly the key element in their lives." More specifically, "once American
Indian groups . . . saw themselves as parts of larger wholes and used this as a
major feature of their own group identities, then multi-ethnic contexts became essential to the understanding of these groups" (Cohen 1978:383).
Trosper (1981:247) has made the assertion more pointedly: "American Indians have transformed themselves from a diverse people with little common identity into an ethnic group."

These claims are similar to those made by Spicer and Castile. In this view,
the social identities available to native North American peoples in the twentieth century are largely the products of Indian-Anglo interaction. Because
native peoples have had to accommodate their presentations of self to Euro-
American images of Indians in order to accomplish the desired social work
of their encounters with Anglos, they have come to construct social identities
that conform to Anglo expectations. These expectations, as Berkhofer and
Trigger have noted, are formed from preconceptions of a singular Indian
identity that is defined by a paired contrast with a Euro-American self-
identity.

Boundaries between Indians and Anglos have emerged as a significant
focus in recent ethnographies explicating Indian identities in contemporary
settings (e.g., Braroe 1975; Scollon and Scollon 1979; Blu 1980; Lithman
1984). Each of these studies has employed a sophisticated theoretical appa-
ratus predicated either implicitly or explicitly on the contrasts and interac-

tions between a dominant Anglo society and a subordinate category or group of native persons. Blu (1980:5), for instance, in writing of the Lumbees' struggle for official recognition as an Indian people by the federal government, cast the problem of being Indian in the twentieth century as one of conforming to Anglo expectations: "Lumbees have to cope with the images that Whites have about Indians in general in such a way that Lumbees can be included in the category 'Indian' (by changing the characteristics of the category, or by making their own characteristics fit, or both)." Blu shows how the Lumbees have created a distinctive identity for themselves in reference to the dual "Black/White" racial categorization of the American South. Blu describes this as a process in which the Lumbees use claims to a shared historical charter, rather than biological characteristics, to symbolize their unique economic and political status (Blu 1980:215). Not surprisingly, the most potent historical symbols invoked by Lumbees in their quest for Anglo recognition of their Indian identity are historical contacts with Euro-Americans found in documentary references and treaties (Blu 1980:217).

As Blu's study of the Lumbees demonstrates, ethnicity theory necessarily focuses on interethnic contexts or landscapes. Although ethnic categories and groups reflect cultural differences, they do so as people use these differences to mark their uniqueness, based on economic and political self-interest, with respect to other categories and groups (Barth 1969). Only certain cultural features are selected as ethnic boundary markers.

The symbols or images used for marking ethnic boundaries are ones that are, in some sense, agreed on by persons of all the ethnicities involved in the interaction (Barth 1969:38). While claims to ethnic identity are acts of self-definition, these are definitions which also make sense in the wider multiethnic context. Thus the "language" of ethnic symbolism may be thought of as a kind of lingua franca. In situations of dominant-subordinate relationships, it seems likely that the symbols used to mark the ethnicity of a subordinate group will be constructed primarily by members of the dominant society as they set the terms for interethnic interaction. This is clearly the case with respect to an Indian ethnic identity in the context of Anglo-American society. If this is so, then it is important to ask to what extent identification in multi-ethnic contexts comes to affect the ways in which members of ethnic groups identify themselves to one another. This is where the various theories of ethnicity disagree.

Barth treats maintaining an ethnic boundary as a separate undertaking from using shared cultural conceptions to construct social identities within ethnic groups. This is what Gumperz (1982b:5) calls "interactive" group formation, in which one ethnic group "is distinguished from another by its similarities and overlapping networks." In this model, people selectively re-emphasize existing social relationships and cultural symbols as a way of mobilizing a common interest group.[8] The relationships and symbols used for interethnic boundary marking will not necessarily be those used for in-tracommunity social organization.

A contrasting view of ethnicity, however, makes an explicit connection between setting up external boundaries between ethnic groups and con-structing social identities within those boundaries. Gumperz (1982b:5) de-scribes a process of this kind as "reactive" group formation, in which an ethnic group defines itself through the reassertion of "historically established distinctions from other groups within a common national polity."[9] In this model, changing political and economic conditions define membership in social groups on the basis of common interests. These newly constituted units then robe themselves in distinctive ethnic identities (Bentley 1987:25), which may or may not replicate continuous cultural communities.

This is the perspective taken by Braroe (1975) in his study of another Cree community in Canada. Braroe takes the view that Anglos determine the conditions for most of their encounters with Indians. The problem for the Indians, then, is how to work within those Anglo-defined dimensions to maintain and elevate their devalued social selves. Braroe (1975:141) argues that this ongoing social situation between Indians and whites shapes not only the nature of Indians' behavior in the presence of Anglos but also their conceptions of and attitudes toward those "things they themselves feel to be characteristically and essentially Indian." Thus native people are seen as using their perceptions of Anglos' expectations and images of Indians to construct boundaries around their own distinctive native world and to de-cide what belongs in that world and what does not. As Braroe represents the situation in the community he studied, the only choices are between Indian and white. Because of their interactions with Anglos, Indians must play the whites' game, but Anglos rarely if ever concern themselves with native ex-pectations and strategies. Even in situations of miscommunication, white conceptions and behaviors toward Indians are depicted as the indirect bases for Indian conceptions and behaviors. In the moral economy of Braroe's community, Anglos control the common infrastructure upon which are built all symbolic superstructures.[10]

Lithman (1984), in a study of a Manitoba Indian reserve community, takes a similar position. Like Braroe, he contends that Indians' distinctive social identities are a result of their interactions with Anglos (1984:60). Thus he claims that Indians use their interactions with Anglos "to form a conception of what they [the Indians] are" (1984:61). Lithman (1984:110) concludes that native communities are maintained in Canada as a consequence of the structuring of Indian-Anglo interactions and "the indignities which Indians have to endure in most instances of such interaction, resulting in a desire to withdraw from interactions with Whites." Lithman (1984:171) argues that interaction among members of an Indian community, the values and traditions of that community, and the community's sense of itself as a historical entity are guided by Indian-Anglo interaction.[11] In this manner, ethnicity theory, like acculturation theory, establishes a paired contrast that produces its own result.

A DIFFERENT PERSPECTIVE

In contrast to approaches that emphasize Indian-Anglo interaction in the maintenance and elaboration of contemporary Indian communities, several recent studies have emphasized Indian-Indian interaction.[12] Philips's (1983) study of communicative means on the Warm Springs Indian Reservation in Oregon is founded on an explicit contrast between Indian and Anglo. Unlike the Scollons and Braroe, however, she does not use Anglo forms and strategies to define Indian forms and strategies, nor does she claim that interethnic contexts of interaction are key to the self-identities of native peoples. Philips argues that Warm Springs Indians employ separate models for Indian-Anglo interaction and Indian-Indian interaction: "It is through Anglo-Indian contact that the Warm Springs Indians' sense of identity as 'Indian' and not White is fed and maintained. But it is the largely Indian network of interaction that sustains the culturally distinctive ways of regulating communication in face-to-face interaction" (1983:23).Where other ethnographies proceed from Anglo perceptions of Indians, Philips's study entails separate analyses of Warm Springs Indian and Anglo conventions of interaction, such as turn-taking, attention structures, discourse structures, rules for appropriate discourse, and cultural knowledge. Warm Springs Indian identities and ways of expressing them do not mirror Anglo identities and communicative means. Consequently, the Indians whom Philips depicts are not the antitheses of Anglos, either implicitly as the comparison is drawn by the ethnographer or explicitly as mandated by Anglo-dominated contexts of interaction.

Following Barth, Philips (1983:38) is careful to distinguish between the use of symbols to represent and maintain boundaries between Indians and Anglos and the construction and maintenance of "a culturally distinctive social milieu" by Indian people in their encounters with one another. Although her study does not describe in detail the ways in which Warm Springs Indians structure interaction with one another as a community, it is clear that the identities associated with participation in Indian contexts of interaction are different from those associated with participation in Anglo-dominated contexts.

Two other recent representations of Indian peoples that share this approach are Loretta Fowler's ethnohistorical studies of the Arapahoe (1982) and the Gros Ventre (1987). Fowler's critique of ethnographies that use an acculturation framework is especially apt here, and it may be extended to apply to studies focusing on Indian–Euro-American interaction in general:

> The acculturation framework often presents native peoples as essentially passive, or at best unsuccessful; change is viewed not as resulting from resourceful and creative acts or choices but as capitulation to pressures from the wider society. The underlying assumption is that eventually "natives" will assimilate or, if they do not, become hopelessly disorganized, marginal people. Ethnographers who take this approach tend also to overemphasize the shaping of Indian culture and history by social contacts with and adoption of ideas of non-Indians. They ignore the interactions among different Native American groups with varying lifestyles and the ways in which these peoples' ideas and actions are changed by such contacts. (Fowler 1987:6)

Fowler (1982:6) recognizes that native communities must adapt to constraints on social action imposed by the Anglo-dominated political economy, in which they have increasingly become "encapsulated" since their initial contacts with Euro-Americans. At the same time, though, she argues that native communities have remained somewhat independent, adapting to changing social conditions not under their control by creating culturally acceptable innovations that they can control. Fowler's accounts of the Arapahoe and Gros Ventre communities focus on how the members of each have adapted to changing constraints on social interaction in order to maintain a traditional sense of community. The ways in which Arapahoes and Gros Ventres have managed this, although responsive to external social conditions, are not predictable on the basis of those conditions. Instead, the innovations have been constructed in accord with ongoing cultural traditions and are best understood as continuations of those traditions rather than as artifacts of Indian–Euro-American interaction.

The contrast between the Arapahoe and Gros Ventre communities is particularly instructive in this respect. Each was organized at the beginning of the nineteenth century into age-grades with a politico-religious authority structure centrally focused on a set of sacred objects. Each became dependent on mounted bison hunting and the Anglo-dominated trading economy, and each developed intermediary leaders who were themselves dependent on symbols and proceeds of relationships with Euro-American traders to maintain their authority within the native community. However, with the collapse of bison populations (and the drastically decreased significance of Indian peoples to the Euro-American economy on the Plains), Arapahoes and Gros Ventres were forced to accept reservations in the 1870s. Each community adjusted to the changed social conditions in different ways. While confinement to a much smaller geographic range caused both communities to abandon the more elaborate age-grade system of social organization, Arapahoes maintained the authority of junior-senior respect relationships, while Gros Ventres did not. Intergenerational conflict became a dominant theme in the Gros Ventre community, while consensus politics, directed by tribal elders, remained the dominant theme among Arapahoes. Although both Arapahoes and Gros Ventres have attempted, with some success, to represent themselves to Euro-Americans as moving toward the Euro-American goal of assimilation, Arapahoes have done so while maintaining their traditional religious system, while Gros Ventres have done so in part by abandoning their traditional religious beliefs and rituals.

This is not to say, though, that the Gros Ventre community has become somehow less Indian than the Arapahoe community. Indeed, Fowler's study shows that Gros Ventre people have maintained a distinctive identity in the midst of changing social circumstances by redefining and reusing shared cultural symbols and by constructing differing and often contradictory versions of their history.[13] Gros Ventres have maintained their traditional emphasis on prominence, primacy, and conspicuous generosity by changing the traditional forms in which these values have been expressed: "Being Gros Ventre was not dependent on a particular set of ritual symbols, ceremonial forms, or a pattern of structural alignments that ordered behavior. Rather, it emanated from the interpretations that made changes both meaningful and acceptable and enabled Gros Ventres to make creative transformations of their world in their own terms" (Fowler 1987:22). In this process, Gros Ventre people have relied on the community they share rather than on their interactions with Euro-Americans in order to "be Gros Ventre," even though they often disagree about what "being Gros Ventre" means. While members of traditional native communities often find themselves in the position of responding to changing social conditions dominated by Euro-Americans, their responses are their own.[14] This is an important lesson for anthropologists who attempt to study contemporary Indian peoples. As Fowler notes, "An approach that emphasizes the powerlessness of Indian people—the political economy of Indian-white relationships—and overlooks the way the exploited population interprets and reacts to those relations distorts the process by which Native American societies change" (Fowler 1987:9).

This is also the point of Fowler's study of the Arapahoe.[15] While Arapahoes have maintained their traditional way of structuring authority through generational respect and continue to center that authority structure on traditional beliefs and symbols of power, they too have taken note of changed (Anglo-dominated) social circumstances and have adapted to those circumstances:

> The Arapahoes resolved problems of legitimation of authority and advocacy of tribal interests by interpreting new social realities in ways that were culturally acceptable as well as adaptive. Symbols emerged that worked to revitalize or reassert traditional values and relationships, yet at the same time reassured whites that the Arapahoes were neither dangerous nor uncooperative. At the same time, old symbols took on new meanings that both reinforced traditional understandings and motivations and made innovation culturally acceptable. (Fowler 1982:5)

What Fowler's studies bring out most clearly is that native peoples have, since contact with Euro-Americans, engaged in two separate though interlocking enterprises. One is their interaction with members of other communities—more and more with Euro-Americans—and the other is their interaction with one another. As traditional bases for polity and subsistence have been disrupted, some degree of political and economic sustenance derived from interactions with Euro-Americans has been necessary to support the activities of traditional native communities. The need to secure that sustenance has made it increasingly necessary for American Indian peoples to deal with the Euro-American political economy and in doing so to represent themselves to Euro-Americans in ways that make sense to non-Indian members of the politically and economically dominant population. In this fashion, native peoples have managed to survive as discernible entities within the matrix of Euro-American society.

At the same time, changes in the social conditions surrounding native communities have necessitated changes in the ways in which those communities are constructed; that is, in social relationships and in cultural beliefs and symbols. These changes, however, have been structured along traditional lines that make sense to members of the native communities, not in ways sensible to, or imposed by, members of the Anglo community. In this way, native peoples have continued to construct moral communities within which members' interactions are organized and facilitated.

In studying the history of American Indian peoples since the arrival of Columbus, it is necessary to attend to both Indian–Euro-American interaction and Indian-Indian interaction, and it is crucial to understand the points at which these two dimensions articulate. The alternative, as we have seen, is to mistake articulation for causality. Causality is a mechanical process whose results cannot be negotiated by the participants in social situations. Articulation is a creative human act in which people make choices every day as they try to make sense of their social world.

AFTER COLUMBUS

Can we, then, speak of the "American Indian experience" since Columbus with any degree of generality or uniformity? On one level, we can indeed engage fairly safely in such summary statements, not because all Indians or Indian communities are the same but because of the demonstrated similarity in Euro-American images of and policies toward Native Americans. To a considerable extent, Euro-Americans have spent the last five hundred years constructing a uniform set of expectations and social conditions around Indian communities in North America. Indeed, the BIA is the culmination of an approach to American Indians that knows no local cultural uniqueness and that blindly applies uniform federal policies with little regard for diversity among native communities.[16] The pervasive stereotypes that Anglos have formed about native peoples also are evidence for the utility of some sort of general model, as members of different native communities have been lumped into the same general category, "Indian," and treated as if they possessed similar characteristics.

To the extent that dependency and ethnicity theories focus on the general conditions of Indian life in America created by Euro-Americans, they constitute useful frameworks for studying those community outlines visible to outsiders. Given the fairly uniform colonial and federal policies to which they have been subjected, most Indian peoples have faced many of the same economic and political conditions. Not surprisingly, different Indian peoples have made many of the same accommodations to similar external conditions, including reservation life, allotments, treaty claims, and most recently, tribal sovereignty. Often, either through formal means, such as the American Indian Congress of the late nineteenth century and the American Indian Movement of the present century, or through informal interaction, these external responses to Euro-American domination have been coordinated across community boundaries.

Similarly, given a limited set of Euro-American expectations for their behavior, Indian people have faced many of the same problems in interacting with local Euro-American populations and have resolved those problems in many of the same ways. These interactional strategies—which include silence, retreat from direct confrontation, and the intentional representation of ignorance—have contributed to the stereotypes that many Euro-Americans have of "Indians," even as they have aided native people in accomplishing their immediate situational goals in interacting with Anglos. From the outside looking in, then, there is some truth to the claim that Euro-Americans have created an ethnic category, "Indian," through their treatment of native peoples in a singular, uniform fashion.

Considering the often desperate situations in which American Indian peoples have found themselves as a result of this treatment, we might also ask why these peoples have endured as distinct communities. In part they have had no choice, because Euro-American prejudices have denied them access to economic and political opportunities. In greater part, though, the traditional social and cultural worlds have persisted because the Indian people who take part in them have found them preferable to the Euro-American social and cultural alternatives. Here again a certain paired contrast between Indian and Euro-American does apply, as native communities do indeed offer their members qualities and possibilities that the mainstream Euro-American community does not.[17]

It is when we ask *how* native peoples have persisted in North America and have maintained their traditional communities that general models break down and Anglo-imposed uniformities and contrasts lose their explanatory power. Examining the process of intracommunity organization and its response to external change is necessarily a two-part study. First, we must determine the external conditions affecting the traditional community and the ways in which members of the traditional community have dealt with members of the dominant society who control those conditions. Second, we must determine the consequences of those external changes for intracommunity relations and for how community members reorganize to maintain a sufficient frequency of social interaction. These are questions that require different scales of sociological analysis.

The analysis of the native community in an interethnic setting and its external relations to the dominant political economy requires a macro-sociological scale. We are concerned here with collective interests, expectations, images, and interrelations among enduring social units. At this level, ethnicity and dependency theories have much to tell us about the contrasts between Indian and Euro-American. Blu's work on the Lumbee, for instance, tells us a great deal about how a native people can manipulate their historical relations with Euro-Americans, and Anglo racial categorizations, to construct their own social identity within the interethnic fabric of the

American South. Similarly, Bee (1982) and Jorgenson (1978) have specified the general outlines of the inescapable dependency of native peoples on the Euro-American political economy as a result of the historical processes of the last five hundred years. In the case of both ethnicity and dependency theories, we are dealing with identities and relations across community boundaries rather than with the construction of identities and relations within a shared community.[18]

The analysis of the organization of interactions among members of a native community requires a micro-sociological scale. Here we are concerned with how individual members of a community construct their identities and relations with one another in such a way as to constitute a shared social and moral unit. These individual acts of sharing certainly accommodate changes in prevailing political, economic, and territorial constraints on social interaction but do not directly mirror the external relations that create those conditions.

Thus Fowler's accounts of the histories of the Arapahoe and Gros Ventre communities are concerned with changing patterns and occasions of social interaction as a result of external changes in the social conditions of life on the northern Plains. Fowler makes it clear that changes in intracommunity organization were calculated primarily for the purposes of Arapahoe–Arapahoe and Gros Ventre–Gros Ventre interaction, not on a general Indian–Euro-American model. Contrasting Indian and Euro-American behavior makes no sense at this level of analysis; it only serves to conceal more fundamental processes of community maintenance and change.

THE COMANCHE COMMUNITY

If anything is clear about the last three hundred years of Comanche–Euro-American relations, it is that we have not understood Comanches' relations with one another very well. Euro-American governments and settlers had little motivation to do so, and, indeed, had a compelling economic and political interest in intentionally misrepresenting the internal organization of the Comanche community. In the anthropological literature of the last hundred years, Comanches have at best been a debating point, a problem for more general anthropological categories and concepts. As a stock example of individualism, Comanches have better served anthropological theory than anthropological theory has served Comanches. It is perhaps time to turn the proposition around and ask what anthropological concepts and frameworks are useful in understanding Comanche social organization apart from the external categories of "Plains Indian" and "Indian."

The traditional anthropological concepts of "culture" and "society" do not appear to be very serviceable in this connection. Both carry with them considerable baggage in anthropological studies. For better or for worse, the term *society,* much like the term *tribe,* implies some sort of unified structure connecting Comanche people into a single social entity with consonant political, economic, and territorial functions. This is, however, a Euro-American assumption about social organization that may not hold true. The term *culture* has been used by many Americanist anthropologists to include not only conceptual frameworks like a language or belief system (to which it is most properly applied) but also social action and patterns of social life. This application has been so broad and so pervasive (including most of the early ethnography done with Comanches) that the term is useless for a discerning analysis. Even in its proper domain, *culture* signifies only part of the process of mutual association that is at the heart of Comanches' relations with one another.[19]

What is most conspicuous about the enduring enterprise of "being Comanche" is the ability of a people to continue to associate with one another, not the preservation of a specific territory, language, or social structure through which to do so. Comanches have used a variety of social and cultural forms to remain in communication with one another, changing these forms as the external conditions surrounding their lives have changed. In short, they have maintained an ongoing community. While the term *community* is not itself a neutral one in anthropology, it has a somewhat less intuitive ring than either *society* or *culture.*

The analytic definition given the sociolinguistic concept of a speech community in the last twenty-five years makes it a particularly apt model for what Comanches share, and have shared, that makes them Comanche rather than Cheyenne or French. Gumperz (1972:16) has defined the concept of a speech community in the following way: "To the extent that speakers share knowledge of the communicative constraints and options governing a significant number of social situations, they can be said to be members of the same *speech community.*" Hymes's definition is similar: "A speech community is defined, then, tautologically but radically, as a community sharing knowledge of rules for the conduct and interpretation of speech" (1974:51). Both Gumperz and Hymes note that a community of this sort may well be socially diverse, not necessarily corresponding to wider social units such as an ethnic category or a state. The sociological utility of the concept of a speech community, however, is that it denotes a specific social unit rather than a cultural framework, such as a language, that may be shared across social units. Hymes (1974:47) puts the problem for the analyst using the concept of a speech community in this way: "One starts with a social group and considers the entire organization of linguistic means within it, rather than starting with one partial, named organization of linguistic means, called a 'language.'" Over time, a community may alter or replace the social and linguistic means used by its members to interact with and understand one another and yet remain the same historical entity.

Membership in the same speech community requires neither territorial integrity nor shared political and economic interests (though these are both conditions that may contribute to the formation and elaboration of a community).[20] Instead, membership in such a community requires knowledge of shared communicative means. The maintenance of a speech community depends on continued social interaction among its members and continued agreement among those members about, in Hymes's words, the "definition of situations in which, and identities through which, interaction occurs" (1974:47) in addition to knowledge of the linguistic means used to signal those situations and identities. Thus, as Gumperz notes, a speech community is "held together by frequency of social interaction and set off from the surrounding areas [that is, from other communities] by weaknesses in the lines of communication" (1972:101).

In characterizing gradations in the lines of communication—in defining where a community begins and ends—Gumperz (1982a) distinguishes between "linguistic competence" and "communicative competence." He notes that a knowledge of grammar (that is, linguistic competence) is not the same as a knowledge of contextualization conventions (that is, communicative competence). This distinction leads to a disjunction between meaning and interpretation. Linguistic competence enables one to discern meaning in an utterance or a sequence of utterances such as a story, but it is communicative competence that enables one to interpret what is intended by an utterance in a particular social context. At the outer margins of a community, it is possible to participate minimally in social life with only a linguistic competence. This is, after all, what many American tourists do in Great Britain. However, full participation in a community requires a communicative competence that includes a knowledge of social context and interactive convention, as well as of linguistic structures.[21]

The Comanche community is, and has been, a social unit, though not a formally structured one, defined by the ability of individual Comanches to interact with one another on a regular basis. Comanches have maintained their community by maintaining lines of communication with one another.

In this way, the definition of the Comanche community, and its continuity from precontact times to the present, is founded on a shared communicative competence.

Membership in the Comanche community has, at least since the early eighteenth century, depended exclusively on communicative competence and has not included other criteria such as birth. Thus Comanches were able to supplement their population in the nineteenth century by incorporating into their community captives who had learned to communicate and interact appropriately. Conversely, those in the twentieth century who have been "born Comanche" (that is, who have a father or mother who is recognized as a community member) but who have not learned to communicate competently (generally because they have been raised outside the community) are not considered "real Comanches" by other community members.

At the same time, Comanches have had to learn how to interact with Anglos. Comanche-Anglo interaction may be understood as a function of different communicative competencies and of restrictive social conditions on Anglo community membership that have kept Comanches from fully entering that social world. Although Comanches may, and do, participate with considerable communicative competence in Anglo contexts, there remains in southwestern Oklahoma an unspoken barrier to recognizing them as equally privileged members of the Anglo-dominated community.[22]

Comanches' land, labor, and capital have been consistently undervalued in the local economy, used by Anglo farmers and merchants when needed and discarded when not. The unique legal status of Indians in the United States kept Comanches from voting until 1924 and still places them in a grey area with respect to law enforcement and judicial jurisdiction. As Sarah Pohocsucat put it in 1967, "Lots of Indians would tell you you can't be a white man, you'll always be an Indian."[23] Membership in the surrounding Anglo community requires something more than just communicative competence. Considerations of social and cultural background (birth, economic status, and religious belief, for example) also are conditions for membership.

Obviously, the concept of speech community has now been extended to a broadly sociological, rather than a narrowly sociolinguistic, meaning. Although the sociolinguistic definition of *speech community* was developed as a way of using social dimensions to illuminate linguistic data, this concept is more generally applicable to the broader study of the regulation of social interaction (Hymes 1962, 1964). Face-to-face interaction, after all, is an exercise in communication, and natural languages are not the sole means by which communication may be accomplished. Edward Sapir, for one, recognized that cultural frameworks, including natural languages, are based within, and to some extent depend upon, the broader dimensions of social interaction in which they are used: "The true locus of culture is in the interaction of specific individuals and, on the subjective side, in the world of meaning which each one of these individuals may unconsciously abstract for himself from his participation in these interactions" (Sapir 1949:515).

These same ideas also may be found in Comanches' comments about their own community, such as those of Haddon Nauni in 1985: "A Comanche, everything he does, he doesn't do without basis or meaning. Whatever we do or are involved in has a purpose. If they can't do something that has mean- ing, then they just won't do it. He participates as one of us. He knows all the meanings." To know all the meanings is to know how to signal, and read, representations of social intention and social identity in encounters among Comanches. Through communication of this kind, Comanches have orga- nized and maintained their traditional community for the last three hun- dred years. As will be seen, Comanches have adapted to changing social conditions that have constrained their ability to be physically present to one another by altering and innovating the means they share for intracom- munity interaction. Comanches have used changing languages, social identi- ties, and social situations to realize a variety of actual social units and gather- ings as a way of maintaining their traditional community.

A VOCABULARY FOR INTRACOMMUNITY ANALYSIS

A vocabulary for analyzing what goes on within a community may be found in the works of Erving Goffman. Goffman created a sociology of interaction in which he established a basis for the formal study of the techniques people use to negotiate their encounters with one another. Although Goffman gave little consideration to the communities implied by those shared techniques, the conceptual framework he created is well suited to the analysis of (to use Hymes's phrase once again) the social situations in which, and social identi- ties through which, interaction between community members occurs.

Goffman was primarily interested in the study of everyday social encoun- ters, or the field of social life.[24] Goffman defined this field as "the realm of activity that is generated by face-to-face interaction and organized by norms of comingling" (1971:ix). The study of social life is the study of the types of gatherings used by a community to regulate and build upon the fact of copresence. Thus, when members of the Comanche community gather in the same place, such as at a powwow, they use standard expectations for appropriate behavior to organize their mutual interactions. These standard expectations both define the community that Comanches share and enable

Comanches to subject constituent units of that community—such as social identities, relationships, and groups—to social sanction.

In Goffman's definition, the study of social life is not synonymous with the study of social structure, the usual anthropological gloss upon social organization. Social structure is the field of longstanding social institutions that endure through time and across space despite changes in personnel (Goffman 1969:140).[25] A Comanche military society, for instance, was an element of social structure, as is a Comanche dancing society today. Both are examples of social institutions that continued to exist despite a complete turnover in membership over time or periods during which members were absent from one another's presence. As Goffman (1961:8–14) noted, the processes of group formation and maintenance are distinct from the processes of social interaction and should be treated as such analytically. Thus we should not attempt to explain the organization of a specific gathering of a Comanche dancing society at a powwow simply by referring to the organization of the dancing society as a unit of Comanche social structure, or vice versa.[26] Instead, Goffman (1961:7) believed that social interaction can best be understood by identifying the types of processes and units in which it occurs. He argued that conventional social representations of self and of social intention—often tied to specific kinds of gatherings and situations—are employed strategically so as to effect or enhance desired social outcomes (Goffman 1959, 1969). These are the means members of a community use to construct social situations and communicate within those contexts (in short, communicative competence).[27]

In studying the processes of social interaction, Goffman (1959, 1963a, 1963b) focused on the close identification of a participant in a social encounter with his or her social "face," and the ways in which people try to protect that face from various forms of risk. These facades, when properly sustained, are instrumental in accomplishing social work because they are read or interpreted by other participants as valid statements of both social worth and social intention. To lose face is to lose value in the eyes of one's community and consequently in one's own eyes as well, to become both morally and socially useless, bringing into question the validity of one's membership in the community. To the extent that one is brought up to value the community of which one is a member, this is a powerful sanction indeed. Thus the social presentation of self is neither strictly mercenary nor instrumental but is instead always constrained by displays of self-esteem. The "honoring" that goes on among participants at contemporary Comanche powwows is a good example of this, as both those being honored and those doing the honoring add value to their faces. As will be seen in subsequent chapters, Comanches have taken advantage of the attention to face in public gatherings such as powwows as a means of organizing their community in the absence of formal social structures and institutions.

In studying units of social interaction, Goffman developed an extensive taxonomy of types of gatherings in which processes such as face or impression management are situated. That taxonomy begins with a distinction between unfocused and focused interaction:

> Unfocused interaction consists of those interpersonal communications that result solely by virtue of persons being in one another's presence. . . . Focused interaction occurs when people effectively agree to sustain for a time a single focus of cognitive and visual attention. . . . Those sustaining together a single focus of attention will, of course, engage one another in unfocused interaction. They will not do so in their capacity as participants in the focused activity, however, and persons present who are not in the focused activity will equally participate in this unfocused activity. (Goffman 1961:7)

Unfocused interaction is based, simply, on copresence, and it occurs, both consciously and unconsciously, in any gathering of two or more persons. Gatherings are bounded by the spatial and temporal limits that constrain the ability of people to be present to one another. Indeed, immediate presence is the minimal definition of a gathering and may simply refer to passers-by on a sidewalk (Goffman 1963a:18). The spatial and temporal boundaries that limit unfocused access to others define the social situation (Goffman 1963a:18).

Focused interaction, in contrast, assumes some degree of involvement in a conscious, cooperative activity. Some or all of those physically present to one another may become participants in a social encounter by engaging in a shared structure of purposive communication (Goffman 1961:8). While a number of encounters may occur, both sequentially and simultaneously, in the same gathering of people, as at a party, encounters are defined by the continuity of focused interaction, not by the continuity of a specific focus or topic.

A Comanche powwow is a good example of both unfocused and focused interaction. Everyone present at a powwow is visually accessible to one another, and how one is dressed, whom one is seen speaking with, whether one actively participates in the dancing, whether one honors another or is oneself honored, all these contribute to unfocused impressions given off without focused involvement. One might also engage in focused interaction during a powwow, such as a conversation in which the cooperative management of a topic or sequence of topics requires the competent involvement of those participating. Observing and responding appropriately to the singers and dancers in the powwow arena is also an example of focused interaction, requiring knowledgeable involvement even if the observer does not himself sing or dance.

Often, gatherings (and the social encounters that may result from them) are situated in more encompassing social frameworks, which Goffman called social occasions: "This is a wider social affair, undertaking, or event, bounded in regard to time and place and typically facilitated by fixed equipment; a social occasion provides the structuring social context in which many situations and their gatherings are likely to form, dissolve and re-form while a pattern of conduct tends to be recognized as the appropriate and (often) official one" (Goffman 1963a:18). Social occasions equip participants with frameworks that guide the structure of focused interaction and the interpretation of unfocused interaction. A Comanche powwow is certainly a social occasion. The focused involvement within the powwow arena and among the observers surrounding the arena is structured by a set of beliefs about what is appropriate to powwow gatherings, hence the elaborate attention paid to one another's faces in the honoring ceremonies that are interspersed with the dances. Unfocused interaction also is interpreted through that conceptual framework. Drunkenness, for instance, is regarded as inappropriate and harmful to one's face during the "traditional" dances that take place in the afternoon and evening of a powwow but is tolerated as acceptable behavior during the "49," or social dancing, which takes place after midnight when the powwow proper has concluded.

Some social occasions, and the gatherings and situations within them, may be private, "soundproof regions where only members or invitees attend" (Goffman 1963a:9). Thus, a family gathering, such as might occur at Christmas, is a private region of social interaction. Private encounters are premised in part on a calculated disregard for face. This is because they are surrounded by conditions that force participants to disregard breakdowns and transgressions in face-to-face interaction. Long-term investments in kin and friend relationships, for instance, tend to mitigate any short-term refusal to cooperate in social interaction (Gumperz 1982a:209).

Two stories told about how Comanches' family and friends treat one another make this point. The first is about a warrior who borrows the favorite horse of a friend. He rides the horse to death, and instead of going back to his friend and somehow accounting for the horse, he simply laughs the next time they encounter one another. The friend says nothing. The second story is about a son-in-law who borrows a folding chair from his in-laws to use at a powwow. He doesn't return the chair, later using it when fishing at a farm pond and absentmindedly leaving it there. When the father-in-law finds the chair and brings it back to the house, the son-in-law simply laughs. The in-laws say nothing. In each of these stories, relationships are tested through the strategic risk of face. By not calling the face of another into question, the friend or relative is tacitly indicating that there exist compelling reasons outside the immediate social encounter for a relationship to be continued despite some disagreement or perceived inequity.

By their very nature, public gatherings transcend the more close-knit networks of family and friends that hold the nuclei of private encounters together. Indeed, to extend the analogy, public gatherings are complex arrangements of those more stable molecules. These arrangements are both responsive and vulnerable to changes in historical and social circumstances, especially as those circumstances constrain the ability of community members to be present to one another. Powwows within the Comanche community are open to any member who wishes to be present. Thus they are, in Goffman's definition, public regions, "freely accessible to members of that community" (1963a:9). Comanches who violate expectations for appropriate behavior at powwows, such as by becoming publicly drunk during the evening dances, cannot depend on compelling personal relationships with everyone present to limit the damage to their social faces. As Gumperz has observed, public situations "rarely provide the conditions where breakdowns can be disregarded" (1982a:210). Although Gumperz is referring to breakdowns in communication, this may be extended to breakdowns in social interaction as well.

In addition to impression management, public gatherings such as powwows also may have consequences for the social identities of those present. A social identity is by definition a public identity by which one is known in the community at large. Social identities are emblematic of the organization of the membership of a community (Goffman 1963a:103; Goffman 1969:140). Simply by being present at a powwow a Comanche communicates a strategic choice that may have long-term consequences for his or her social identity within the community. Prior to World War II, for instance, powwow attendance aligned one with a particular faction in tribal politics.

Public gatherings may have consequences for both longstanding relationships and groups by means of the social identities that are signaled through participation in them: "It is a fact that the individual's relationship to gatherings and social occasions sometimes tells us something about his relationship to broader units of social life" (Goffman 1963a:220; see also Goffman 1961:14). Goffman described how this may happen with respect to relationships:

> When a person begins a mediated or immediate encounter, he already stands in
> some kind of social relationship to the others concerned, and expects to stand in a
> given relationship to them after the particular encounter ends. This, of course, is
> one way in which social contacts are geared into the wider society. . . . It is often
> the person's social relationship with others that leads him to participate in certain
> encounters with them, where incidentally he will be dependent upon them for
> supporting his face. (Goffman 1967:41–42)

The same may be said for membership in a social group or category. An individual's social relationships and memberships may result in, to use Goffman's phrase, recurrent occasions of focused and unfocused interaction (1967:136). In a small, face-to-face community, such as that which Comanches share, such social identities are not easily shirked (Goffman 1971:191–193). This is because most encounters among members are not between strangers (which Goffman called "anonymous relations") but between participants with shared knowledge of one another (which Goffman called "anchored relations"). In communities of this sort, physical presence is a vital element in community participation, and the fact of presence at a particular gathering tends to persist in the memories of other members long after that gathering has ceased to exist as a social unit.

This is not to say, of course, that physical presence and face-to-face interaction play an insignificant part in the Anglo community. However, Anglos are members of all manner of groups and categories in which physical presence has little or no necessary role. It is possible, for instance, to be a staunch supporter of a political party, to contribute money, and to work for candidates entirely through the mail or over the telephone. It also is possible to believe and participate strongly, even passionately, in an evangelical church without ever leaving one's living room. It is not possible, however, to "be Comanche" over the phone, or by mail, or through watching television. Membership in the Comanche community requires participation in gatherings of other members of the community. Such participation need not be frequent, but community members are required somehow to "stay in touch" with the community through physical presence at some public gatherings in order to remain in good standing.

THE INTERSECTION OF SOCIAL LIFE AND SOCIAL STRUCTURE

Public gatherings are vital to community maintenance. They can be used to signal identities in constituent social units of the community and also to hold participants, both as individuals and as members of networks and groups, to standards of conduct that emphasize the community they share. Both these functions—the public signaling of social identity and the public concern for face—are useful in maintaining the larger community as a social unit.

Social identities that categorize participants (either in egocentric relationships or in endocentric memberships in collective entities) represent the alliances and memberships that obligate and empower social action within the community. Thus, social identities enable participants to identify themselves as belonging to those social units and provide a framework in which members may conceptualize the internal social arrangements and divisions of their community. This is certainly true of the public gatherings in which Comanches participate. As Haddon Nauni explained participation in pow-wow gatherings in 1985, "That arena [the circular dance area] is your people, your society. Be proud, but also be humble."

The motivation to preserve moral worth in public gatherings exposes relationships and memberships in constituent social units to regulation in the larger unit of the community. This regulation subjects the self-interest of egocentric relationships and closed social groups to the common interest of the whole community. In this way, the community at large may regulate private conduct that is essential to, or endangers, its continuity.

Together, these two functions tie constituent social units to the larger social unit of the community. Without such linkage, a community would have no means of enforcing agreement on shared standards for social interaction and would gradually dissolve into its constituent parts. By linking participation in public social occasions with social identities, and by subjecting that participation to the public concern to preserve one's own and others' face in gatherings unsupported by compelling personal ties, communities as social units are provided with the means of organizing and regulating their memberships without a formal, centralized social structure. In this way, the organization of social life may intersect with the organization of social structure.

Because of the conspicuous lack of an overarching formal social structure in the Comanche community, the main business of Comanche social organization was, and still is, accomplished at the level of social life, as people interact in social gatherings. This is the glue that anthropologists have consistently overlooked in Comanche social organization. Public gatherings constitute a means for individual Comanches to express their identities as members of the Comanche community (in other words, a means of being Comanche) and in constituent units of the community. Public gatherings also enable the Comanche community to regulate its constituent social units (relationships, groups, and categories), as well as the behavior of individual Comanches. As the social conditions that constrain Comanches' ability to be physically present to one another have changed, so too have the public social occasions used for the purpose of community maintenance. A history of the organization and maintenance of the Comanche community, then, is a history of the changing forms of public gathering.

2

The Nomadic Community, 1706-1875

Careless of the future, they [the Comanches] are indifferent to the benefits that accrue from the recollections of the past. The revolving day embodies all their concerns. . . . It is, however, presumable, that their wandering mode of life and the remoteness and seclusion of the country through which they have ranged since time immemorial, have mainly contributed to perpetuate both the identity and the independence of a tribe.

David G. Burnett, 1818

I do not know whether the greatest enemy of them [the Spanish provinces on the southern Plains] is the savage Indians or the impression which conjectural opinion and mistaken reports have made.

Teodoro de Croix, 1777

By now it is a truism of anthropology that the words we use, and the semantic categories they signify, influence the ways we perceive the world and act in it. While most people who read this book will not know individual Comanches, and even fewer will have firsthand knowledge of the Comanche community, nearly all will know the sign "Comanche" and will associate with it a category of Native Americans who are defined by the same distinctive features. That sign and the category it marks are the result of nearly three centuries of Euro-American perceptions and interpretations of what it is to "be Comanche."

Although this book is yet another of those Euro-American exercises, it is one that attempts to sort out extracommunity claims about identity from intracommunity claims and thereby to differentiate between the social construction of the native community and the cultural reification of that historical process by the surrounding, economically dominant Anglo community. To begin to get at the internal organization of the Comanche community, we must examine the signs and categories Euro-Americans have used to distinguish Comanches and also the history of Comanche–Euro-American relations, which has shaped the uses of those signs. Once this background is understood, we can evaluate contemporary and retrospective Euro-

American accounts of Comanches for what they can tell us about the organization of Comanche-Comanche relations.

COMANCHES PRIOR TO EUROPEAN CONTACT

Those peoples whom Euro-Americans label Comanche originated from Numic populations (often referred to under the rubric Shoshonean) in the Great Basin, centered in present-day Nevada, Utah, and Idaho. Numic peoples probably moved first onto the northwestern periphery of the Plains— the present-day Wyoming and Montana—before moving south into present-day Colorado and New Mexico, where they first encountered Europeans (Shimkin 1986). Comanche oral tradition recognizes a Basin origin, explaining the separation from Shoshone relatives as the result of either a dispute over the distribution of meat from a hunt or an epidemic.[1]

Because of the close linguistic relationship between Comanche and Shoshone (indeed, many Comanche speakers say the two are mutually intelligible), most scholars have assumed that Comanches had only recently diverged from Shoshonean stock when they first came into contact with Europeans on the southern Plains early in the eighteenth century (Mooney 1907:327; Wallace and Hoebel 1952:6; Lamb 1958; Miller 1970; Thurman 1980:60). The idea of a relatively recent Basin origin has often been used as an explanation for differences between Comanche forms of social organization and those of other Plains peoples (see Oliver 1962), and so has become an indispensable component of most Comanche histories. Wallace and Hoebel (1952:6–9), for instance, explain Comanches' lack of the typical "Plains Indian" forms of social organization (military societies, tribal councils, descent-based social groups) by their "late arrival" on the Plains. In this interpretation, Comanche ethnogenesis resulted in large part from the attraction of Spanish horses and trade goods. The idea implies that without a European presence in North America there would have been no Comanches.

Other scholars, however, have argued that Comanches may have exploited the Plains proper for a considerable period before they came into contact with Europeans (e.g., Shimkin 1940, 1986; Kavanagh 1986; Shaul 1986). Shaul (1986), for instance, has suggested that the linguistic similarity of Comanche and Shoshone is a function of a longstanding tradition of contact between the two communities of speakers, thus effectively masking what could be a much longer period of geographic separation. Although difficult to prove, it is entirely possible that Comanches were active on the Plains for some centuries before European contact. This interpretation places

MAP 1. The Southern Plains. Comanches frequented Spanish markets in Santa Fe and Taos during the eighteenth century. In the nineteenth century, the federal government established the Comanche and Brazos agencies as reserves from which Comanches could trade with Texans until 1859. The Upper Platte and Upper Arkansas agencies also served as contact points between Comanches and Anglos before and during the Civil War. The Kiowa, Comanche, and Apache Reservation was established by treaty in Indian Territory in 1867. All Comanche bands resided on it after 1875. (Map by Christine Schultz)

formative emphasis on the period during which Numic bands exploited the northwestern Plains area rather than on European contact. It suggests that Comanches had already established the tradition of an enduring community by the time they moved onto the southern Plains and into the European range of vision. Tah-pon-y, a Comanche interviewed by Hugh Scott in 1897, supported the idea of an early Comanche presence on the southern Plains: "When Comanches first came down here, they came down on foot—they had neither horses or dogs—they packed their property on their backs. Five generations of old men have died since [Comanches] came to this country and I am the sixth. I am 64 years old."[2]

One attraction of the Plains to proto-Comanche bands would have been the bison herds supported by the Plains grasslands, in contrast to the sparser Basin environment, which required a more diverse hunting strategy and probably a smaller human population density (Steward 1938). While an improvement over the Basin environment, the western margin of the Plains area initially used by those Numic bands possessed limited resources, with smaller, less predictable herds of bison than could be found on the southern Plains (Bamforth 1988). Comanches probably derived their subsistence from bison and other herd animals, from small game, and from an extensive inventory of flora found on the Plains (Carlson and Jones 1940). They were also participants in the extensive prehistoric trading networks of North America, perhaps using their Shoshonean connections to tie into western networks (Wood 1980; Shaul 1986).

It is difficult to speculate about the initial forms of Comanche social organization for the protohistoric period, that is, between the time various Numic bands departed the Basin and their first contact with the Spanish at the beginning of the eighteenth century. Our bases for such speculation are what we know historically of the social organization of the Numic peoples who remained in the Basin area and what we know historically of later forms of Comanche social organization. We cannot, however, simply draw a line between these two points and obtain an accurate picture of the proto-historical Comanche community. First, we cannot assume that the material circumstances of economic life in the historical period, so heavily influenced by the European presence in the New World, were at all equivalent to the circumstances of the protohistoric period. Second, our images of native social organization for the historical period may be defective, biased by self-reference to Euro-American forms of social organization. An immediate sense of this problem can be gained from a brief consideration of what we "know" about Shoshonean social organization in the Basin area.

Traditionally, the Basin area has been represented as supporting only a minimal level of human social organization, and this is one of the stereotypes that has informed anthropological conceptions of Comanche social organization on the Plains. At the same time, however, the Basin area is known to have been characterized by cooperative hunting strategies such as the Magic Antelope Surround, in which large numbers of participants are needed to drive a herd of antelope into a corral (Lowie 1909, 1924; Steward 1938). The degree of organization implied by the surround is somewhat at odds with the typically minimalist characterization of Basin social structure. While the Basin environment clearly could not support large gatherings of hunter-gatherers for extended periods, periodic cooperative efforts such as the surround suggest that Basin peoples did in fact engage in more complex forms of social organization. It is only our ethnocentric preference for "permanent" corporate forms of social organization that causes us to label Basin societies as less complex. As will be seen in our more detailed consideration of historical Comanche social units, transient social gatherings can be just as effective means of social organization as enduring social groups.

THE SIGN "COMANCHE"

One of the earliest documentary notices of Comanches as such occurs in a report by the governor of New Mexico written on August 18, 1706: "The extensive province of Navajo is the seat, establishment, and dwelling-place of numerous rancherias of heathen Indians of this name. It extends about one hundred leagues from south to north to the boundaries of the numerous nations of Yutas, Carlenas, and Comanches."[3] This report locates Comanches in substantial numbers on the northeastern frontier of present-day New Mexico, and the reference is so matter-of-fact that a prior Spanish acquaintance is suggested. How long that acquaintance had existed is uncertain, but Comanche bands may have been among the fifty-four nomadic peoples listed by Vargas in a 1694 description of native communities surrounding Spanish New Mexico.[4] Prominent in Vargas's account were the Utes, who had been known to Europeans since the early seventeenth century and in whose company Comanches are believed to have become known to the Spanish (Loomis and Nasatir 1967:18–20).

Prior to 1694 the Spanish were distracted from observations of native peoples of the interior by the Pueblo Revolt of 1680, in which the native peoples of New Mexico regained control over the northernmost Spanish province in the New World. Spanish domination was restored by Vargas between 1692 and 1700, partly by force but also through compelling economic circumstances. Many of the nomadic peoples not directly colonized by the Spanish in the region, including the Utes, had become entangled in the Spanish economy of New Mexico and supported the return of Spanish officials and traders after the revolt (Espinosa 1936:186–187; Espinosa 1939:88).

The Spanish provided a market for various Plains goods (including bison hides and captives) and were an important source of European goods (including metal items and horses).

The Spanish called these nomadic peoples Norteños, or Nations of the North, a category of native peoples (including those who would come to be called Comanche) on the northern frontier of the Spanish provinces. The Spanish also categorized Comanches as among the Indios Bárbaros, a term used to identify native peoples who had not been incorporated into the Spanish colonial system. When, however, the Spanish began to compete with the French and British in developing spheres of influence within that region we think of today as the southern Plains and which the Spanish referred to as the *interior,* more specific categorizations of its native peoples became necessary.

The Spanish began to distinguish Comanche peoples from other nomadic peoples of the northern frontier when Comanches began to take part in Spanish activities on the southern Plains, including raiding Pueblo settlements in alliance with Ute bands in 1707 and participating in Spanish markets in those same settlements in 1709 (Thomas 1935:16, 61; Kenner 1969:28). The sign the Spanish adopted, "Comanche," like those which have come to stand for so many American Indian peoples, is not one devised by the people to whom it has been applied. Opler (1943) has suggested that "Comanche" was derived by the Spanish from a Ute word, /komantcia/, taken to mean "my adversary" or "anyone who wants to fight me all the time."[5]

Because they perceived Comanche people as a singular category, the Spanish and later the Anglo-Americans viewed their actions as linked, and they consistently tried to force Comanches to approximate their image of a unified tribe, both in their reports of Comanche social life and in their dealings with Comanche bands and leaders. This was the case even when Euro-Americans recognized that Comanches did not constitute a single polity (e.g., Bolton 1914, 2:166). To the extent that Euro-American control over economic and military resources was crucial, Comanches' self-interest periodically caused leaders and bands to go along with that singular image.

At other times, Euro-American observers on the southern Plains were not certain of the social identities of the peoples they described in their reports and letters. This confusion resulted both in multicultural residual categories like Norteños and Indios Bárbaros and in misidentification. A term that is often used in French accounts of the southern Plains and which later turns up in Spanish and Anglo-American accounts is Padouca. This is most likely a residual category that was used to label different Plains peoples at various points in time. La Harpe, for instance, uses Padouca to refer to Comanches in 1719, but Gaignard uses the term in 1770 to refer explicitly to Apaches (Bolton 1914, 2:87; Smith 1951, 1959). French explorers may have expected to find Padoucas on the Plains because of stories of a large bison-hunting tribe there reported to La Salle in 1680 (Hyde 1959:25). The Spanish and Anglo-Americans later incorporated the term into their geographies of the region because of the earlier French reports.

The power of such mythical categories was not limited to the eighteenth and early nineteenth centuries. Some Anglo-American historians (e.g., Grinnell 1920; Secoy 1951; Hyde 1959) took the label as evidence of an actual sociopolitical unit on the Plains and expended considerable effort in trying to identify the "true" Padoucas. Similarly, the name Comanche also has had enduring consequences for Anglo perceptions of the people thus labeled. As we will see, some scholars have gone to great lengths to rationalize the singular category that it implies with anthropological theories of social and political organization. If these people were indeed all Comanche, what did that common identity mean for their mutual social relations?

This question has been answered in a variety of ways. Wallace and Hoebel's attempt is perhaps the most widely known:

> "Tribe" when applied to the Comanches is a word of sociological but not political significance. The Comanches had a strong consciousness of kind. A Comanche, whatever his band, was a Comanche. . . . By dress, by speech, by thoughts and actions, the Comanches held a common bond of identity and affinity that set them off from all other Indians. . . . In this sense, the tribe had meaning. The tribe consisted of a people who had a common way of life. But that way of life did not include political institutions or social mechanisms by which they could act as a tribal unit. There was, in the old days, no ceremonial occasion or economic enterprise that pulled all the far-flung bands together for a spell, be it ever so brief. There was no chieftain or group of chieftains to act for the tribe as a whole. There was no tribal council. (Wallace and Hoebel 1952:22)

Had the Spanish not preferred to make connections among different bands of Comanche speakers, subsequent Anglo-American and scholarly accounts might be very different. Rather than dealing with the historical and sociological problem of a single people collectively labeled Comanche, we might instead be dealing with the academic problem of a half dozen or more peoples who spoke the same language but who had been given different ethnic designations.[6]

Some Euro-American observers did take note of different Comanche band or divisional identities when this suited their purposes in trade or diplomacy. Kotsoteka, Yamparika, and Jupe were the most frequent designations during the eighteenth century, and Yamparica, Penetaka, Quahada, Tenewa, and Nokoni were the most frequent designations during the nineteenth. These Comanche divisions were comprised of allied residence or local bands that operated in contiguous areas. But even these smaller-scale social units were, as we will see, problematic glosses on the internal organization of the Comanche community.

In either case, whether as a single tribe or multiple divisions, the problem is of our own making, an artifact of the history of Euro-American relations with, and images of, the people or peoples in question.

COMANCHE–EURO-AMERICAN RELATIONS, 1706-1875

Whatever their precontact movements and modes of subsistence, Comanche encounters with Spanish settlers and French traders on the southern Plains introduced them to new economic possibilities. Comanches recognized early on the value of horses in trade with Euro-Americans and other Plains peoples, and they oriented their use of the southern Plains around raiding and trading activities that focused on the horse as an economic commodity. By 1719, Comanches were reported as mounted warriors, suggesting that they were able to acquire sufficient numbers of horses to make the transformation from a pedestrian lifestyle to a mounted nomadic one early in the first half of the century (Chappell 1906:254). Comanches were reported to be trading horses to the French in 1724 (Folmer 1937:125–127), and a Comanche village was described as possessing "a number of horses" in 1739 (Folmer 1939:170).

Horses were, of course, to become a significant component of the overall prereservation Plains economy (Haines 1938; Ewers 1955; Roe 1955; Holder 1970). Comanches have long been known as among the most active Plains peoples in trading horses from the south and southwest (where they were relatively available) to the northern Plains (where they were not), and they were also among those Plains peoples with the highest ratios of horse wealth per person (Thurman 1980; Osborn 1983; Hanson 1988). The horse was valued because it facilitated movement over long distances and thus made bison hunting more efficient.

The large Comanche horse herds that begin to be described by the mid eighteenth century, though, were not simply for bison hunting. Indeed, it can be argued that the requirements of maintaining such sizable concentrations of stock mitigated their efficient use in pursuit of the bison. The degree to which Comanche movement and social organization quickly became dependent on the acquisition of horses may be seen in a Spanish document of 1749 quoted by Pichardo, writing in the early part of the nineteenth century:

"They were dispersed, with their large droves of horses, for which reason they could not live together, having to seek sufficient pasturage and water for their horses" (1931–46, 3:317).

By midcentury the horse trade may have replaced bison hunting as the dominant economic fact of Comanche life, further entangling Comanches in the developing Euro-American political economy. As the organization of the Comanche community came to focus on raiding and trading during the eighteenth century, the Comanche subsistence base may also have been changing, with Comanches acquiring food supplies by trading horses rather than by using those horses to hunt bison or by pursuing traditional plant gathering.[7] While hunting and gathering remained a significant source of Comanche subsistence up to the reservation period, postcontact nomadic Comanche life on the Plains was not synonymous with those activities. As will be seen, the gradual disappearance of the bison herds beginning early in the nineteenth century caused Comanches to adjust, but not to abandon, their activities on the open Plains.

The horses on which those activities were based were acquired in part through trading with the Spanish and in part through raiding Spanish settlements. Early Spanish accounts describe both activities in a seemingly contradictory pattern that would prevail for most of the eighteenth century (Thomas 1935:26–27). The apparent contradiction was in the Spanish toleration of Comanche raids. Only rarely did Spanish authorities deny Comanche bands access to Pueblo markets because of raiding activities. This suggests that the Spanish were dependent on Comanche trade to a degree that made some losses due to raiding seem an acceptable cost of doing business.[8] Where the Spanish did attempt to exert some control over Comanche activities was in the frequency and conditions of Pueblo trade fairs, which were the largest sources of European goods available to southern Plains peoples (Twitchell 1914, 2:205, 210, 227; Kenner 1969). Arguably, Comanches used raids to circumvent these Spanish controls, which regulated both the availability of horses and other goods and their prices. Trading opportunities with the French and with other Indian communities also lessened the consequences of Spanish regulation. The Spanish decision to establish the province of Texas as a barrier to French incursion onto the Plains provided Comanches with additional economic opportunities that were alternatives to New Mexican markets and goods (Thomas 1935:36).

The Spanish, though, were not simply the innocent sources of European goods and horses. Spanish traders, when not closely supervised by colonial authorities, tended to take advantage of Comanches who attended the Pueblo trade fairs (Thomas 1940; Simmons 1977). Those traders also made a market for captives, in which captured Indians were exchanged for horses (Hackett 1923–37, 3:486–487; Simmons 1977). While many contemporaneous accounts and even most historical studies emphasize the "ferocity" and "barbarity" of some Indian actions toward Euro-Americans on the southern Plains, some justification for Indians' hostility may be found in the dishonesty of Euro-American markets and the slave trade that Euro-Americans supported.

Between 1719 and 1746, French traders also were intermittently active among Comanche bands. The French trade threatened Spanish interests on the southern Plains, thus further reinforcing the Spanish interest in maintaining economic relations with Comanche bands even in the face of repeated hostilities (Thomas 1940:135). French traders were important sources of firearms for Comanche bands, which Spanish traders were prohibited from providing (Kenner 1969:38).[9] French traders were providing guns to various native peoples on the southern Plains at least as early as 1727 (Thomas 1940:16–17). Comanche bands did not always tolerate these traders, who also were supplying the Comanches' Apache and Osage enemies, but nevertheless had consistent access to the goods they provided through Caddoan and Wichitan village peoples (Thomas 1940:16–17; Loomis and Nasatir 1967:20–21).

In 1746 and 1747, Comanches came into more direct, regular contact with French traders. By that time, Comanches had driven their Apache enemies south, out of the trading sphere exploited by the French, and so were more tolerant of a regular French trade in which horses and hides were exchanged for guns and ammunition. The French used a people whom they called the Jumanos (most likely Wichitan villagers) to broker their relations with Comanche bands (Bolton 1964:155). Unlike the Spaniards with whom the Comanches interacted, the Frenchmen who contacted Comanches were independent hunters and fur traders, not government agents (Bolton 1964:162). Individually, they had been attempting to penetrate the Plains for thirty years and had been trying to initiate a trade with Santa Fe since 1739, only to be rebuffed by the Spanish (Loomis and Nasatir 1967:52–61). Allying themselves with Comanches was the next best economic alternative to participating directly in the Pueblo markets. As a result of this contact, Comanche bands were described by the Spanish as possessing and skillfully using a substantial supply of firearms by 1752 (Thomas 1940:118).

Spanish as well as French colonial authorities had identified Comanche bands as the key to dominating the southern Plains trade (Loomis and Nasatir 1967:101). Consequently, the reports they received of Comanche-French cooperation caused the Spanish considerable consternation (Twitchell

1914, 1:148–151). Not only were Comanches being provided with guns, they were also sponsoring French encroachment into the interior of the southern Plains. The Spanish response to this was not military but economic. To lure the Comanches away from their French trading partners, the Spanish governor of New Mexico offered greater access to the Pueblo markets in 1751 (Thomas 1940:25). After some negotiation, and a few hostile engagements, Governor Vélez Capuchín managed to arrange an accommodation with most of the Comanche leaders whose bands operated in the area contiguous to the province of New Mexico (Thomas 1940:118–125; John 1975:321–328). In exchange for continued economic relations, the band leaders undertook to curtail the raiding activities of their followers. This peace lasted until 1760. Subsequently, another peace was arranged from 1762 to 1766, and two other, short-lived accommodations in 1771 and 1774 (Thomas 1940:35–37, 41; Bolton 1970:123).

Meanwhile, farther east, Comanches continued to trade with French agents and to raid Spanish settlements in Texas (Thomas 1940:37; Bolton 1970:87, 109). The trade with Frenchmen based in Louisiana may have been an important source of horses for the British colonies on the East Coast, perhaps rivaling in importance the Comanche trade in horses with other Indian peoples of the Plains.[10] After the French officially ceded their Mississippi valley territories to the Spanish in 1763, many independent French traders remained and continued to do business with Comanches and their village allies (Bolton 1970:121, 124). By 1768, British agents had also begun trading with Comanche bands (Thomas 1940:38). During this period, Comanches had ceased to be allies of the Utes, who may have become competitors as brokers in the New Mexico–Texas–Louisiana trading chain that the Comanches dominated.

Comanches were quite successful in playing off Spanish and French interests, which later took the form of New Mexican and Louisianan interests after the French withdrawal. By raiding in Texas, they acquired horses and captives, which they subsequently traded to village peoples and French and British agents for guns and ammunition. They also traded captives and hides to the Spanish in New Mexico for horses and European goods. When they could get away with it, Comanches also raided in New Mexico. When this threatened to deny them access to Pueblo markets, they reached accommodations with the provincial authorities. Even when the Spanish wanted to cut Comanches off from trade entirely, the marginal nature of the New Mexican and Texan economies prevented them from carrying this policy to its logical conclusion. Further, traders from Louisiana and later St. Louis were always eager to do business with Comanche bands when the Spanish were not.[11] The Spanish were not unaware of these facts, and in 1754 they began to attempt to link their New Mexican and Texan Indian policies (Bolton 1964:169–170).

It had become clear to the Spanish colonial authorities that the best means of influencing Comanche actions was through trade. A policy of pursuing a Comanche-Spanish accommodation was formally approved in 1778 (Thomas 1940:53–54). The councils that created this policy recognized that the Comanche peoples did not constitute a single political unit. As the minutes of the council at San Antonio de Bexar noted, the term "Comanche nation" was "applied generically to various groups of Indians" (Bolton 1914, 2:166), but the very existence of a generic term suggested the utility of a unified category to the Spanish. Instead of reaching separate arrangements with each Comanche band, they chose to use trade to force the Comanches to resemble a single nation and so to respond better to Spanish interests on the southern Plains. An added motivation for this decision was the growing Spanish frustration with their sometime Apache allies, whose raids were even more troublesome than those of the Comanches. Apachean peoples, whose bands ranged deep into Spanish territory, had become obstacles to provincial consolidation. The Spanish wanted to co-opt the Comanches through trade and use them to drive out the Apaches, gambling that the Comanches, whose bands dominated the periphery of the Spanish provinces, would not take up permanent residence in New Mexico and Texas (Thomas 1932:64–65).

For their part, the Comanches may have found accommodation with the Spanish to be an economic necessity. Longstanding French and native sources of trade were disrupted in the early 1780s as more native peoples moved onto the southern Plains and Euro-American conflicts elsewhere decreased the flow of trade goods (John 1975:590–591). Croix's report of 1781 described the benefits of accommodation for Comanches: "They can have everything at the hands of the Spaniards. In a few years they would see in their country the procreation of horses in the same abundance as that of deer and buffalo, and then not needing these animals, the acquisition of firearms in barter for hides and herds would be less difficult for them" (Thomas 1941:112–113).

By 1783, Comanches were making overtures to the Spanish, attempting to establish a temporary peace that would see them through the difficult times (Thomas 1932:71–73). However, the Governor of New Mexico, Juan Bautista de Anza, consistently refused to make a treaty that did not link the actions of all Comanche bands with respect to the Spanish. Thus it was not until 1786 that the Comanches were able to develop a broad consensus among the various bands that satisfied the Spanish terms. Anza actively shaped that consensus, both through economic and military actions that denied Comanches access to trade and through Spanish contacts with Comanche leaders.

The Spanish actively promoted the career of one Comanche leader—Ecueracapa—in order to construct the idea of a supreme command among the previously autonomous Comanche bands. Anza (Thomas 1932:302) encouraged Ecueracapa to combine Spanish assistance with his "natural authority" within the Comanche nation to "take charge of the [Comanche] government and absolute direction of its national interests." In effect, Anza proposed that Ecueracapa approximate a formal political structure among the autonomous Comanche bands. The Spanish record explains the logic of this: "[B]y means of his [Ecueracapa's] person, elevating him above the rest of his class, we would be able, perhaps, to submit subtly all his nation to the dominion of the king without using violent means contrary to his sovereign intentions" (Thomas 1932:302). This benefited the Spanish in that, ideally, it tied all Comanche actions together and made all Comanches responsible for preserving the peace upon which the alliance, and trade, depended.

The Spanish invested Ecueracapa and other Comanche leaders allied with him with physical symbols of the alliance, including sabers, Spanish flags, and a staff of office. At the same time, Comanche bands were given greater access to Pueblo markets, where the regulated prices were readjusted in their favor (Thomas 1932:305–306, 318–319). The meaning of these actions was clear: Continued economic good for the Comanches depended on the coordination of Comanche relations with the Spanish. Subsequently Ecueracapa made this argument during an extensive tour of Comanche bands, successfully creating a consensus that supported the Comanche-Spanish accommodation he had negotiated with Anza.

That accommodation was an arrangement that worked out better for New Mexico than for the Spanish province of Texas. Comanches made considerable efforts to preserve their good relations with the authorities in New Mexico, but they were attentive to Texas authorities only when the benefits of trade in that province outweighed the benefits of raiding (John 1984). As Texas governor Domingo Cabello y Robles noted in 1786, Comanches had established a trade in horses stolen in Texas and sold in New Mexico (Faulk 1961:179). The peace with Anza did not inhibit Comanche raids in Texas; instead it supported continued raiding by increasing Comanche access to New Mexican markets, which were to grow into the comanchero trade of the nineteenth century. At the same time, the greater significance of Louisianan markets and the as yet unstudied impact of an eastern Anglo-American market for horses also promoted Comanche raiding in Texas and Mexico. For most of the remaining period of Hispanic influence on the southern Plains, the differing economic interests of New Mexico, Texas, and Louisiana prevented Spanish and, later, Mexican and American officials from cooperating in a concerted policy that would effectively use trade to regulate Comanche behavior within the region.

Instead of taking Comanche raiding in Texas as a violation of the linked peace, Spanish officials rationalized the differing economic strategies with which Comanches approached New Mexico, Texas, and Louisiana as representing two separate, geographically static Comanche "nations," east and west (Bannon 1970; John 1984). Thus, in the first two decades of the nineteenth century, Spanish officials engaged in frequent references to eastern and western Comanches as if they were organized polities (Twitchell 1914, 2:586, 596).[12] Rather than a political distinction, however, the "eastern" Comanches represented the source of horses in Texas and Mexico and the "western" Comanches represented the trade in horses in New Mexico, each economic mode reflecting a different temperature in Comanche–Euro-American relations.[13]

There is no evidence that this dual economic division resulted in any corresponding dual political division in the internal organization of the Comanche community. Comanches, though, took advantage of the reputation that western leaders had among the Spanish as "peace" chiefs by bringing one, called Oso Ballo, to negotiate with colonial officials in Texas in 1811 when the temperature of Comanche-Spanish relations in the province was particularly hot (John 1984:362–363). By 1812, Spain had lost the ability to control trade in Texas in the face of Anglo-American traders from the east and insurrectional movements from within, so it effectively lost whatever leverage it had held over Comanche behavior in the province (John 1984:364). Anglo-American traders, in particular, enlarged the eastern market for horses stolen in Texas, resulting in an increase in Comanche raids through the 1820s (Kavanagh 1986:85).

The changing character of the southern Plains in the early part of the nineteenth century ensured that Comanches in New Mexico preserved the outward appearances of a centrally controlled polity to 1821, as northern Plains and eastern Woodlands peoples crowded in and Comanche fortunes became more closely tied to Spanish markets. As vacancies occurred in the "supreme command" the Spanish had engineered, Comanches nominated new leaders to manage their access to Pueblo markets (Kavanagh 1986:68–69). During the 1820s, however, the centers for this trade moved from the market towns and pueblos to the Plains, as New Mexican traders found it worth their while to go to the Comanches (Kavanagh 1986:91–92; Kenner 1969:80). This allowed Comanches to relax the care with which they had treated New Mexican settlements as symbols of opportunity for trade, and they increased their raiding activities in the province (Twitchell 1914, 1:346–347).

By the 1830s, Comanches also were increasing their raiding activities in Mexico south of the Rio Grande. These raids had begun as early as 1819 and grew more frequent through the 1850s (Kenner 1969:69). The forcible separation of Texas and later New Mexico from the administration of the Mexican government worked to the advantage of Comanche bands. Mexican authorities could not pursue Comanche raiders into Texan and U.S. territory. Once again Comanches made opportunistic use of Euro-American administrative categorizations to facilitate their economic activities.

The remaining influence on the southern Plains in the first half of the nineteenth century was a growing Anglo-American presence. First came traders seeking to capitalize on the Louisiana Purchase of 1803, and then came colonists moving into the Mexican province of Texas. Anglo-American traders were attracted to the southern Plains by both hides and horses. John Sibley, an American agent commissioned to capture the southern Plains trade from the Spanish, wrote in 1807 that horses and mules were "to them [the Comanches], like grass they had them in such plenty" (Sibley 1922:74). Anthony Glass, an Anglo-American trader who wintered with a Comanche band in 1808–09, noted that the band had three times as many horses and mules as people and was forced to move frequently to find new pasture as a result (Flores 1985:67–68). This was similar to Spanish observations of Comanche band movements from 1750 on. The dynamic of Comanche participation in the Euro-American economy—trading horses for manufactured goods—was clear. Sibley, for instance, quotes a Comanche leader trying to interest Anglo-Americans in trade: "We are in want of merchandize and shall be always" (1922:61). The merchandise that they wanted ran from guns and ammunition to blankets and looking glasses (Kavanagh 1986:334). Some of these items were used by Comanches, and others were traded away to other Indian communities.

The Anglo-American trade from the east, like the New Mexican trade from the west after 1821, was conducted by individual enterprise, not in organized markets as the Spanish Puebloan trade had been. This meant that Comanches did not have to satisfy colonial governments with the appearance of a coordinated peace, as they had had to satisfy the Spanish in 1786. It also meant that Euro-American traders could trade with Comanches with little regulation from colonial authorities, obtaining horses that had been raided from settlements in their own territories and providing Comanches with guns and ammunition even at times of tense relations.

The appearance of large numbers of Anglo-American settlers in Texas in the early 1820s was both hindered and assisted by Comanche activities. Between 1822 and 1827, Comanche raiding in Texas was supported by Anglo-American traders (Kavanagh 1986:85). At the same time, those same traders were supplying horses to the settlers whom Comanches were raiding (Wallace and Hoebel 1952:292; Kavanagh 1986:252). Some Anglo-Texan officials recognized that the primary motivation for Comanches in their relations with Anglos was trade (Wallace and Hoebel 1952:293–294). Like the Spanish and French before them, these officials attempted to link the actions of autonomous Comanche bands into a collective polity through their economic relations with Euro-Americans. A Texan-Comanche peace was arranged from 1827 to 1832, and subsequent treaties and armistices were entered into in 1838, 1843, and 1850 (Winfrey and Day 1966; DeMallie 1977; Kavanagh 1986). Each of these accommodations was based on the Comanches' interest in trade and the Anglo-Texans' interest in the continued expansion of their settlements. Like the Spanish, Anglo-Texan agents tried to deal with the various bands through strong Comanche leaders whom they invested with "paramount" political authority and symbols (Kavanagh 1986).

This tactic was only partly successful. Unlike the Spanish in the previous century, Texas officials could not effectively regulate Comanche-Anglo trade, which motivated Comanche actions, and were unwilling to curtail frontier expansion. Comanches such as Buffalo Hump could be satisfied for a time by promises of increased trading opportunities, but they were constantly being pressed to give up more of their hunting territories to Anglo settlement (Schilz and Schilz 1989). By 1846, when Texas joined the Union, the northward and westward movement of settlers was bringing Texans into conflict with Comanche bands.[14] Most of the bands based their operations beyond the settled frontier, residing on the Upper Platte from 1846 to 1855. In 1855, Cheyenne and Pawnee movements southward pushed the Comanche bands to the Upper Arkansas, where they remained until 1864.[15]

For Texan settlers, and also for other Anglo-Americans who read the increasingly popular newspaper and dime novel accounts of life on the western frontier, Comanches became the scourge of the southern Plains, even though many of their raiding activities were covertly supported by Anglo traders, mostly based in Texas.[16] In the popular imagination, the name Comanche took on a fearsome quality. Anglo settlers in Texas viewed Comanches with alarm, reacting to the presence of those few Comanche bands that remained in Texas in ways that promoted conflict.[17]

The popular Anglo image of Comanches and the economic interaction of Comanches and Anglos in early-nineteenth-century Texas illustrate the two main tendencies in Euro-American–Indian interaction noted in chapter 1. In general, Texans viewed Indians as the opposite of "civilized" Anglo-Americans, that is, as bent on the wanton destruction of frontier homesteads and homesteaders. Meanwhile, in those specific instances in which Indians were instrumental to the furthering of Anglo economic interests, trade with those same "uncivilized barbarians" was tolerated and, indeed, defended from the criticisms of federal authorities. No less an icon of frontier Texas than Jesse Chisholm was identified as having traded guns to Comanches in 1856, a time when Anglo animosity toward Indians on the Texas frontier was perhaps at its most vociferous.[18]

The image of ruthless Comanche warriors killing and taking captive the Anglo settlers was used to justify first Anglo occupation of their lands and later the establishment of an independent Anglo-American government and militia to protect the frontier better (Kavanagh 1986:107–108). It was during this period that narratives describing the experiences of Anglo women and children taken captive by Comanches became a popular genre of literature, contributing to the Comanches' reputation for ferocity and savagery.[19]

Their reputation, however, masked the integral redistributive role that Comanches played in the political economy of the Great Plains and the American Southwest among various Euro-American interests during the eighteenth and nineteenth centuries. Through their trading relationships with peoples of the northern Plains, Anglo traders, and the so-called comancheros of New Mexico, Comanche bands were important sources of cattle and horses. Comanche trade was crucial to the New Mexican economy from the mid eighteenth century to the early 1870s and was a significant element of the Texan, Louisianan and Missourian economies up to the Civil War (Kenner 1969).

The Comanches' role as middlemen in the multicultural Plains economy allowed them to survive what would otherwise have been catastrophic changes in the Plains environment.[20] By 1847, Comanches were experiencing considerable difficulty finding bison and other herd animals.[21] As Special Agent Neighbors noted in a report to the Indian commissioner, "buffalo and other game have almost entirely disappeared from our prairies."[22] While this scarcity may have been partly a consequence of Anglo hunters, the phenomenon was general throughout the Plains in the late 1840s and may have resulted from an underlying ecological cause (Richardson 1933:172–177; Fowler 1982:21–22). In response, Comanches and other Plains peoples shifted their economies more toward raiding and trading (Fowler 1982:24–25). Agent Neighbors observed in a letter of November 21, 1853: "The great excuse now given for their acts of plunder is that they cannot subsist of any other means." As a result, Comanches came more and more into conflict with Texan and U.S. military forces. By the 1840s, Texas settlers had come to view Comanches more as a threat to their economic success than as a source of goods.[23]

The Comanche bands that raided into Texas and Mexico were known, by the Indian agents at least, as the "upper" or "northern" Comanches. In contrast, those bands that spent considerable time in Texas under peaceful circumstances were known as the "lower" or "southern" Comanches.[24] The distinction between upper and lower Comanche bands was largely an administrative convenience to distinguish between the actions taken by different Indian agencies, each reporting to a different superintendency, one responsible for Indian relations in Texas and one for Indian relations on the central Plains.[25] This administrative distinction, however, had significant consequences for Comanche-Anglo relations from 1847 to 1858, at which point all Comanche bands were moved north of the Red River. In many respects, the "upper" vs. "lower" Comanche distinction was similar to the earlier "eastern" vs. "western" distinction made by the Spanish.

The upper, or northern, Comanche bands were portrayed as responsible for most of the raiding activities of the 1840s and 1850s in Texas and Mexico (Wallace and Hoebel 1952:302–303; Winfrey and Day 1966, 3:88; Thurman 1980:64). The lower bands were portrayed as relatively peaceful, engaging in "lawful" trade with Anglos. The policy of the Indian agents in Texas was to encourage the nonraiding activities of the lower bands. At the same time, Texas Indian agents frequently advocated the use of greater military force to curb the raiding activities of the upper Comanche bands. The Upper Platte and Upper Arkansas agents were, however, more concerned with the behavior of Comanches within their administrative territories, so they frequently gave out presents, rations, and annuities to promote good relations to the same upper Comanche bands that the Texas agents accused of raiding Anglo settlements south of the Red River.[26]

Once again, Euro-Americans rationalized Comanche actions into two categories, each reflecting a different economic motivation based on the dynamics of the Euro-American political economy. For those Comanches living in Texas, it was necessary to come to some accommodation with the Anglo population to allow continued trade. Ultimately this accommodation took the form of reservations, established in 1855. These were meant to provide enclaves where Comanches would be protected from increasingly hostile Anglo settlers and on which Comanche-Anglo trade was carefully regulated.[27] While the reservations became the base for those so-called lower Comanches directly engaged in trade with Anglos, they never attracted more than 450 Comanches at any one time (Neighbours 1975:163; Thurman 1980:64). Comanches living outside of Texas had to reach an accommodation with the Upper Platte and Upper Arkansas agents so that they could have access to licensed traders, retain a safe home range for their families, and be relatively free from military interference.

In each case, however, the accommodations were reached between band leaders and government officials. It was in the interest of the Comanche leaders to maintain good relations with the Anglo authorities of their territories; indeed, the ability to maintain access to trade and shield their followers from Euro-American pressures may be thought of as one of their primary attractions as leaders. Comanche leaders, however, did not constitute the whole of the Comanche community. The Comanches who populated the bands did not labor under the same administrative divisions as the Indian agents and did not recognize the same upper and lower divisions. Instead, they moved about between bands and U.S. territories as changing economic circumstances dictated. Agent Neighbors described the relations of the so-called lower and upper bands in 1853:

Altho the Comanches are divided into several bands, they keep up continual intercourse with each other, and are equally engaged in their depredations and war parties. Whenever a chief from one of the upper bands starts to Mexico or to any point on our frontier, they send runners to the lower bands, and all their warriors join him, so they are in fact but one people. Consequently, altho the chiefs with whom we have intercourse may be disposed to remain friendly, it is impossible for them to restrain their warriors, and if a depredation is committed, it is impossible to reach the individuals from the fact that as soon as the depredation is committed, he leaves his band and joins his relations in one of the upper bands so that in the present arrangement there is no responsibility.[28]

In this instance, the Euro-American propensity for categorizing Comanche actions into general classes worked in favor of the Comanches. A small group of Comanche "chiefs" and their followers were able to remain in Texas and exploit the possibilities of Anglo trade there as lower-band Comanches, while the larger population of Comanches based their families outside the jurisdiction of Texas authorities and took advantage of the opportunity to raid into Texas and Mexico. Individual warriors moved between upper and lower bands according to their own interests. As will be seen later in this chapter, the decentralized structure of the Comanche community made this fluid situation possible. Ultimately, though, the economic benefits of Comanche trade lessened as the Anglo population of Texas and the eastern United States became able to supply themselves with horses, and in 1858 Anglo settlers, through the constant harassment of reservation residents, forced the federal authorities to remove all Comanches to north of the Red River.[29] In late 1858, both lower and upper bands were reported to be actively raiding Texas settlements.[30]

Relations with Comanches during the Civil War were a fairly low priority for both the United States and the Confederacy (Wallace and Hoebel 1952:303).[31] The Indian agency correspondence files and annual reports for the period of the war tell more of the disorganization of the Indian service than of Comanche activities. During this period Comanches continued to raid into Mexico and Texas and to engage in trade with Anglos on the Upper Arkansas and into New Mexico (Wallace and Hoebel 1952:305; Thurman 1980:65).[32] The Civil War nevertheless was a watershed in Anglo-American–Comanche relations. At its conclusion, Anglo-American settlers were poised to overrun the southern Plains. Prior to the war, Comanches had been a necessary, if difficult, factor in western development. After the war they became, in Richardson's (1933) term, a barrier.

Postbellum federal Indian policy on the southern Plains was largely a response to increased raiding by Comanches, Kiowas, and others for cattle in Texas and Kansas, supported by New Mexican traders. These raids threatened economic expansion and, unlike the prewar period, did not bring sufficient economic benefits to other sectors of the Anglo-American economy. Between 1865 and 1867, Indian agents and military commanders competed with one another for influence over the Anglo-American response (Hagan 1976:23–25). The Indian Office, represented by Agent Leavenworth and abetted by prominent New Mexicans who benefited from the comanchero trade, attempted to negotiate an accommodation with Comanche leaders. The War Department, allied with Texan, Kansan, and Coloradan settlers who were ready to raise militias to crush the remaining "wild" Indians, wanted to initiate a systematic military campaign. Faced with these two alternatives, Comanche leaders entered into treaties in 1865 and 1867 in which they agreed to give up nomadic hunting and raiding in exchange for government annuities and reservations (Hagan 1976:21, 39). These were promises easily made at the time because the federal government was not yet in a position to establish and maintain a Comanche reservation. Comanches could once again satisfy Euro-American fears without materially altering their way of life.

The volume of the comanchero trade in 1868 and 1869, however, forced further U.S. action. Between 1868 and 1875, the military took the field to contain Comanche raiding (Hagan 1976:51–56). Despite the image perpetuated by countless movies, though, Plains Indian resistance to the increasing Anglo presence on the Plains in the late nineteenth century was undercut by economics, not military defeat. The Treaty of Medicine Lodge in 1867 provided inducements, in the form of annuities, for bands to accept reservations in Indian Territory.[33] These inducements became increasingly attractive as Anglo hunters accelerated the decline of the bison herds that had begun in the 1840s and as authorities finally brought the comanchero trade under control in New Mexico and Colorado (Richardson 1933:172–177; Kenner 1969:201–209). Though Comanches continued to raid Texas as late as 1875, they were outnumbered by the cavalry units and militias that patrolled the open Plains and, perhaps more telling, they no longer constituted a significant economic force (Winfrey and Day 1966, 4:365, 369–372).

From 1869 to 1875, Comanche bands gradually took advantage of treaty inducements while expanding the range of their hunting, raiding, and trading activities (Wallace and Hoebel 1952:313). Comanches used the agency and reservation in Indian Territory in much the same way they had used the Texas Indian agency and reservations—as a refuge from attack and as an alternate source of subsistence. By 1871 a core of Comanche leaders and their followers were operating on the Staked Plains to the west of the reservation, drawing personnel from bands on the reservation for hunting and raiding.[34] When subsistence or military pressures became too great, those personnel flowed back to the leaders of reservation bands, who had established beneficial relationships with Indian agency officials that included periodic rations.

At last, in 1874 and 1875 the subsistence pressures became too great for Comanche bands outside the reservation. During the winter of 1874–75, nearly all the Comanches came in to the reservation and stayed (Wallace and Hoebel 1952:328). This constituted, for the first time in their history, a gathering of the whole Comanche community. As a result of two outbreaks of smallpox and one of cholera in 1816, 1839–40, and 1849, and the increased difficulty in finding food over the previous three decades, there were fewer than 1,600 Comanches present (Ewers 1973:108; Hagan 1976:139).

Curiously, while Wallace and Hoebel note the increasing economic dependence of the Comanches on Anglo sources, they nevertheless portray the battles of Adobe Walls and Palo Duro Canyon in 1874 as the decisive events in Comanche-Anglo relations prior to the reservation period (Wallace and Hoebel 1952:325–327) despite the fact that few Comanches were killed in these encounters, and no territorial advantages were won or lost. Wallace and Hoebel's descriptions of the military confrontations, however, are full of the sort of drama with which western movies conclude: "This time there were to be no peace councils, no presents. The Comanches were licked" (1952:327).

As some members of the present-day Comanche community recount their history, however, those last nomadic bands of Comanches came in to the reservation during the winter of 1874–1875 not out of a sense of military defeat but because they could not find anything on the Plains to eat. The problem that Comanches faced in the winter of 1875 was how to continue to provide a subsistence base for their community.

ANTHROPOLOGICAL CONCEPTIONS OF "COMANCHE"

Anthropological images of Comanches have focused almost exclusively on the prereservation period. Despite the attempts of Euro-American governments in the eighteenth and nineteenth centuries to treat them as a single political entity, Comanches during the prereservation period are an especially apt example of the incongruity of social group and cultural community. Indeed, it is for that disparity that Comanches chiefly have been known in the anthropological literature.

Ralph Linton and E. Adamson Hoebel, who together conducted the first extended field research with Comanche people, in 1933, have been primarily responsible for shaping the anthropological image of Comanches.[35] Their accounts of Comanche social organization have emphasized Comanches' minimal use of formal structures and institutions to organize their community. Linton's (1936, 1949, 1955) explanation of Comanche social organization was that Comanches, as a people, possessed a minimal culture and survived by opportunistically incorporating elements from other cultures in response to changing social conditions. Kardiner's (1949) psychological analysis of Comanche society, based on Linton's fieldwork, emphasized the relatively permissive child-rearing practices of prereservation Comanche families as a basis for that social individualism and cultural plasticity.

Wallace and Hoebel sharpened Linton's depiction of Comanches by suggesting a tension between "Comanche notions of individual rights and tribal standards of right conduct" (1952:224).[36] This view was derived not only from Linton and Kardiner but also from Hoebel's (1940, 1954) work on Comanche "law," which he characterized as "individualism checked at critical points by social care for other individuals" (1954:176). Hoebel attributed the individualism to the Comanches' Shoshonean roots and the social care to the necessity for cooperation in larger groups in the Plains environment (Hoebel 1940:129; Wallace and Hoebel 1952:33).

Because Hoebel's works have come to be regarded as the standard accounts of both the Comanches (e.g., Hoebel 1940; Wallace and Hoebel 1952) and the Cheyennes (e.g., Llewellyn and Hoebel 1941; Hoebel 1960), the two peoples have frequently been contrasted, with "Comanche" signifying a minimal, individualistic form of social and ceremonial organization, and "Cheyenne" a centralized, institutionalized form (see Hoebel 1954, 1977; Lowie 1954; Eggan 1966; Driver 1969; Edgerton 1985). Hoebel has described Comanches as "politically naive" (1954:142), their cultural background as "meager" (1954:128), and their religious practices and beliefs as "vaguely defined and almost wholly devoid of ceremonial structure" (1954:129). He has also offered the generalization that "Comanches underformalized their conception of their own behavior" (1940:6).

Hoebel and other Plains scholars have been at some pains to try to explain this state of affairs, especially because it contrasts with the more formal, institutionalized model of "Plains Indian" social organization that has been the accepted anthropological wisdom for most of the twentieth century (see Wissler 1914, 1926; Kroeber 1939; Lowie 1954; Oliver 1962). In describing the internal organization of the prereservation Comanche community, anthropologists have either described Comanches as an exception to the classic model of postcontact Plains social configuration—stubbornly resistant to the changing social conditions surrounding their everyday lives—or attempted to force what we know of Comanche social organization into the structures of the classic model. Anthropologists of both camps have written of the "Comanche Problem," the "Comanche Anomaly" or the "Comanche Exception," indicating their preference for generalized categories and models in describing American Indian peoples.[37] The explanations offered for the Comanches' lack of centralized social institutions have focused mainly on the Shoshonean background of Comanche peoples (e.g., Mooney 1907:327–328; Hoebel 1954:29; Oliver 1962:71–76) and the unique ecological parameters of the southern Plains (e.g., Colson 1954; Tefft 1960, 1964; Bamforth 1988).

Shoshonean peoples of the Basin area already were known in anthropology for the small size of their social units and their minimal social structure (Lowie 1909, 1924; Steward 1938). By arguing that Comanches had only recently been separated from their Shoshone relatives, some anthropologists have claimed that Comanches did not have the time to develop a more formal social structure (Oliver 1962). Other anthropologists argued that Comanches had no motivation for developing a more formal social structure because the southern Plains was better stocked with bison than the central and northern Plains, making hunting an easier, smaller-scale task (Colson 1954). Recently, Bamforth (1988) has defended the classic Plains model by arguing that Comanches did conform to it. Bamforth's argument is the inverse of Colson's, holding that the southern Plains had less dense and less predictable bison populations than the northern Plains and so was less likely to support larger, more centralized social units for long periods. Thus Comanche social units were predictable from the Plains environment they inhabited. Like other explanations of Comanche social organization, this has the same intellectual objective of preserving the concept of "Plains Indians" as a general category.

When considered in the light of Comanche–Euro-American relations prior to 1875, however, none of these explanations holds up. As we have seen, for at least 175 years Comanche actions were tightly bound up in the fabric of the Euro-American-dominated Plains political economy. Comanches were neither isolated nor insulated from the historical processes that constrained the social organization of other Plains peoples. And while the Comanche economy included bison as a significant component, Comanche social organization after 1700 was not predicated exclusively, or even primarily, upon the constraints of bison hunting.

REVISIONIST IMAGES OF SOCIAL AND CULTURAL STRUCTURE

Recently, three scholars have produced revisionist studies of the Comanches, one focusing on religion (Gelo 1986) and the other two on social organization (Thurman 1980, 1982, 1987; Kavanagh 1986). These scholars assume that Linton and Hoebel painted too simple a picture of the Comanche cultural and social worlds. Their studies attempt to detail previously unnoticed structures in Comanche beliefs and social organization, thus locating Comanches more securely in a "Plains" context. Gelo argues for a unified Comanche religion underlying a variety of ritual expressions, past and present. Kavanagh and Thurman attempt to reconstruct a more integrated and structured system of relationships among the nomadic Comanche bands prior to the reservation period, arguing for a previously unnoticed tradition of Comanche political organization.

These scholars have recognized the disparity between the individualistic, minimalist stereotype of Comanche society and belief and the historical fact of a shared Comanche community. At the heart of this disparity is the apparent disjunction between the mutually exclusive, autonomous bands in which people resided and interacted every day and the inclusive linguistic and cultural community that subsumed the various bands. Gelo, Thurman, and Kavanagh have tried to eliminate that contradictory appearance by discovering underlying cultural and social structures that tend to validate the singular image of the Euro-American category, "Comanche."

Gelo attempts to apply Lévi-Strauss's style of structural analysis to the symbolic dimensions of Comanche ritual and so to uncover an underlying (and relatively unchanging) Comanche cultural framework. The difficulty with this approach is that it lacks articulation with Comanche social organization. Gelo does not concern himself with the ways in which cultural frameworks are used by Comanches in everyday social interaction. In many respects, Gelo treats his version of "Comanche religion" as an artifact separate from the social reality of the Comanche community, a strategy that allows him to substitute Euro-American models of Comanche "culture" for the people themselves.[38]

Kavanagh's arguments for a more centralized and institutionalized Comanche social organization are based primarily on the Euro-American practice of attempting to promote and legitimate particular Comanche leaders as "principal chiefs" or "generals-in-chief." Kavanagh (1986:280) suggests that the ability of a leader to get along with Europeans was crucial to the success of Comanche social groups in the eighteenth and nineteenth centuries. Thus, in Kavanagh's (1986:291) interpretation, Euro-Americans became one of the sources of the power and authority of Comanche leaders. These leaders were maintained in office by gifts of physical symbols that represented them as the authorized conduits of Euro-American power, prestige, and most important, trade goods. In this way, Spanish, Texan, and Anglo-American governments encouraged Comanche bands to act as larger-scale political units, which have become known as the primary divisions of Comanche society (Kavanagh 1986:281–291). Each of these divisions, such as the Yamparika or the Penetaka, was comprised of the smaller local or residence bands that were the primary social groups in which Comanches lived and moved during most of the year.

Working from contemporaneous documents, Kavanagh (1986:309) has reconstructed the successions of principal chiefs for different divisions, using as his criterion the official conferral or denial of such recognition by a Euro-American colonial administrator (see Kavanagh 1986:293–294). He offers these reconstructed successions as evidence that Comanches did move toward the same kind of formal, centralized, institutional social organization found among other Plains peoples. The divisions gave Comanche social organization the coordination Kavanagh believes was needed to enable Comanche leaders to extract and control the maximum benefit from Euro-American trade.

Thurman (1980:49), like Kavanagh, also argues that, by the nineteenth century, Comanches were organized much like any other "typical Plains tribe." Thurman (1982:578) bases this conclusion on evidence he adduces to indicate that Comanches had soldier societies and head chiefs, and frequently held Sun Dances. He proposes that Comanches were organized into "supraband" polities (i.e., divisions), each of which Thurman (1987:554) defines as a "tribe" made up of smaller subsistence bands, with military societies organized in each polity, cross-cutting membership in the subsistence bands. Each of these suprabands had a head chief, the leader of one of the constituent subsistence bands who was recognized as such through validation and practice rather than in any formal selection process.

Like Kavanagh, Thurman (1980:52) does not attempt to link the divisions or suprabands apart from the occasional recognition of a principal chief. Thurman's argument for a more structured Comanche social organization differs from Kavanagh's, however, in that Thurman emphasizes ecology as the prime motivation for nineteenth-century Comanche social organization, while Kavanagh emphasizes Euro-American contact and trade. Thurman (1980:50) points out that the acquisition of horses made larger gatherings possible. It is this development that, in Thurman's view, made the divisional or supraband polities the most significant unit of Comanche social organization and that made Comanche social organization much like that of other "typical" Plains societies. In a sense, Kavanagh's interpretation also turns upon the acquisition of horses, but he locates the significance in the political economy of trade that horses made possible, not in the mobility they offered.

By evolving Comanche social organization from Shoshonean bands to Plains tribes or suprabands, Kavanagh and Thurman make Comanches fit into anthropological expectations for mounted nomadic peoples. Both Kavanagh and Thurman take the divisions or suprabands to be the moving force in Comanche history, defining territories, raiding activities, Euro-American relations, and forms of internal social organization. Kavanagh's "Big Man" theory of Comanche politics works well with respect to Comanche–Euro-American interaction. Comanches used Euro-American expectations about strong central authority figures to negotiate their economic transactions and political relations with Euro-American agents more successfully. Several recent studies of Plains communities (Fowler 1982, 1987; Moore 1988) have emphasized the importance of intermediary leaders in Indian–Euro-American relations on the Plains, as native economies became increasingly dependent on Euro-American trade in the late eighteenth and the nineteenth centuries. The question, though, is whether the status of Comanche leaders or "Big Men" in relation to Euro-Americans accurately reflects the internal organization of Comanche social units.

The division has always seemed promising as the basic structure of Comanche society (see, e.g., Mooney 1907; Lowie 1915, 1954; Hoebel 1940; Linton 1955). Divisions have received considerable attention from ethnohistorians as glosses upon the activities of the subsistence bands they are taken to subsume. Often, where the actions of Comanche peoples are not linked under the rubric "Comanche" they are attributed to a collective "Yamparika" or "Penetaka" or some other division. In anthropological summaries of Comanche society, the divisions have been used as a handy gloss on the internal organization of the larger community. Divisional or supraband categories are, however, most often cited without examination of how they were used by Comanches to organize their relations with one another. And where some effort has been made to characterize the sociological significance of Comanche divisions, as Thurman and Kavanagh have done, the assumption is that these social units functioned in the same way as higher-level band organizations among other "typical" Plains peoples.

In revising Comanche history, Kavanagh and Thurman have resorted to two of the classic images of the Euro-American conception of Plains Indians: paramount chiefs and tribes. While evidence for both may be found in Comanche–Euro-American relations from 1700 to 1875, there remains some question as to whether similar evidence exists in Comanche-Comanche relations. Attending to Comanches' relations with one another will tell us more about what it is, and has been, to "be Comanche" than will attending to Comanche-Anglo interaction and the external bounding of the Comanche community. Of course, as Fowler has emphasized, it is important to keep in mind that intracommunity innovations are also adaptations to changes in external, Anglo-dominated social conditions, especially as those conditions constrain intracommunity interaction.

REINTERPRETING THE SIGN "COMANCHE"

As we have seen, in describing the internal organization of the Comanche community during the prereservation period, anthropologists have either held Comanches out as an exception to the classic model of postcontact Plains social configuration, stubbornly resistant to changing social conditions, or have attempted to force what we know of Comanche social organization into the structure of the classic model. Certainly the social conditions in which all Plains peoples were caught up during the eighteenth and nine-teenth centuries significantly changed the constraints on group formation and social gathering. It has been argued, for instance, that horses made possible larger social units on the Plains (e.g., Holder 1970; Thurman 1980; Moore 1988) and that participation in Euro-American trade required differ-ent patterns of interaction (e.g., Fowler 1982; Moore 1988). To assert that Comanches were immune to the evolving Euro-American-dominated politi-cal economy of the Plains is simply to ignore history.[39] Indeed, the studies of Hoebel and Linton, which portray Comanches as Shoshones on the Plains, are artifacts of a period in anthropology in which little account was taken of the historical dimension of the social worlds of native peoples.

At the same time, however, one would be equally mistaken to assert that Euro-American contacts so dominated the social lives of Plains peoples as to cause each community to organize the interactions of its members according to the same general model.[40] In giving priority to Comanche–Euro-American interaction in the organization of political relations within the Comanche community, Kavanagh and Thurman replicate the time-worn Eurocentric belief that contact with Europeans caused Indian peoples to reorient their social worlds to the interethnic boundaries between Euro-American and Indian. In arguing that Comanches were organized in unified tribal polities, Kavanagh and Thurman simply plug them into traditional scholarly models of Plains social organization. These models were them-selves influenced by Euro-American concepts of politics, society, and struc-ture in which authority is distributed in a hierarchy of social units as leaders and members both act within a codified framework of rights and obliga-tions.[41] While it is probably impossible to reconstruct Comanche social or-ganization as it existed before European presence, it is possible to describe how Comanches adapted to the growing Euro-American influence on the social conditions of Plains life in ways that were distinctively Comanche.

COMANCHE SOCIAL UNITS

Those peoples whom Europeans called Comanches called themselves /numina/ meaning "the people," a designation based on their perceived dif-ferences in the conventions and style of social interaction from other peoples, both Indian and European. As already noted, this common identity was a symbol of a shared cultural community that informed social interaction but not of a structured organization of the nomadic bands within which Com-anches interacted.

Comanches participated in at least five social units. The first was comprised of those relatives who resided in the same camp, usually an extended rather than nuclear family. The second was the residence, or local, band, made up of men and their extended families who were allied with a particular leader or headman. The third was the division, which was comprised of residence bands exploiting the same territory. The fourth was the focused-activity group, which was formed for a specific activity and which dissolved at the conclusion of that activity. The fifth was the Comanche community as a whole, defined by a shared communicative competence.

Extended families were formed around senior men, often two or more brothers, and constituted private areas of social interaction (Hoebel 1939:447). When personal ties failed to overcome breakdowns of communication within an extended family, the unit broke apart rather than resolving the conflict (Hoebel 1940). Otherwise, extended families acted as social extensions of the senior men. While an extended family sometimes was coterminus with the residence band, there was a marked advantage in two or more extended families cooperating in the same residence band, creating a larger work unit (Wallace and Hoebel 1952:23). Reported band sizes range all the way from the essentially private region of the extended family (ten to thirty persons) to public aggregations of several hundred individuals (Hoebel 1940:11). In 1772, De Mezieres described Comanche residence bands as follows: "[Comanches] divide themselves into an infinite number of little bands for the purpose of seeking better pastures for their horses, and cattle [bison] for their own food. This explains why they separate from their chiefs, following out their individual whims, and doing damage which the others can neither prevent nor remedy when it comes to their notice" (Bolton 1914, 1:297).

Whether as a single extended family or as an alliance of extended families, the primary choice in group affiliation that Comanches made was with respect to their residence band. The residence band constituted those persons who were accessible to one another on an everyday basis for most of the year. Divisional affiliation and focused-activity-group participation, in contrast, represented discrete gatherings of residence band members for limited periods.[42] These latter two social units were largely functions of residence band membership, because participation in both depended on geographical proximity as determined by residence-band movement and location. Burnett described divisions and residence bands in 1818 as follows:

These three great national parties [divisions], are subdivided into captaincies or villages, to each of which is appointed a chief, whose distinction seems to consist rather in name than authority. His name, however, gives title to the flying village, and is useful in this respect, as some sign of discrimination is necessary and they can derive none from locality. These subdivisions are various and contingent, each member being at liberty to withdraw from one village and unite with another, as caprice or convenience may dictate. (Wallace 1954:124)

Residence bands were held together by the relationship between a successful, popular leader or group of leaders and those who chose to follow him or them (Wallace and Hoebel 1952:23, 210–212). There was, in this, no self-reproducing social structure in which individuals succeeded to or inherited structurally defined roles or offices, although some of the reputation (and social following) of a popular leader might attach itself to a kinsperson or associate (Wallace and Hoebel 1952:211). Kills Something explained how a man became a leader in this way in 1933: "No one made him such; he just got that way" (Wallace and Hoebel 1952:211).[43] There is evidence that particularly popular leaders sometimes dominated a number of residence bands (see John 1975; Kavanagh 1986), but this, too, was based on personal reputation rather than an institutional structure.

Hoebel noted that "personal power was the recognized basis of social relations between men" (1954:137),[44] but what Hoebel called "personal power" was in fact social face. In his descriptions of Comanche leadership, Hoebel (1940) repeatedly made the point that a Comanche war leader became one through feats in battle, with no formal installation, term, or even office. In other words, Comanche war leaders were those men who engaged in public behavior that enhanced their moral worth in the eyes of their fellows. Among such behavior was counting coup, refusing to retreat in the face of an enemy, and going to the aid of a dismounted comrade (Hoebel 1940:34–35). Each of these actions, when committed in the presence of other Comanches, contributed to the reputation of a warrior and carried over to a man's reputation once he retired from warfare. However, should a recognized leader decline to undertake any of these actions, he would lose face and his position of leadership: "A war chief whose nerve failed him in a dangerous position could retreat—by giving up his right to wear the bonnet. He could cast it off and flee for his life. But he was a man without status thenceforth, for he could never again regain the bonnet and its rank. Life certainly would have been miserable from that point onward. Men hailed him as 'elder sister'" (Hoebel 1940:35).

Neighbors (1853:130) observes that only actions in public gatherings contributed to or detracted from a war leader's reputation. Actions in private regions did not affect one's public face unless they were publicly commented upon in a manner that made them unavoidable challenges to one's moral worth. The same applied to "peace chiefs," who were men who engaged in public displays of generosity (Hoebel 1940:18), thereby enhancing their moral worth in the eyes of others. Again, to behave otherwise in public gatherings would be to lose face and forfeit the recognition of other band members.

Although Hoebel attempts to make a case for an institutional distinction between "war leaders" and "peace leaders," these might better be labeled "focused-activity-group leaders" and "residence-band leaders," with some overlap between the two categories. Individual warriors with a reputation for bravery could put together focused-activity groups for raiding or military purposes without possessing any special authority outside of those groups (Hoebel 1940:22). At the same time, no strict rule prevented a so-called war leader from also functioning as a peace leader for a residence band, and those Comanches with stronger reputations probably did so (Hoebel 1940:20). Certainly a successful war leader had to be not only brave but also generous in the distribution of the spoils of a successful raid or military encounter. Similarly, a man who lost face by not demonstrating qualities of bravery would not likely be recognized as a residence-band leader or peace chief.

Euro-American misconceptions of "eastern" and "western" Comanches during the period between 1800 and 1820 and of "upper" and "lower" Comanche bands during the 1840s and 1850s give us perhaps the best insight into whatever distinction Comanches did make between their leaders. The "western" and "lower" Comanche leaders were primarily intermediaries who specialized in trading the spoils captured by focused-activity-group leaders. As such, peace was indeed the policy of the "western" and "lower" Comanche leaders, but it was peace with Euro-Americans, not the civil regulation of intracommunity relations that the term "peace chief" sometimes is used to imply. In contrast, "eastern" and "upper" Comanche leaders were more frequently engaged in forming focused-activity groups for raiding. Though many of these leaders also were responsible for residence bands, they derived the larger part of the economic support for their followings from goods obtained in raids rather than from service as middlemen in Indian-Anglo trade.

Raiding, however, together with military activity focused around revenge, was clearly an individual enterprise, not an extension of residence or divisional memberships (Wallace and Hoebel 1952:250–251). Of course, participation in a raid would be limited to those men in close proximity to each other and would include many warriors with the same residence band and divisional identities. A revenge party would be further limited to the deceased's relatives, many of whom would be members of the same residence band. Still, the point is that participation in these activities was neither restricted nor compelled by band membership but was structured according to interpersonal relationships among warriors. As Ruíz observed in 1828, "For the duration of the campaign the Comanches follow the warrior who organized the venture. At the end of war they are free to go where they please, although many leave before the campaign's end. They are not responsible to anyone. The ones who continue fighting gossip about these deserters" (1972:13).[45]

Raiding or war parties did not even require the presence of an established leader but might be made up solely of young warriors out to make their own reputations.[46] Euro-American archives are full of observations of small-scale focused-activity groups undertaking economic and military operations on their own initiative, regulated primarily by their shared standards for public interaction. While divisional gatherings were undoubtedly useful settings in which to recruit participation in these activities, participants often crossed divisional boundaries.[47] Although little information is available on Comanche military societies, they were probably organized on the basis of repeated patterns in focused-activity-group formation that cut across residence band boundaries.[48] As Cabaya told Hugh Scott in the late 1890s, "The Comanches have soldier bands that are common to all the Comanches and when they went to war a man took a pipe around to the different bands. . . . When we came together the soldiers had their own dances[.] [E]ach company might have men from every Comanche band in it."[49]

Comanches did participate in larger-scale military activities, usually focused around the reputation of a particularly popular leader. Often participation in these campaigns cut across divisional lines. The Battle of Adobe Walls (1874), the last concerted Comanche effort against Anglo forces, was an example of this type of activity. Those Comanches who participated did so out of a belief in the power of the leaders of that action, among whom were Eschiti and Quanah (Wallace and Hoebel 1952:324–325). Large numbers of Comanche warriors had participated in prior major military actions, again primarily out of respect for the publicly demonstrated moral worth of the leaders of those engagements (John 1975:412–413, 685–688).

Though perhaps to a lesser extent than the more prominent residence-band and focused-activity-group leaders, all Comanche men were held to the same public standards for the enhancement and maintenance of face. Public displays of bravery and generosity were rewarded with the esteem of other band members and were counted separately from actions in private social settings. Obviously, Comanche social organization depended to a great extent on the desire to maintain and enhance one's face in public contexts.

As David Burnett noted in 1818: "Goodness, however, in their [the Comanches'] system of ethics, is a qualified term that has reference to acts of public benefit and renown" (Wallace 1954:126).

Participation in residence bands and focused-activity groups was supported in part by social conditions that mitigated breakdowns in social interaction. These conditions were of two kinds: kinship relations and an institutionalized form of friendship through which kin terms were extended. The Comanche kin-term system recognized persons as kin within the following dimensions: (1) three generations senior and two generations junior in lineal depth; (2) no limitation in the collateral relationships that might be recognized through any of those lineal relatives; and (3) one marriage relationship for affines, who might be recognized through either lineal or collateral relatives. As Gladwin observes, a Comanche could, if sufficiently motivated, identify some genealogical link with any other Comanche and thus "gain admittance to the in-group of the addressee, and the mutual support and esteem there expected" (1948:77).

From a practical point of view, though, this network was limited by the shorter lifespan of those who led a nomadic existence, which tended to narrow the lineal depth of kin networks; by prohibitions on mentioning the name of a deceased relative who might be the key to "discovering" a kin relationship; and by a disinclination to go over genealogies within the family so that children might be aware of kin whom they had never met (Gladwin 1948:76). Further, there were advantages in having a smaller kin network. Since Comanches were prohibited from marrying anyone recognized as kin, a smaller network resulted in a larger number of potential spouses (Wallace and Hoebel 1952:140). Also, kinship entailed social obligations that compelled supportive interaction and thus limited individual choice and the movement of personnel among social units.

Institutionalized friendships between persons of the same sex allowed Comanches who resided together or cooperated in political or economic activities but who were not genealogically related to signal a similarly compelling obligation to support mutual interaction not only with one another but also among their respective extended families (Gladwin 1948:91–92). This was probably the primary means by which extended families were linked within a residence band, thus extending some sense of a supportive private region of interaction throughout the entire band. As Gladwin (1948:91) notes, though, there is evidence that these friendships were not always life-long, with new friends replacing old as the self-interest of those involved changed.

While private regions dictated by kinship and friendship relations no doubt held together many Comanche social units, such as extended families and smaller residence bands and focused-activity groups, it was the public regions of Comanche social life that held together larger social units and made possible adaptive, often necessary, changes in social organization. Public regulation of social interaction also served to reinforce the threads of private relations out of which were knitted the fabric of Comanche social life. When a breakdown did occur, as might happen even among kin or friends, one always had the option of pulling up stakes and moving to another social unit or forming a new unit (Wallace and Hoebel 1952:23). This put a premium on forms of social organization that subjected members to shared standards of interaction, connecting them as participants in the same social unit and thus supplementing the many different private bonds that connected them as individuals.

The importance of impression management in intragroup organization is well documented in Hoebel's (1940) study of Comanche political organization and "law-ways."[50] Although Hoebel was trying to represent a codified version of Comanche social organization, the examples he adduces are clearly reflections of standards of social life arising from units and processes of public interaction rather than rules of social structure institutionalized in enduring social units and relationships. For instance, in discussing "adultery and wife-stealing," Hoebel (1940:49–65) consistently encounters a distinction between public and private knowledge of one's wife's misbehavior. It was only when knowledge of adulterous activity became public,[51] thus threatening the "face" of the husband in intraband interaction, that it became necessary for the husband to publicly restore his sense of moral worth by demanding some sort of recompense from the other man: "Adultery and taking another's wife were direct attacks upon the prestige of the wife's husband. Both acts were unmistakable challenges which could not be ignored by the man who would maintain enough face to make life livable. Ridicule was the weapon used by society to cause a man to proceed after the cause for action had become public" (Hoebel 1940:50).

In the examples given by Hoebel's informants, the actions taken by "wronged" husbands are often dramatically public, demanding the attention of the entire band.[52] When an intermediary was drawn into domestic disputes—almost always to aid the husband against a more powerful man in the band—this was accomplished by appealing to the intermediary's self-esteem: "A war leader who refused to accept the request for aid in prosecution was to be deemed unworthy of his rank, for it was imputed he feared the defendant. No war leader could admit fear" (Hoebel 1940:64).

In contrast to transgressions committed in public contexts, adultery or homicide committed within the bounds of a family unit (that is, among persons who shared compelling personal ties and thus occupied a private region of interaction) was a private matter that had no public dimension even when known to everyone in the band. For instance, a man could kill his wife and face no public retribution because this was considered a private, family matter (Hoebel 1940:73). Even when transgressions such as adultery and assault were committed among male kin,[53] kin relations were sufficiently compelling to resolve the breakdown in interaction, and the failure to address the transgressions publicly was not counted as a threat to one's face. However, when transgressions that could not be glossed over occurred among kin, publicly redressing the loss of face was often considered more damaging to one's face than the initial transgression. In some of these instances, Comanches committed suicide instead (Hoebel 1940:112–117). If, though, persons whose faces were publicly at risk were impervious to community opinion, Comanches had no resort to other, formal means to enforce those standards. Thus, while Comanches disapproved of incest, those individuals who were willing to ignore the risk to their faces could blithely engage in openly incestuous relationships (Hoebel 1940:108–110). Similarly, Comanches accused of sorcery could avoid public sanction by denying the accusation and relying on the subsequent damage to their faces for protection, as other Comanches were unwilling to take on someone with a reputation for antisocial power (Hoebel 1940:91–92).

While this may seem a less compelling form of social organization than one in which rules and roles are more formally spelled out, there is evidence that it was in fact a smoothly functioning, tightly ordered system. There is, for instance, the observation of David Burnett in 1818:

> Notwithstanding the extreme laxity of their [the Comanches'] whole economy of government, and their entire exemption from legal restraint, they live together with a degree of harmony that would do credit to the most refined and best organized societies. The little bickerings and jealousies and inordinate strivings for thrift and distinction, that disquiet and mar the social circles of refinement, are unknown to the rude and simple children of nature. (Wallace 1954:125)

Smithwick, in writing of a three-month stay with a Comanche residence band in 1837, had a similar impression of Comanche social organization: "They were the most peaceable community I ever lived in. . . . I did not hear a single wrangle among the adult members" (1983:130).

In contrast to residence bands and focused-activity groups, Comanche divisions were not social groups. Instead, the divisions may be better understood as discrete gatherings focused around activities associated with larger-scale public social occasions, including performances of the Sun Dance.[54] Participation in these gatherings was channeled through the constituent residence bands; that is, one was a member of the division with which one's residence band and leader were affiliated. Each of the divisions was associated with a distinct territory within the Comanche range on the southern Plains, although these ranges or territories were not exclusive and often shifted (Wallace and Hoebel 1952:22).[55] Territory, to Comanches, was not some absolute plot of ground but was rather a matter of proximity. Divisions were comprised of residence bands that, because of territorial proximity, tended to have more frequent ties of kinship and marriage. Geographic proximity was important because it determined which residence bands (and their members) were potentially present to one another for a given divisional social occasion. As Robert Coffey put it in 1985, "In their travels they'd meet. Every clan had their territorial place."

Divisional identities most likely denoted shared participation in activities that were part of the round of seasonal nomadic movements, including hunting encampments and ceremonial performances. These activities took advantage of similar patterns of movement within the Comanche range, while activities like raiding often took Comanches outside of their accustomed ranges. Thus geography was an important factor in divisional participation.[56] Geography also explains why divisional identities did not persist beyond the opening of the reservation in 1875. They were based on social conditions constraining mutual presence in a nomadic context and were not realized as formal, self-reproducing social institutions (Hagan 1976:153–156). Once Comanches were established within the smaller reservation territory, they no longer required the mechanism of divisions to regulate nomadic residence units and their leaders.

Prior to the reservation period, however, some mechanism for regulating the competition for personnel and leadership was necessary in the absence of mutually exclusive social units, such as descent groups. The activities of popular leaders and the social units at their direction were ultimately regulated by divisional gatherings. The public nature of these gatherings and the cooperation required to organize them subjected those leaders and the social units they personified to standards of conduct that emphasized their own and others' moral worth. This public regulation also occurred in a more limited fashion within each residence band, as noted above. Focused activities, such as performances of the Sun Dance or councils of leaders called to discuss specific matters, would have entailed considerable cooperation from members of a number of residence bands, thus necessitating requisite concern for the faces of all involved.[57] Wallace and Hoebel, citing both twentieth-century informants and historical records, describe a council meeting of residence-band leaders within a divisional gathering as follows: "The entire meeting was conducted with strict formality and with a degree of courtesy that could hardly be exceeded. . . . Sometimes there were vast differences of opinion among the men, yet each was heard gravely and respectfully; and no matter how earnest the debate might become, no man ever interrupted the speaker, nor did anything like wrangling occur" (Wallace and Hoebel 1952:214).[58]

Divisions were important to Comanche social organization because, without the social regulation they offered, there were no public constraints on the actions of individual Comanche leaders and residence bands with respect to other leaders and bands. Comanche reliance on the reputation of a leader or leaders to hold an everyday nomadic group together meant that movement of personnel between bands was the rule rather than the exception (Wallace and Hoebel 1952:23). A Comanche leader who did not cooperate in mutual expressions of moral worth at a divisional gathering risked losing face, followers, and influence. In the absence of divisional gatherings, the Comanche community would have dissolved into residence band communities, each pursuing its own interests. Consequently, Comanches paid careful attention to divisional identities. These identities were explicitly signaled by differences in material culture such as dress, in dialect, and in cuisine, among other symbols. Whenever Comanches moved between residence bands affiliated with different divisions, people adopted the symbols of their new division: "[I]t was mandatory upon an individual to follow the customs of the group with which he lived in order to be socially accepted by his new associates, and this despite the frequent exchange of band allegiance and the interband marriages" (Wallace and Hoebel 1952:24).

Respect for divisional symbols was not simply a matter of inertial custom or the ease of social acceptance. Instead, these symbols were ritual markers of the public cooperation that existed within each division. Displaying the symbols and changing them when one changed divisions signaled a willingness to subject one's face to public regulation in that division. It was also a way of asserting one's social value as a participant in divisional gatherings. As noted above, some Comanche leaders were able to acquire a degree of authority that approximated control over a division or supraband or over the whole Comanche community. This control, however, was based on personal relations between a leader and his many followers and denoted the leader's ability to gather personnel for a specific activity, such as a raid or a council, rather than the formation of an enduring social group.

The limitation of Comanche leadership to personal authority creates a difficulty for Thurman's (1980) assertion that divisions or suprabands were the controlling polities of Comanche social life, and also for Kavanagh's (1986) claim that Comanches were united in multiband political alliances from the mid eighteenth century on. To be exercised effectively, personal authority requires physical presence.[59] The enduring fact of Plains ecology, however, was the constraint it placed on large gatherings, first through the distances over which pedestrian bands had to travel to be present to one another, and second through the limits of Comanche horse herds, which were among the largest on the Plains and which required considerable amounts of fresh grass each day (Bamforth 1988; Moore 1988:150–169). Divisional or supraband gatherings were effective arenas for political and other focused activities for short periods, but because there is no evidence of self-reproducing or institutional structures linking subsistence bands and establishing formal positions of leadership, divisions or suprabands are better understood as focused gatherings than as longstanding social groups.

The leaders who from time to time represented divisions or suprabands to Euro-American authorities were intermediaries with limited authority. They dealt with Euro-Americans on specific matters relating to Comanche–Euro-American interaction and were not "paramount" or "principal" leaders in the way that we usually employ these terms. In 1843, for instance, when a representative of the Texas Republic arrived in the village of a prominent Comanche leader to negotiate a truce, he was told that the leaders of the other bands associated with the division must be present to make a binding agreement (Winfrey and Day 1966:272). Hildreth, writing of the Dodge Expedition of 1831, quoted a Comanche leader, Ta-we-que-nah, on a similar process of consultation before reaching a political consensus: "I wish to be at peace with you. There are many bands of Comanches, I shall visit them all this year, and will say to them what you have said to me" (Hildreth 1836:170). Even when agreements were made with leaders to whom the authority for such an action had been delegated, it was necessary that they make subsequent contact with other leaders to ratify the accommodation informally (as Ecueracapa did in 1786).

Within the Comanche community, the authority of leadership was even weaker. Kavanagh (1986) is unable to demonstrate that the divisional leaders who were chosen as "principal" chiefs by Euro-American authorities, and who exercised considerable control over Comanche-Anglo relations, had equal authority or power with respect to Comanche-Comanche relations. Indeed, when Kavanagh (1986:149–150) does refer to the internal workings of the Comanche community, he is forced to make a distinction between the external authority of "officially recognized" Comanche leaders in dealing with Anglos and the lack of authority those same leaders had in dealing with the interaction of Comanches with one another.

Examples of the limited authority of Comanche leaders may be found throughout their relations with Anglo-Americans in the nineteenth century, a period in which Comanche leaders controlled access to more economic resources than at any previous point in their history (Kavanagh 1986). Burnett summarized thirty years of experience with Comanches in 1847: "The authority of their chiefs is rather nominal than positive; more advisory than compulsive; and relies more upon personal influence than investment of office" (Winfrey and Day 1966, 2:87). Also in 1847, Agent Neighbors stated that there is no principal chief of all the Comanches.[60] Again, in 1848 Neighbors observed that "the authority of the chief extends only to the personal influence he may exercise."[61] By 1857, federal agents were unable even to approximate the kind of alliance that the Spanish had accomplished with the Comanches. "Their chiefs have but little control," Neighbors reported, "and I have never known them to make a treaty that a portion of the tribe do not violate its stipulations."[62] As late as 1872, Agent Tatum observed that "Comanches have no head and controlling chief, but each one independently of the others so far as it suits him."[63]

Because they lacked institutional authority to regulate intracommunity relations yet controlled access to economic resources, Comanche leaders present an interesting problem for traditional anthropological interpretations of Plains social organization. Comanche social organization must have operated in a markedly different way from our usual expectations of a more structured relation of power to authority.

THE INTERSECTION OF PRERESERVATION SOCIAL LIFE AND SOCIAL STRUCTURE

As we have seen, the units of Comanche social structure (relationships, residence bands, divisions, and activity groups) were closely tied to the personal identities of the individuals who participated in them. While often compelled by ties of kinship and friendship to participate in a particular unit, Comanches acted as individuals, not as filial or descent groups nor as age sets or common-interest associations. They moved from residence band to residence band and from raiding party to raiding party as their own best interest and personal obligations dictated. Within those groups, social relations were regulated by conventions of face-to-face interaction, most prominently by strategic considerations of face.

Divisional gatherings were the fulcrum for the organization of the social groups (autonomous residence bands and focused-activity groups) among which Comanches divided their community. Contrary to conventional anthropological expectations, however, divisions were organized as gatherings for the regulation of public commingling, not as corporate social groups. Their great advantage was that they exposed prominent Comanches who were leaders of residence bands and focused-activity groups to public sanction, both through the care that a leader had for his social face and through concern for maintaining and enhancing membership in the groups that were his power base. At any given moment in the prereservation period, Comanche leaders—not the activity groups, named bands, and divisions that they dominated—were the fixed markers in the Comanche social world. These leaders competed with one another for participants in their residence bands and focused-activity groups as well as for influence in divisional gatherings. Marcy provides a classic description of this competition from the 1850s:

> Although Sanaco is acknowledged by all to be the ruling spirit of the Southern Comanches, and claims and holds that position in their united deliberations [i.e., divisional gatherings], yet his band and that of Ketumsee are otherwise separate and independent. Ketumsee is an ambitious and astute leader, pursuing a discreet and complacent policy in the government of his followers calculated to enhance his popularity, and he has already alienated several of Sanaco's band, who have transferred their allegiance to him. This has engendered a feeling of ill will and jealousy between them which causes each to be suspicious of the motives of the other. (Marcy 1866:210)[64]

It was this competition that regulated the organization and actions of Comanche social units within the larger Comanche community, as leaders behaved in ways that maximized their followings while preserving their ability to make alliances with one another for limited purposes.[65] Thus, Comanche social structure is best understood as the strategic movement and organization of personnel among different social groups, regulated by means of periodic multigroup gatherings rather than a static organization of Comanches into longstanding, mutually exclusive divisions.

The movement of personnel across divisional boundaries also resulted in a frequency of interaction that preserved the lines of communication within the larger social unit of the Comanche community. Shared linguistic and social standards were maintained by the frequency of divisional movement. As a result, it was unnecessary for Comanches to gather as a whole "tribe" or community on a periodic or annual basis to reinforce those shared standards. Differences in symbols associated with the different divisions, such as variations in dress and food preparation, were emphasized, but as markers of divisional identities, not as weaknesses in the lines of communication.

Changes did occur in Comanche-Comanche relations as a result of their increasing contacts with Euro-Americans during the eighteenth and nineteenth centuries. These alterations, though, were not imposed by and did not directly conform to Comanches' interactions with Euro-Americans. They were elaborations on already existing Comanche frameworks for conceptualizing constituent social units and regulating social interaction within those units. As others have noted, Euro-American trade, especially the availability and use of horses, significantly altered the opportunity for movement and mutual presence on the Plains (Ewers 1955; Oliver 1962; Fowler 1982; Moore 1988). Horses made possible larger and more frequent gatherings of personnel and probably also required a greater frequency of movement for sufficient pasturage (Thurman 1980; Moore 1988). Comanche–Euro-American trade promoted raiding into territories dominated by Euro-Americans and also the rise of Plains leaders who were intermediaries with or brokers for Euro-American government officials and traders (Fowler 1982, 1987; Moore 1988).

In their relations with Euro-Americans, Comanches were consistently guided by economic considerations: how plentiful were bison and other game, where goods were available and vulnerable to raiding, where markets existed for those goods, and what inducements Euro-American governments were prepared to offer for restrictions on Comanche activities. These considerations caused Comanches to come onto the Plains in the first place; to raid Spanish-dominated pueblos; to reach a series of accommodations with the Spanish administrations in New Mexico and Texas; to try to maintain a negotiated presence in Anglo Texas; to raid those Texas settlements; to accommodate Indian agencies on the Upper Platte and Upper Arkansas; to negotiate a treaty for annuities and a reservation; to resist the authority of the reservation agency over their actions; and finally to move onto that reservation. In nearly all these actions, Comanches were responding to the economic opportunities and constraints that the expanding Euro-American presence on the southern Plains dictated. Arguably, these changing conditions had five primary consequences for Comanche-Comanche interaction: (1) an increase in the size and frequency of divisional gatherings, (2) an increase in the influence of individual Comanche leaders, (3) an increase in the formation of focused-activity groups, (4) an increase in movement between residence bands and thus between divisions, and (5) changes in the territories associated with specific divisions.

As Thurman (1980:49–51) has observed, the reported size of Comanche camps in the early nineteenth century varied from small residence bands of about twenty people up to quite large gatherings of more than a thousand and estimated horse herds of more than 20,000 head. These latter were clearly divisional gatherings. There also is evidence from the early nineteenth century that such gatherings occurred both in summer and in winter, and from 1786 on, there are references to occasional gatherings of two or more divisions that Euro-American observers often designated as "councils." Council meetings of this kind would have functioned as public occasions for social regulation in ways similar to divisional gatherings. Sometimes these gatherings were at the behest of Euro-American agents (as, for instance, the 1786 gathering at which Ecueracapa was delegated to enter into an accommodation with the Spanish), and sometimes they were in reaction to Euro-American actions (such as the 1874 gathering as a prelude to the raid on Adobe Walls). In a community in which authority was personalized (rather than institutionalized), it is only logical that wider influence depended on larger gatherings and that the two should covary.

There is little evidence, though, to suggest that there was a corresponding increase in residence band size. Ecueracapa, at the height of his influence and at a time when bison herds were yet undiminished, was reported to be leading a residence band of 157 lodges (perhaps 400 to 600 people) (Thomas 1932:322). This was probably near the limit of what the Plains environment could support. The acquisition of horses and firearms could make bison hunting more efficient but could not improve the availability of grass and firewood. The residence bands that came onto the reservation between 1870 and 1875 were made up of 300 people each at most, with the majority being much smaller (Wallace and Hoebel 1952:327–328).

In addition to the political basis of larger divisional and multidivisional gatherings, there was also an economic basis to the increased, multidivisional influence of individual Comanche leaders in the late eighteenth and nineteenth centuries. As Kavanagh has amply documented (1986:258–265), Euro-American presents and trading constituted a considerable economic input into the Comanche community. Comanche leaders between 1786 and 1867 had many more goods at their disposal than did those of previous periods. These goods undoubtedly were used to heighten the influence that particular leaders enjoyed, both through their redistribution and through the control that leaders exercised over access to them.

The Comanches' expanding role in trade also increased the opportunities for initiative in achieving leadership. Comanche trade in horses, and later cattle, was supplied by focused-activity groups. The increased number of raiding opportunities during the nineteenth century allowed any Comanche warrior who could form a group to engage in this sort of free enterprise. Particularly successful organizers of such expeditions would have attained both the reputation and the economic means to become influential in longer-term social units (i.e., residence bands and divisions). Arguably, the decrease in bison populations in the nineteenth century made raiding and trade more important economic activities for Comanches. Thus the formation of focused-activity groups became more frequent and the economic role of intermediary leaders more central to the formation of residence groups.

The increased economic significance of focused-activity groups also meant that Comanche warriors shifted their participation from one social unit to another more frequently. Any increased movement between social units would only have further emphasized the importance of regulating competition among those units and the personal authority of their leaders. Lacking a centralized framework to organize the distribution, rights, and duties of its members, the Comanche community relied on public gatherings such as divisional occasions to accomplish this regulation.

It should be noted, however, that competition was not always successfully regulated, nor was cooperation among bands or across divisions always accomplished. For instance, a barrier to a Comanche-Spanish accommodation between 1778 and 1786 was the reluctance of some bands, under the leadership of Toroblanco, to give up raiding Spanish settlements. When divisional councils failed to regulate the actions of Toroblanco and his followers, he was assassinated by Ecueracapa's agents (Thomas 1932:299). Although only one individual was eliminated, this had the effect of fragmenting the opposition that had formed around Toroblanco's personal reputation, and a treaty consensus then became possible around the surviving reputation of Ecueracapa.[66]

The success of divisional and multidivisional gatherings in achieving interband cooperation depended largely upon the economics of the time. During those periods in which economic conditions were much the same for all Comanche bands, consensus was more easily achieved. At other times, consensus was difficult to accomplish, even within the same division. For instance, in the early nineteenth century in Texas some bands saw economic benefit in maintaining trade with Texans, while others saw economic benefit in raiding Texan settlements (John 1984; Kavanagh 1986:68–81).[67]

Finally, the historical process of the postcontact Plains must have had consequences for the territories associated with specific divisions. Inevitably, each time Comanches shifted the focus of their movements, they had to adjust the territories of the different divisions. These adjustments were ad hoc, determined mainly by the proximity of residence bands to divisional gatherings and perhaps also by the existing relationships between residence-band leaders. While this view in no way discounts the functions that divisional gatherings provided in Comanche social life, it does suggest that divisions were more situational, and more opportunistic, than most scholars have been prepared to admit.[68]

The remarkable feature of prereservation Comanche social organization was not its lack of formal structure or complexity but the sophistication of the interactional conventions used by Comanches to order their social world. Most Euro-Americans would be hard-pressed to function in a world with few explicit laws or defined positions and institutions of authority, let alone to excel at the same time in a rapidly changing political economy. Comanches used their distinctive means of social organization to out-compete a succession of Euro-American regimes on the southern Plains for the better part of two centuries.

3

The Reservation Community, 1875-1901

The Kiowas and Comanches are fast passing away, and unless they become civilized and embrace the Christian religion, it is not likely they will last much beyond the present generation. Agent Lawrie Tatum, 1871

They had to start doing something else. They had to look to other things to do instead of going out onto the Plains.

Leonard Riddles, 1985

During the nineteenth century, Anglo-Americans used reservations as legal vehicles to obtain ownership of large expanses of land in exchange for much smaller areas, as well as a means of restraining the movements and activities of nomadic Indian communities. For Comanches, though, a reservation held quite different meanings. As we saw in the previous chapter, Comanches had some experience with reservations in Texas in the 1850s. There, they used the reserves as protected enclaves to maintain trade relations with Texans and to evade Anglo military pursuit. Comanches initially used the Indian Territory reserve provided under the 1867 Medicine Lodge Treaty in much the same way.[1] What made the Indian Territory reservation different—and ultimately more attractive to Comanche bands—was the promise of semiannual annuity payments and the distribution of biweekly rations. These were attractive inducements because of the decline in the Anglo market for horses and cattle and the depletion of bison on the Plains.

The economic and political utility of nomadic Indian bands to Anglo-Americans had supported Comanche activities for the first three-quarters of the nineteenth century, but that utility had come to an end (Kenner 1969:201). By the 1870s, Anglo settlements in Texas became more densely populated and so were less vulnerable to opportunistic Comanche raids, though some raiding did continue through 1875 (Wallace and Hoebel 1952:328). The comanchero trade in horses and cattle, which had flourished between the Comanches and New Mexican traders, was suppressed successfully by the U.S. government between 1867 and 1872 (Kenner 1969:176).

The increased Anglo presence on the Plains also threatened Comanche subsistence activities. Large-scale Anglo hunting of bison had begun in 1872, dramatically reducing the availability of bison for food and flooding the bison-robe market, which had previously been dominated by Indian hunters (Richardson 1963:299–300). While bison populations had been declining throughout most of the nineteenth century, the slaughter that occurred in the 1870s made nomadic life on the Plains difficult to sustain. Further, as Anglo-American settlers'moved onto the Plains, their farming and ranching activities altered the movements of other game upon which Comanche hunters also depended.

Between 1869 and 1875, Comanches responded to these pressures by making increasing use of the reservation, with periodic small ventures outside its boundaries. By 1875 nearly the whole of the Comanche community—1,521 people—were counted as reservation residents.[2] In 1901, when the reservation was dissolved into allotments, the Comanche population was 1,409.[3] In the intervening years, the Comanches had led a precarious existence on the margin of the ever-expanding Anglo political economy.

Anglo expansion and Comanche uncertainty were built into the treaty that established the reservation. It carried a termination date of 1898 for federal annuities due the Comanches. By that time the Indian Office expected Comanches to have entered the mainstream of Anglo society. In accounts of Comanches' reservation experience, the assimilationist objectives of Anglo policy frequently are characterized as the agenda of the Comanche community itself: "The cultural change demanded of the Comanches was too rapid and too great for simple adjustment. They were called upon to pass within the span of a single life from the Stone Age to that of steam. Men trained for war and raiding and communal hunts found themselves idle, faced with the problem of adopting the white man's way of life" (Wallace and Hoebel 1952:328–329). The sale of the last jointly owned reservation lands in 1906[4] is construed as the end also of the Comanche community: "Verily, the phase of reservation life had passed, a short interlude of 40 years. The Comanches had entered the White Man's Road. They were Lords of the Southern Plains no longer" (Wallace and Hoebel 1952:353).

The Comanches did adapt to (rather than adopted) Anglo-dominated social conditions during the reservation period, creating social units to take account of changing constraints on their ability to interact with one another. The Comanche community that existed at the end of that period, just prior to allotment in severalty, was different in many ways from the Comanche community that gradually settled onto the reservation territory from 1870 to 1875, but it was still distinctively Comanche.

THE SUN DANCE OF 1874

The sequence of events that has come to symbolize the "desperation" and final "defeat" of the Comanches, leading directly to the reservation era, was the Sun Dance and the subsequent "outbreak" of 1874 (see Hoebel 1941; Wallace and Hoebel 1952; Fehrenbach 1974). This sequence begins with the vision of a Comanche medicine man, Eschiti,[5] which, he claimed, foretold that the performance of the Sun Dance would deliver Comanches from Anglo domination. This dance was performed in the early summer of 1874, with members of nearly all the remaining Comanche bands in attendance. As a result of the dance, a group of Comanches and other Plains peoples attacked a small group of Anglo-American bison hunters at Adobe Walls (Richardson 1933:373–374; Wallace and Hoebel 1952:319–326).

By the time of Eschiti's vision in 1874 the range of Comanche bands had been greatly restricted by Anglo settlement, and nearly all the Comanches were near enough to participate in the Sun Dance that it authorized. The events surrounding Eschiti's vision increased the flow of warriors from reservation bands to those bands organized around a core of Comanche leaders, categorized by Anglo officials under the rubric of the Quahada division, that operated on the Staked Plains west of the reservation. Eschiti's claims also attracted Kiowas and Cheyennes (Wallace and Hoebel 1952:325), whose range also had been narrowed to reservations in Indian Territory and the southwestern margin of the Plains.

Wallace and Hoebel (1952:319–320) portray this as the first, and last, Comanche attempt at tribal solidarity. It was the first, they assert, because it was the only time that Comanches performed the Sun Dance and the only time that most, if not all, bands were gathered in the same place.[6] It was the last because the Battle of Adobe Walls, which followed the Sun Dance, undermined Eschiti's claims for his vision: "The Sun Dance had failed them and they felt their power-giving spirits had all but forsaken them. Their accustomed guardian spirits, and even the Sun, lacked sufficient power to turn back the whites and to preserve their old tribal way of life" (Wallace and Hoebel 1952:331).

The experience, in Wallace and Hoebel's view (1952:344–345), caused the Comanches to become resigned to the inevitability of reservation life, immunized them to later revitalization movements such as the Ghost Dance, and forced them to abandon their traditional belief system. The same sequence of events that Wallace and Hoebel credited with breaking the spirit of the Comanche community can, however, be interpreted in a very different way. It may also be seen as a consequence of the economic pressures surrounding the community and as a transitional stage in the Comanches' continuing innovation of their community. Comanche-Anglo tension on the reservation began not with Eschiti and his vision but with an order from Washington in late 1873 that the agent halt rations to the Comanches until they surrendered

five warriors who had participated in raids with Quahada bands.[7] This order caused great concern among reservation Comanches, and many considered the withdrawal of rations in the midst of winter an act of war. While
rations were reinstated before the winter ended, the always inefficient
federal procurement system brought only partial distributions.[8] It was in this
context that Eschiti had his vision and Comanches began to talk about a
"medicine camp" or Sun Dance. The encampment appears to have lasted for
several months, from April to June, during which the participants were
uncertain as to the actions they might take.[9] The early idea was to raid the
Tonkawas in retribution for assistance rendered to the U.S. cavalry units
that had pursued Comanche bands in the previous year. As the encampment
wore on, raids on Anglos also were discussed.[10] Finally, in late June, Comanches became much disturbed about the destruction of bison by Anglo
hunters, and this focused the encampment on the notion of raiding the bison
hunters' camp at Adobe Walls.[11]

As Kavanagh (1986:228) has pointed out, Eschiti's rhetoric was at least a
century old. What was unique about the gathering it authorized was the
wide participation across divisional lines, which Wallace and Hoebel as well
as Kavanagh interpreted as an incipient nationalist movement. The Sun
Dance of 1874, though, is better explained by Comanches' new proximity to
one another than as a belated attempt to use shared religious beliefs to forge
a unified political entity. With geographical compression, divisions lost their
primary function of regulating residence bands sharing the same territory.
Comanches compressed the previously separate divisional gatherings into a
single occasion, the 1874 Sun Dance, to organize their community in a way
that adapted to the new social conditions they faced.

The uncertainty of federal rations and the decline in trading opportunities
had created an economic crisis. Sufficient goods were not available to maintain the existing Comanche organization of residence bands, focused-activity
groups, and their respective leaders. The older leaders of reservation bands
dominated the distribution of the few goods that were available from the
agency. The leaders of Quahada residence bands and of focused-activity
groups outside the reservation, many of whom were of a younger generation
than the reservation leaders, faced the collapse of the New Mexican market
that had supplied their livelihood and prominence.

The Sun Dance in 1874 was an attempt by this latter segment of the
Comanche community to compel reservation bands and their leaders to cooperate in an armed challenge to the Anglo-American policies that had
effectively constrained Comanche activity. The public occasion of the Sun

Dance made it less likely that the leaders would refuse to cooperate in a stand against Anglo authority, because of their concern for face, and this was backed up by the intimidation of military society police who tried to force reservation leaders and their bands to attend the gathering (Kavanagh 1986:174–175). New Mexican traders supported the efforts of the Comanches who organized the camp because it was to their advantage to preserve nomadic trade on the western margin of the Plains. Meanwhile, older Comanche leaders, anxious to preserve their access to agency goods, tried to use their role as intermediaries to make a deal between the agent and the camp participants.[12]

Although the goal of the Comanche faction that formed around Eschiti has been described as the annihilation of the Anglo-Americans, the discussion of actual targets for attack was much more selective, suggesting a realistic political strategy behind the rhetoric. Tonkawas and bison hunters were each marginal tools of Anglo-American Indian policy. Striking successfully at either held the promise of getting the attention of the Anglo authorities, perhaps without the heavy hand of military suppression.[13] There would then be an opportunity to renegotiate the economic conditions of Comanche life.

In the end, the medicine camp did not command the consensus of the entire community, and the bison hunters at Adobe Walls had new, long-range rifles (Wallace and Hoebel 1952:325). After the failure of that raid, the "outbreak" was increasingly driven by the military's response rather than by Comanche design. Comanche bands were pursued by cavalry units through the summer and fall. The winter of 1874–75 brought another round of subsistence pressures, and most bands came in to the reservation (Hagan 1976:112). The remaining Quahadas, numbering more than 400, came in the following June, not through military defeat but voluntarily (Hagan 1976:117–119). Their horses and weapons were taken from them, and few economic opportunities remained beyond the reservation to cause Comanches to leave again.

ECONOMIC CONDITIONS OF THE RESERVATION PERIOD

Within the reservation, Anglos controlled the distribution of nearly all the economic resources upon which Comanches depended. Rations were handed out at Fort Sill once every two weeks or when available until 1879, when the agency was relocated to what is today Anadarko.[14] Later, in the 1890s, when Comanches had become more sedentary because of agricultural activities, subagencies were placed around the reservation.[15] Rations took the form of beef on the hoof and basic foodstuffs such as flour, sugar, and coffee.

Comanches initially supplemented their government rations with winter bison hunts, which provided them with meat superior to what they were given at the agency and brought in income through the sale of robes. The last of these hunts was in the winter of 1878–79, when the Comanches were unable to locate any bison.[16] Their rations, however, were not adjusted to take account of the loss of bison meat from the annual hunts.[17] This forced Comanches to make up the difference by engaging in some limited agricultural activities and by raising cattle. After the failure of the 1879 bison hunt, both the agent and the Comanches recognized that cattle in addition to those issued sporadically as government rations would be vital for Comanche survival (Hagan 1971, 1976). Periodically, the agent was authorized to purchase a number of cattle to be distributed among families.[18] In addition to providing meat, this also gave the agent a means of rewarding the more cooperative families and individuals. Comanches also managed to acquire cattle on their own initiative. Various cattle trails between Texas and Kansas went across reservation land, and Comanches enforced their legal ownership of the reservation by levying an informal toll on each herd that crossed their land (Hagan 1971). Comanches benefited as well from strays, and as late as the 1890s they were known to raid neighboring Chickasaw herds.[19]

Stock raising was the most successful indigenous subsistence venture during the reservation period. In 1875 there were two Indians per head of cattle on the reservation (Stahl 1978:106). By 1885 that ratio had been reversed, with individual Comanche herds ranging from one or two cattle to 200 head (Stahl 1978:108).[20] By 1892 reservation herds numbered more than 25,000 head, or five head for every Indian (Stahl 1978:108). At allotment, the ratio was down to 4:1, but this still amounted to more than 17,000 head (Stahl 1978:108).

Comanches also began growing some of their own food. Agricultural activities were undertaken mainly by the heads of residential units (extended families and nuclear families), who were responsible for the subsistence of others. Comanches who became especially prosperous hired Anglo labor to farm their fields (Hagan 1976:182). Production gradually expanded throughout the reservation period, but Comanche agriculture was neither intensive nor full-time and never approached the levels required by the Comanches for their annual subsistence (Hagan 1976:181–182). For instance, at its high point in 1899, 15,800 reservation acres were under cultivation, or almost four acres per person, but because of a drought, production was only a half of what it had been on just 5,000 acres in 1895 (Stahl 1978:109).

The other significant economic input into the reservation community was cash. At the beginning of the reservation period, Comanches had little access to money and little need of it. While the Treaty of Medicine Lodge promised Comanches a financial settlement in exchange for their claims to much of the southern Plains, the government used this money to obtain rations and other goods and also counted it as administrative overhead. Comanches derived some income from the sale of bison robes and cattle hides to Anglo traders,[21] and in 1879 the agency, unable to find reliable Anglo freighters, began hiring Kiowas, Comanches, and Apaches for that work.[22] This placed between $5,000 and $10,000 in Indian hands each year. Selected Comanche leaders, such as Quanah Parker, were given nominal government positions in exchange for their cooperation. This provided them with monthly salaries that enabled the leaders to reward their supporters (Hagen 1976:186–187).

By far the largest cash input, though, came from Texas cattlemen. Beginning in 1885, Comanches entered into lease arrangements with Texas ranchers for reservation pastures. This arrangement lasted until 1906 and provided each Comanche with a semiannual "grass" payment. The periodic disbursement of grass money attracted a number of licensed Anglo traders to the reservation.[23] The payments also fueled Comanches' gambling activities, mainly in a card game called "Monte" and horse races, which increased dramatically in 1882 and which were a constant source of complaint by agents thereafter.[24] Though it was periodically suppressed,[25] gambling was a significant activity both within local communities and in larger gatherings, such as occurred at the biweekly distributions of rations and at the semiannual payments of grass money.[26] While Anglos were sometimes involved, most of these activities were conducted among Comanches or between Comanches and other Indians.

The payment of grass money probably went a long way toward securing Comanche subsistence for the remainder of the reservation period. The money allowed Comanches to buy their own supplies from licensed traders on the reservation, who let Comanches run up bills and then used their official relationships with the agency to collect on those debts. This gave Comanches an alternative to government rations and allowed some to continue a nomadic existence within reservation boundaries.

Despite the various economic resources Comanches developed after 1875, they had not become self-supporting by the end of the reservation period in 1901.[27] Had they done so, their resistance to allotment might have been more determined. Instead, Comanches were faced with the threat of an end to their rations with the lapse of annuities after 1898 and continued rations only at the discretion of the agency (Hagan 1980:186–187). Without either continued federal rations or some financial settlement for the opening of their lands to Anglo homesteading, their economic base would have eroded. It is in this economic context that the negotiations over allotment are best understood.

At the beginning of the reservation period, the land occupied by Comanches was not yet desirable as farmland. For nearly thirty years, agent after agent pointed out the poor quality of the soil. By the early 1880s, however, the Anglo-American desire for free farmland brought pressure on the federal government to open up large tracts of Indian land to homesteaders.[28] Under the Dawes Act, passed by Congress in 1887, the federal government was empowered to purchase the bulk of reservation lands from the various Indian tribes, leaving each tribal member with a 160-acre allotment and opening the millions of acres that remained to Anglo homesteaders. The Cherokee Commission was set up in the 1890s to negotiate with tribal peoples on the value of their reservation lands and the implementation of allotment. This was accomplished in the Jerome Agreement, named for the chairman of the Cherokee Commission. This agreement, supposedly reached in 1892 with Comanches, Kiowas, and Apaches, was later much disputed by some members of those communities. For eight years, petitions were circulated, delegations visited Washington, and lawyers were engaged by various interests, Anglo as well as Indian, in an attempt either to implement or to circumvent the Jerome Agreement (Hagan 1976:236–237).[29] Congress did not authorize allotment to begin among the Kiowas, Comanches, and Apaches until 1900.

Despite the long process of opening up the reservation,[30] one is struck by the inevitability of allotment and the absence of militant resistance to its implementation among Comanches. Certainly some Comanches—and even more so Kiowas—did oppose the policy and did press their case both within their communities and with the federal government (Hagan 1976:205–207, 263–264). However, the main concern of the Comanche negotiators (even those who later opposed the agreement) was that cut-rate prices were being offered for their land (Hagan 1976:206–207). Very little appears to have been said about the consequences of the sale beyond the financial settlement (Hagan 1976:264).[31] For Comanches, the issue in the Jerome negotiations was continued economic survival after the lapse of treaty-mandated annuities after 1898. Comanches realized that, even with the food they were able to grow themselves, the cattle they were able to obtain, and the grass money payments, they could not survive without some replacement for the annuity income and could not depend on continued agency rations.

This is not to imply that Comanches were unaware of the value of the land they occupied. Certainly those Comanches, such as Quanah Parker, who interacted often with Anglos were well aware of the significance of reservation land. Quanah had attained much of his prominence, at least in Anglo eyes, by arranging the lease of reservation pastures in the early 1880s (Wallace and Hoebel 1952:347–348; Hagan 1980:181–182). From an intra-community perspective, however, status was attained in other ways than through the ownership of land.

Ultimately the identification of the Comanches with their reservation territory became the salient index by which they were known to Anglos in the late nineteenth century. The symbols of reservation land (controlled by Indians) and of "open" land (controlled by Anglo homesteaders) became the focal points in Indian-Anglo relations. There existed both formal rules prohibiting Anglos and Indians from entering each other's domains and informal practices for the conventional violation of these rules (Hagan 1976:151–152, 237, 268). Comanches traded at Anglo stores across the Red River in Texas, and Texas cattlemen found their way to reservation pastures.

The arrival of grass payments and Anglo cowboys had brought the first significant infusion of Anglos to the reservation. In 1878 there were only 150 to 170 Anglos on the reservation.[32] These were agency personnel and licensed traders and suppliers. By 1890, Anglo intruders were a persistent problem.[33] They were mainly people interested in deriving some profit from the agency or the Indians. In the eleven years leading up to allotment, they became more numerous and more difficult to control, and by the end of the reservation period, Anglos were illegally pouring into the reservation in expectation of its opening to homesteading.

ANGLO IMAGES OF COMANCHES

The image that Anglos had of Comanches during the reservation period owed much to the Indians' reputation for raiding Texas settlements and taking captives in the years before 1875. Three examples drawn from interviews conducted in 1937 with Anglos who resided near the Comanche reservation in the 1890s portray the stereotype:

The Comanches were sure enough tough. They would come over from their country and steal everything they could get hold of and would sometimes kill a whole family and take their horses and cattle.[34]

The Indians were all very friendly, except the Comanches. The Comanches refused to accept the ways and modes of the white men and would raid and steal all livestock, horses especially, and kill whole families.[35]

I was in a store in Caddo one day when a bunch came in. I was scared to death, and tried to get out, but they were all around me so I had to pretend I wasn't afraid. They never bothered you if you let them alone.[36]

It should be noted that after 1880 there is no mention in agency reports of Comanches raiding Anglo settlements, let alone killing anyone. To those Anglos who had regular dealings with them, Comanches in the reservation period gave quite a different impression:

[Comanches] from being the most cunning, bloodthirsty, and warlike of all the Plains Indians, have become the most tractable and are making greater strides toward civilization than any tribe of blanket Indians to my knowledge. They are obedient, truthful, and honest.[37]

Comanches were quiet and friendly to the few white people who were among them.[38]

For their part, Comanches were far from naive about the more populous community that was crowding their borders. Through their reservation experiences with cavalry troopers, Indian agents, ranchers and cowboys, licensed traders, missionaries, neighboring Texans, and increasing numbers of intruders, Comanches were able to form fairly accurate expectations about Anglo motives and intentions. Agencies and subagencies were the principal locations for Anglo establishments on the reservation, and thus for Comanche-Anglo interaction. Anglo traders set up shop near these locations to catch Comanches as they were issued rations, annuities, and grass payments. Anglo missionaries established missions and schools nearby as well, though Comanches were not targeted by a mission effort until 1889.[39] Missionaries did not make significant inroads into the Comanche community until after allotment.[40] Comanches also were reluctant to send their children to schools, which were, for the most part, run by missionaries.[41]

While many Anglos considered Comanches "uncivilized" and easy to take advantage of in face-to-face encounters, this was not due to any lack of knowledge of the rough outlines of the Anglo world. Rather, the apparent failure of Comanches to act in their own best interest in Anglo contexts was due to the primary orientation of Comanches to their own community and to contexts and priorities for interactions situated therein. Comanches could behave in economically "foolish" ways at Anglo trading posts without damaging their social faces in the Comanche community (Hagan 1976:242).[42] However, when Comanches chose, they could be both economically and politically successful at manipulating opposing Anglo interests for their own benefit.[43] Quanah Parker was perhaps the outstanding example of this strategy.

Without doubt, Quanah Parker is the Comanche best known to Anglos. The popular image of Quanah is as the last "Chief of the Comanches," a title he himself promoted (Hagan 1980:184). Many accounts of Comanche history (e.g., Wallace and Hoebel 1952:316, 327) retrospectively portray Quanah as a principal Comanche leader in the last resistance of 1874–75. These accounts, and Quanah's own efforts at self-promotion, have given the false impression that the Comanches were united behind a single leader. Quanah was instead a typical intermediary leader who achieved his position by acting as the go-between for other Comanches with Anglo officials. Within the community, Quanah's ability to deal with Anglos, and the material goods he derived from those dealings, made him useful and prominent, in much the same way that Ecueracapa had been in managing relations with the Spanish. Even in this role, Quanah did not emerge as a prominent culture broker until 1884, in the negotiations that led up to the leasing of Comanche pastures to Texas cattlemen (Hagan 1980:183).[44] Through his participation in the leasing arrangements, Quanah came to personify Comanche relations with Anglo-Americans. "[T]here was," Hagan notes, "no question of his role as the principal Comanche spokesman by the late 1880s. There also could be no question about the importance of the cattlemen in his rise. They had given him a cause, exposure in official circles, and substantial income by Comanche standards" (1980:183–184). As Hagan goes on to observe, "No small part of Quanah's prominence in this period was his willingness to go along with every one of the 14 white men who served as agent between 1878 and Quanah's death in 1911" (1980:185).

It has been said that Quanah would have been a leader in any community into which he might have been born (Hagan 1980:189). By the same token, it may also be said that any Comanche leader in Quanah's place during the reservation period would have taken substantially the same stance with respect to Anglos as he did. As the primary Comanche negotiator with the Jerome Commission, Quanah devoted considerable effort to raising the price per acre for Comanche land, but he never seriously attempted to block allotment.[45] In the end, the Comanches, with assistance from the Texas cattlemen who were leasing their pastures, were able to stall allotment for nine years, nearly four years beyond the 1898 deadline, prolonging the receipt of government rations until 1901. They also managed to retain 480,000 acres in joint ownership with Kiowas and Apaches for continued lease as pasture.

Just as Quanah's career as an intermediary leader typifies Comanche-Anglo relations during the reservation period, Quanah's personal life represents the maintenance of the Comanche community. While presenting Comanches to Anglo officials as receptive to assimilation, Quanah steadfastly retained a polygamous household even when this threatened his standing with Anglo officials (Hagan 1980:184). Quanah was also intimately involved in the establishment of peyote circles, which by the end of the reservation period had become the primary form of public gathering used to maintain the Comanche community (Hagan 1980:186).

RESERVATION CONDITIONS AND COMANCHE SOCIAL UNITS

The social conditions of the reservation period caused changes in the social units of Comanche life. To some extent, these changes were manipulated by Anglo officials, who controlled access to economic resources. Comanches, however, sidetracked the Indian agents' attempts to use these changes as a means for assimilation. New forms of public gathering were used to link changing social units to the larger community, thus creating ways to continue to "be Comanche."

The Comanches' shift from older forms of social participation to newer forms during the reservation period was not the result of disenchantment with their traditional ways, as Wallace and Hoebel suggest. Instead, they altered their social units and cultural frameworks in order to adapt traditional social processes (such as community maintenance through public gatherings) and cultural beliefs (about power and access to power) to the very different social conditions of the reservation landscape. In response to changing sources and means of economic support, the prereservation residence bands underwent a period of fluctuation in numbers and sizes that transformed Comanche residence units.

After the Sun Dance of 1874 and the failed attack on Adobe Walls, Comanches found themselves gathered during the winter of 1874–75 in one large camp on West Cache Creek. By the spring, that camp had dispersed once again into residence bands, each following a leader in nomadic movements within the reservation boundaries.[46] Once the Quahadas had come into the reservation in the summer, twenty-four residence bands, ranging in size from 18 to 118 members, were identified by the agent, an increase from the fifteen, ranging in size from 24 to 402, listed in 1869–70.[47] In 1878, thirty-three residence bands, ranging in size from 10 to 115 members, are listed (Hagan 1976:154).

The years 1878 and 1879 represented, in many respects, a watershed for Comanche social organization. During those years, Comanches performed their last Sun Dance and their final large-scale bison hunt on the open Plains (Wallace and Hoebel 1952:331). At the same time, the agency changed its policy of distributing rations through residence-band leaders. In a move to accelerate the breakup of those bands,[48] rations were henceforth to be issued to heads of families.[49] Agency personnel referred to the process of breaking up the residence bands as "segregation." Segregation was further promoted among Comanches by the removal of the agency from Fort Sill to Anadarko, forty miles to the north.[50] The move forced Comanches, who were living mainly south of the Wichita Mountains, to make an eighty-mile round-trip journey for rations. That biweekly journey made family groups preferable to residence bands, which formerly had remained in the general vicinity of Fort Sill. Larger prereservation residence bands were simply too large for any purpose except long-term encampments. Thus in 1879–80, thirty-seven residence bands, ranging from 13 to 83 members, are listed.[51]

As the authority of Comanche leaders was undermined by changes in the policy for issuing rations, residence bands retained some utility as economic units. At the same time, the authority of their leaders became even more dependent upon the Anglo agent. As Agent Hunt noted in 1880, "I have allowed relatives to band together and would appoint one of their number a chief or headman and suggest to him to take his people off to some good locality and make permanent houses. . . . The advantage to the man appointed by me was that he become more prominent and controlled the funds derived from the sale of beef hides."[52]

By 1881, when forty-one residence bands are listed,[53] Comanche residence units were much smaller than just two years previously: "Two years ago would have been seen large encampments, often the tribe, scarcely ever less than the entire band, together, while now will rarely be seen more than two or three lodges, but oftener the single family."[54] In 1883, sixty residence bands are listed, with the larger units having only 40 to 50 members.[55] At this point the number of Comanches living as single families (that is, in two or three generational lineal units) in semisedentary locations began to catch up with the number of Comanches moving about the reservation as nomadic extended families (that is, as prereservation residence bands). Thus by 1885 the number of residence bands listed by the agent had declined to thirty-three, with a decrease in the size of most bands from 1883.[56] While patterns of nomadic movement persisted, these became more localized: "These Indians retain much of their roving disposition and except during the cropping season do not camp long in one place, but do not go far from their fields. Few of the Kiowas, Comanches, and Apaches have houses, and most of them live in tents."[57] Andrew Perdasophy, a Comanche who was born in one of these nomadic camps in 1882, described it in this way in 1937: "The Indians are generally known to move very often. The Indian camps were of several families always located near creeks or springs, where there was a good supply of wood and water. In the warmer weather we moved our teepee up on the hills; in the colder weather we would move into low places and near timber, using the timber as wind breaks."[58]

These and other accounts of nomadic Comanche movements during the reservation period suggest that, once a nomadic group found locations that offered the desired characteristics, its members tended to frequent those locations over a period of years. This preference contributed to the gradual formation of geographically localized residence groups. By 1888 a total of 1,564 Comanches were divided into slightly more than 700 domestic units, each of which received a separate ration from the agency.[59] The last census of residence bands, conducted in 1892, listed seventy-five such units, with an average membership of 25 persons (Kavanagh 1989:106). These units were actually extended families who camped together during the summer months but not all of whom resided together throughout the year, which was a very different pattern from the residence bands of just ten years before.

The smaller residence groups that developed during the reservation period, whether nomadic or semipermanent, were based on ties of kinship, marriage, and friendship. Albert Attocknie described such residence groups as being comprised typically of two older men, who may have been either brothers or close friends, their wives and children, and their daughters' husbands.[60] This characterization is confirmed by Comanches today.[61] As Robert Coffey put it in 1985: "Depended on who you stayed around with. Some nomads, some were established. It was just kind of a family, clan here and there." Mr. Coffey's father farmed an acreage with a spring near the present town of Faxon, residing near his close friend and the friend's family.

By the 1890s the agricultural activities of extended and single-family households were the primary indigenous source of Comanche subsistence apart from federal rations and annuities. As a consequence, Comanche residence was becoming more permanent.[62] In 1897 a survey of 253 Comanche families (out of a total of 598 domestic units)[63] who were engaged in some form of settled life showed that more than half of them, 157, were living in houses and farming, while 96 were living on farms without houses.[64] A total of 4,500 acres were being worked, with fields varying from five to twenty acres in size. Just eleven years before, in 1886, only twenty-seven Comanche families had lived in houses, and only forty-eight families had been engaged in farming.[65]

With the decline of residence bands and divisional gatherings, the importance of kinship and friendship networks probably increased. No longer were Comanches moving about among larger, essentially public social units. They now were moving about among smaller, essentially private extended and single-family domestic units. In these latter contexts, kin and friend relationships would have had more interactional value, fitting the visitor into the existing modality of personal relations rather than transforming the private region into a public one. Thus, whereas Comanches had some motivation to minimize kin networks in the public contexts of residence bands and divisional gatherings, they likely were motivated to extend kin relationships during the reservation period. As noted in the previous chapter, Comanche ideas of kinship allowed them to expand their recognition of kin through any genealogical link. With the agreement of those involved, more than one affinal link could be used to create a kin relationship (Gladwin 1948).

Changes in Comanche residence also had consequences for Comanche leadership. The residences found in the 1897 survey appeared to the agent to cluster in three localities: one on West Cache Creek just south of the Wichita Mountains (120 families), another farther south on West Cache Creek (80 families), and the third east of the first two on Medicine Creek near Fort Sill (53 families). These three clusters of Comanche residences may have constituted different political factions, focused around popular leaders, during the late reservation period. Certainly the northern district of West Cache Creek was dominated by Quanah Parker. Residing in the district south of Quanah's were Eschiti, Comer, Howeah, and Moetah, each of whom was a prominent opponent of Quanah on such issues as grass leases and allotments (Hagan 1976:152).[66] Residing in the district north of Fort Sill were White Wolf, Ahdosy, Pieraconic, Otipoby, and Mumsookawat, who also were prominent in reservation-era and postallotment politics, sometimes in opposition to Quanah.

Whether as distinct factions or not, localized residences represented a new kind of community leadership. With the fragmentation of Comanche social units, two changes in Comanche leadership had occurred after 1879. First, a younger generation quickly replaced the older residence-band leaders (Hagan 1980:180–181).[67] This occurred between 1878 and 1885 as the number and size of residence bands changed. Second, after 1885 the influence of that younger generation of Comanche leaders came to depend exclusively on networks of personal relationships within the community and on symbols of authority and economic support bestowed by Anglo officials. Comanche leaders were no longer leaders of organized groups that divided the membership of the larger community. As Agent Hunt noted in 1885:

> The chief has no longer his old-time influence, and indeed, except as chief of the band which was organized for convenience in issuing the ration of beef, the position is almost nominal. The tribes have their chief men who command an influence and who are looked to for advice upon any question in which the whole tribe is interested but none of them can control the tribe or any considerable portion of it. The old chiefs say themselves, their power is gone.[68]

While the power of Comanche leaders may have diminished, their function as intermediaries was still vital both to the community and to the federal government. Comanches needed leaders to ensure their economic base, particularly with annuities due to lapse after 1898 and rations dependent on the good will of the Indian agent. Indian agents relied on community leaders to communicate and promote changing policies. Had Comanche leaders not presented themselves after the disappearance of residence bands, Indian agents would have had to invent them. As it happened, agents had only to select those candidates who were most amenable to cooperation. These leaders benefited personally from their cooperation, redistributing some of the gains to their followers, with Quanah being the most prominent example. Leaders who were not favored by the agents lacked the economic power to attract followers but became the focal points around which those who were dissatisfied with current conditions rallied. Thus, while Quanah gained by far the greatest economic benefits from the agency and had the largest following in the community, he was consistently opposed by other leaders who represented economically dissatisfied constituencies.[69]

CHANGES IN COMANCHE PUBLIC GATHERINGS

The reliance of Comanche residence units and leaders on personal relationships for group membership and authority meant that some form of public gathering was needed to organize those residence units, to sanction Comanche leaders, and to subject the social relationships that supported both group membership and individual leadership to a broader public concern for moral worth. Otherwise, Comanches would fragment among personal networks and political factions, with no basis for a shared sense of "being Comanche." Such fragmentation, of course, was one of the goals of federal Indian policy.

Although most Comanches continued to pursue a nomadic way of life, the limited possibilities for such movement, the shortened distances between residence bands, and the disappearance of the bison removed most, if not all, of the reasons for maintaining divisional identities on the reservation. Divisional units no longer were necessary to provide for cooperation and participation among different social groups over a wide geographical area. Once Comanches were limited to the reservation, it became possible to organize participation in focused gatherings through the social unit of the whole community. There is little evidence of divisions being used for any purpose of social organization after 1875,[70] and there is no statistical evidence that, at the time of allotment, divisional identities were used as a basis for the location of individual acreages.[71]

Military societies also fell into disuse as effective social groups during the early reservation period, probably between 1870 and 1875. The circumstances that had supported these social groups, and gatherings of their members, no longer obtained. No longer were hunting parties, raiding parties, or ceremonial dances in preparation for these activities used as occasions for focused interaction. As Leonard Riddles described this situation in a 1985 interview, "They just saw where their life was going, and saw right off it was a losing battle, and gave up some of their dances. Towards the last, when they were in conflict with the U.S. military, they began forgetting and dropping some of the military societies." Haddon Nauni also spoke in 1986 of the decline of warrior societies, noting that the defeats by the U.S. cavalry "broke apart warrior societies. They just didn't do anything after that."

After 1878, divisional gatherings and military societies ceased to make sense to Comanches as representative forms of their community.[72] Comanches' beliefs about the physical world (populated by bison and other readily available game) and their standards for appropriate interaction with one another (moving about the Plains in residence bands and gathering on divisional occasions) were upset by the changes that had occurred on the Plains between 1867 and 1878. The bison had all but disappeared, and residence bands and divisions no longer served their functions in the geographically concentrated Comanche reservation. With their expectations about the world shattered, Comanches ceased to build public occasions around those expectations.

While in 1874 Comanches had attempted to innovate a multidivisional

Sun Dance as a means of public social organization, these gatherings ended in 1878 after their intracommunity functions were compromised. Comanches' explanations for "putting away" the Sun Dance have much to do with the public nature of those occasions. As Albert Attocknie explained in 1937, "it was also seen that Sun Dance lodge was being built so that people could see in, plainly see all over the lodge."[73] Sarah Pohocsucat also discussed this problem in her 1967 explanation:

> And that [probably the Sun Dance of 1878] was the last medicine lodge they build since they come to the reservation. And sometime later they said they wanted to build one, but they wasn't because they didn't want the white people to come and look at them. My people, the Comanches, when they have their medicine they don't play with it. They want to do what they want and not be bothered with it.[74]

Finally, Leonard Riddles echoed the same reasoning in 1985: "They couldn't go off and be left alone, so they just stopped [performing the Sun Dance]."[75]

The reservation concentrated Comanches in geographical proximity to one another as they had never been before. It also made Anglos consistently present to Comanches as never before. Comanches were now living in a social situation that was not, to use Goffman's term, soundproof. In the first ten years of the reservation, the agents, who were still fearful of military resistance, were particularly sensitive to any large gathering of Indians. Comanches, on the other hand, were sensitive to exposing the public regions of their community to Anglo view.

It is precisely this concern for the Anglo presence that also disqualified agency gatherings as occasions for community maintenance. Comanches gathered at the agency in large encampments on ration days and, after 1885, for the semiannual grass payments. These gatherings continued throughout the reservation period, and the grass payments continued after allotment. Though these were public occasions in which large numbers of Comanches were present to one another, they were devised expressly for the purpose of Comanche-Anglo interaction. Certainly Comanches must have taken advantage of agency gatherings to engage in private, focused encounters with one another, accomplishing social business such as political alliances and marriage negotiations, that could not be transacted within private residence groups. However, just as the open Sun Dance lodge was too vulnerable for continued use, agency gatherings also were vulnerable to Anglo presence, and there is no record of agency gatherings being used as occasions for focused public activities other than gambling and horse racing.

It was under these circumstances, then, that peyote became the basis for a new form of social gathering. Public gatherings centered on peyote rituals became the primary means by which the Comanche social organization was maintained during the reservation period. Because of their innovation as public gatherings, peyote meetings provided Comanches with continued access to power after the Sun Dance and other channels had been put away. Peyote had been known to Comanches for some time prior to the reservation period (Wallace and Hoebel 1952:332). By their own accounts, they received knowledge of it from the Apaches but discovered its use as a medicine on their own (McAllester 1949:14–17; Wallace and Hoebel 1952:334).[76] Before reservation times, peyote was not central to any public ceremony or gathering (Wallace and Hoebel 1952:332). It was but one among a range of organic means used by Comanche specialists to achieve or tap into their conception of the powers available in the world around them. Leonard Riddles made this point in 1984: "Medicine men had quite a bit to do with peyote before its popularity. It was easy for that medicine man to fall right into that peyote."

In 1883 peyote was first reported to the agent as being used in more public ceremonies.[77] By 1888 peyote meetings were common among Comanches.[78] In that year the agent tried to suppress its use, but Comanches would compromise only to the extent of limiting their use to each full moon. By 1890 nearly every Comanche male was a participant in meetings (Wallace and Hoebel 1952:345). In 1985 Robert Coffey described reservation-era peyote participation: "Most of the Comanches, I've heard, attended the peyote. I don't know of any that didn't. Right at the opening of the country for settlement [allotment] nearly every Comanche participated."

Peyote meetings were conducted at night in closed spaces—tipis—while Sun Dances and other prereservation ceremonies had been performed in the open, often during the daytime. In a way that could not be done with the Sun Dance, the shift to enclosed, nighttime ceremonies ensured that the gathering was hidden from Anglo presence.[79] From the confused accounts of reservation-era agents, it appears that peyote ceremonies were never penetrated by agency officials. The use of the tipi also meant that peyote gatherings were smaller than the Sun Dance gatherings had been. On the other hand, they were also more frequent and more easily organized.[80]

The innovation of peyote gatherings during the reservation period maintained many prereservation Comanche beliefs in a new context. Earth, sun, and moon were important symbols in peyote ritual, as they had been in prereservation rituals. There also was a continuing association between high points in the landscape and personal visions and powers.[81] Curing practices, such as eagle doctoring, which had once been conducted in the context of prereservation ceremonial gatherings, such as the Sun Dance, now were conducted under the auspices of peyote gatherings (McAllester 1949:24; Jones 1968:182–183). In this way, peyote gatherings provided the social and geographic framework for cultural practices that once had been oriented around residence bands and divisional gatherings. Thus, for Comanches, peyote was not so much a promise of the return of the days of the bison or an acceptance of the days of the "white man," but the next logical locus of medicine and power once white men had removed the bison and other animals important to Comanche belief and practice and had made an Anglo presence pervasive. As Robert Coffey explained this in 1986, "U.S. government kills all the buffaloes. All these migratory animals becoming extinct. They were looking for something that had power."

Peyote gatherings also created public contexts for the validation of personal accomplishment. Such public contexts were necessary for ritual and political leaders attempting to represent themselves as people with power. While the favor of the Indian agent was an important symbol for a reservation-period leader, claims to traditional kinds of power also were important. Access to power had been important to Comanches in prereservation times in nearly all their pursuits: "In Comanche society," Wallace and Hoebel noted, "practically all males and many old women came to possess medicine. . . . The greater one's power, the greater the prestige he achieved" (Wallace and Hoebel 1952:160).

Peyote was believed to empower the user with visions, experiences in which the user goes off alone, either in fact or in dream, to receive a personal blessing or gift. Persons with such power were believed to be able to make "right" choices and so to make good leaders. In order to validate and use this blessing as a part of one's social identity, it was necessary to express and apply it in a public gathering (McAllester 1949:38). In this relation of private vision to public expression, peyote meetings replicated the model of pre-reservation Comanche belief and practice. Private experiences required validation in a public context in order to be used within the community (Wallace and Hoebel 1952:155–156, 160–161).

Just as Comanches required that the reputations of warriors be validated in public gatherings before 1875, those who claimed to be "strong" peyote men had to demonstrate this by their public behavior in peyote meetings and elsewhere during the reservation period and after. Peyote meetings were regulated by elaborate standards of conduct within the peyote tipi, and there was a marked emphasis on good feelings and respect, thus engendering concern for one another's faces or moral worth (Mooney 1910:442; McAllester 1949:20–21; La Barre 1975:48). Outside the tipi, peyote leaders were held to standards of generosity similar to those expected of prereservation band leaders (La Barre 1975:63–65).

Peyote leaders, or road men, as they were also called because they followed the peyote road rather than the Anglo road, were often political leaders, and peyote circles (that is, groups of participants who frequently went into the tipi together) tended to form around these men much as residence bands had formed around powerful warriors (McAllester 1949:18).[82] Peyote circles became the nuclei for political alliance and power within the Comanche community.[83] These circles, though, were not formal congregations, and peyote leaders or road men frequently were invited to officiate at various circles throughout the reservation. Indeed, the main political benefit of peyote participation came in the form of the networks that arose among different circles, not in the membership of one particular circle.

It was no accident that Quanah Parker was a conspicuously strong peyote man, who officiated at many ceremonies on the reservation, and that rival leaders such as Otto Wells, Mumsuki, and Paddyaker also shared this distinction. Indeed, the establishment of peyote among the Comanches between 1883 and 1888 closely paralleled Quanah's rise as the leading Comanche-Anglo intermediary (Hagan 1980:181–184). Clearly, Quanah used peyote meetings to establish his preeminence within the Comanche community, forming compelling personal relationships that were politically useful. His authority as a leading peyote priest enhanced his authority as an intermediary leader for the Comanches. In 1985 Leonard Riddles characterized Quanah's participation in peyote in this way: "Of course, Quanah Parker probably gave it [peyote] a big push, even though it was brought in by a captured Apache warrior. They had to start doing something else. They had to look to other things to do instead of going out onto the Plains."

Peyote meetings also resembled divisional gatherings, and thus performed an integrative function in that they brought together those Comanches who were in close proximity to one another yet who did not reside or interact in the same everyday social units. Edward Wermy described attendance at reservation meetings in this way in 1985: "They just put the tipi up and would drum and people would follow that sound in the evenings to those meetings." If, as agency reports indicate,[84] peyote was almost uniformly used by Comanches by the 1890s, then peyote gatherings were easily accessible, participation being limited only by proximity and transportation. This also meant that participants at peyote meetings were publicly accessible to the larger community on a consistent basis. Such frequency of social interaction is one of the requirements for the maintenance of a community's standards of behavior among its members.

Although most participants were men, some Comanche women also regularly participated in peyote meetings (Jones 1968). As far as the gathering itself was concerned, women, whether participants in the ceremony or not, were physically present in the vicinity of the meeting—preparing the meeting site, attending to the comfort of participants, and preparing the morning meal after the meeting. Thus, even if they did not actively take part in the focused activity of the gathering, women were engaged in interaction within the larger context of the social occasion (McAllester 1949:19–20).

While the ceremony itself was an elaborate exercise in the presentation of self to others, with ritually mandated care for personal preserves of space, turn, and information within the tipi (see La Barre 1975:43–52), most of the social business relating to the larger community probably occurred in the aftermath, as participants socialized more informally over the traditional morning meal (McAllester 1949:19). Then, as in divisional gatherings, both focused and unfocused interaction would occur among participants, women as well as men: "While waiting for the ritual breakfast, the meeting is again somewhat informal. Several women may leave [the tipi] to help the water-women prepare the food, and younger men may go outside for a stroll and a secular smoke. Old men often lecture younger members on behavior at this time, 'preaching' directly to a relative, and more indirectly to others" (La Barre 1975:52–53). As described here, the peyote meeting is a classic example of informal social interaction at work organizing and regulating a community. The direct sanction of a relative is possible because of the compelling personal nature of kinship relations that mitigate a breakdown in communication. Nonrelatives are sanctioned in a more indirect fashion because of the absence of such underlying support, thus increasing the risk of a breakdown in interaction through damage to the face of the nonrelative. Both kinds of social work, however, have enduring consequences beyond the gathering itself for the reputation or face of the persons involved.

It is interesting that peyote meetings became the dominant form of public gathering in the Comanche community in a relatively short period of time. This suggests, first, that peyote was indeed a logically consistent transformation of existing traditional beliefs, and second, that peyote gatherings fit the social circumstances that constrained mutual presence among Comanches on the reservation.

THE DYNAMICS OF RESERVATION SOCIAL LIFE
AND SOCIAL STRUCTURE

As this chapter has shown, for the first eight years of the reservation period, from 1870 to 1878, the Comanche community was maintained by public gatherings held over from prereservation life. As long as the social conditions of reservation life approximated those of life on the open plains, Comanches maintained many of the same social units they had used prior to the reservation era. As economic conditions changed, however, periodic Comanche-Anglo interaction became vital to Comanche life. This situation gave rise to intermediary leaders, like Quanah Parker, who were instrumental in negotiating new economic arrangements to facilitate community life. Despite the appearance of accommodation that Comanches like Quanah presented to Anglos, the community devised new forms of public gathering to sustain the frequency of interaction among its members.

Comanche social units underwent considerable change between 1879 and 1885, as divisions and residence bands were dissolved into smaller residence groups. For the most part, residence groups became private regions of family relations, ceasing to function as public gatherings. The patchwork of economic resources upon which Comanches depended, and the uncertainty of any one resource from year to year, led many Comanches to take up farming and stock raising. At the same time, Comanche movements around the reservation settled into more localized patterns. Thus, by the end of the reservation period, Comanches had established settled communities. This realignment of Comanche residence units required a consonant realignment of the means by which they were organized within the larger community.

Lacking an overarching social structure, Comanches used peyote gatherings to maintain both their community and many of their traditional beliefs about power. Peyote gatherings conformed to the smaller, more localized nature of Comanche residence units and to the greater frequency of Comanche-Comanche interactions occurring outside residence units. Thus, at the time that Comanches were becoming more sedentary and increasing their agricultural and ranching activities in accord with Anglo Indian policy, they were also maintaining their distinctive community carefully out of the Anglos' line of sight.

The study of peyote use during reservation times and after, however, has usually been compartmentalized under the heading of religion, which emphasizes its psychological benefits to communities under the stress of externally directed change without considering its broader implications for community organization. Wallace and Hoebel, for instance, portray peyote as a source of solace into which Comanches retreated: "It did not solve their problems of adjustment to confinement on a reservation, but it helped to ameliorate their suffering and to prevent total disintegration" (1952:337). This view stresses the cultural dimension of belief while largely ignoring the social dimension of the gatherings. When they do comment on the social dimension, Wallace and Hoebel (1952:332) stress the "group experience" of reservation-era peyote gatherings in contrast to what they describe as the "individual concern" of prereservation Comanche religious belief (Wallace and Hoebel 1952:155), using peyote as an index of Comanche relations with Euro-Americans. This is a good example of the longstanding anthropological interpretation of peyotism as a pan-Indian phenomenon explicable primarily by reference to the general circumstances of Indian-Anglo relations in the latter half of the nineteenth century. Additional examples of this explanation may be found in Slotkin's discussion: "The Peyote Religion is an Indian defense against consequences of White domination. Specifically, my thesis is that Peyotism socially is an example of accommodation rather than militancy; culturally, that it is a case of pan-Indian nativism." Later he observed that the peyote religion "substituted a value system based on an ethic adopted from White mores, but compatible with the Indian culture pattern" (1956:7, 41). McAllester, who in a study of peyote music worked with Comanches in 1940, asserts a similar explanation for the popularity of peyote on the reservation:

> [T]he peyote movement marked the cessation of militant action by the Indians. In place of resistance a philosophy of peaceful conciliation and escape arose. Interestingly enough, peyotism stressed the professed attitudes of the conquering white man—meekness and righteous living—but retained many reassuring elements of aboriginal ritual behavior. The vision, all-important on the Plains, was made easily available by the use of the cactus. (McAllester 1949:85)

While not all anthropological interpretations of peyotism focus on psychological, nativistic, or acculturational explanations (see Aberle 1982; Wagner 1974; Siskin 1983; Stewart and Aberle 1984), nearly all interpret peyotism as an accommodation of some sort with the surrounding Anglo world and the differential social statuses that Anglo-dominated political and economic forces created in native communities. Certainly some echoes of each of these explanations of peyotism may be detected in the Comanches' reservation-era use of the ceremony. Still, these interpretations of peyotism have paid little attention to the social function of the gatherings as such, the public nature of these occasions, and the regulation and organization of social relations accomplished therein. The rapid, widespread adoption of peyotism within the Comanche community can be explained primarily by the prevailing necessities of community organization and only secondarily by such individual considerations as psychological anxiety, relative economic deprivation among community members, political rivalry, and the degree of acculturation.

Through peyotism, Comanches adapted to changing conditions during the thirty-one years of their reservation experience without subscribing to, or approximating, an Anglo model of social interaction. In agreeing to conclude that experience by negotiating the Jerome Agreement in 1892, Comanches were able both to retain their reservation innovations for another nine years and also to provide themselves with another set of economic resources to support the continuation of their community beyond allotment.

4

The Postallotment Community, 1901-1941

I want to continue to live this way, that is, the way we are living now. I want to be satisfied, and the people down there [other Comanches] will be satisfied by our treatment by the government, and I hope it will always be in this form.

Mamsookawat, 1917

In general, it is assumed that Indians are fundamentally responsive to the same situations and interests as other nationality groups where active cultural differences do not interfere. The desire for security, for new activities or interests and for recognition or value in the eyes of their fellowmen must result in common reactions to a given situation. It is apparent that the Indians of the Kiowa Agency are undergoing social changes common to the rural sections of the Southwest as well as presenting problems peculiar to an Indian population.

A. J. Gilkison, 1934

Allotment in severalty was intended to break up Indian communities so that they could not be put back together again by their members. As Comanches chose their 160-acre sections in 1900 and 1901, they had little idea of the new social matrix that was about to form around them. Instead, the choices Comanches made in allotment location reflected traditional notions of the physical landscape and of private relationships. In general, Comanches preferred locations along stream beds for access to water, wood, and shelter from the open plains.[1] Comanches then chose sections of land meeting these criteria near relatives, friends, and affines to whom they were particularly close (Stahl 1978:197–198). Robert Coffey, an original allottee as a child, described these choices in 1986: "Depended on who you stayed around with. Some nomads, some more established. It was just kind of a family, clan here and there."

While the Comanches' allotment choices had some consequences for their ongoing community, the eruption of Anglo homesteaders onto the social landscape was a more significant constraint on participation in the Comanche community, primarily because the homesteaders altered the economic conditions of Comanche social life. When the remaining reservation lands were assigned by lottery, nearly 1,500 Comanches found themselves in the midst of more than 30,000 Anglo homesteaders (Hagan 1976:269). The arrival of those Anglo homesteaders in July 1901 was outside the experience of most Comanches. Sarah Pohocsucat, who was seven years old at the time, described the event:

> One day we woke up and was to rush away to a playground. We saw a big tent. We thought some people had come to camp there, and be going on. So my playmates told me, that they says we wait till they gone—go away. So we waited then after while they started to build frame buildings. My playmates says, "They start building something. What you think they're doing?" Well, I says, I don't know. Well, after while someone went to see what was going on. So they come back and say, "They have a lot of things to see, everything is pretty over there." No tents, in frame buildings. So we go look around and see what was going on. First time I ever see a lot of white people.[2]

Many of the adjustments Comanches made to maintain their community after allotment involved the forms and strategies they employed in public gatherings with one another rather than in the geographical arrangement of private residence units. These changes in public gatherings reflected the new economic conditions that the Anglo homesteaders brought with them during that surprising summer.

POSTALLOTMENT ECONOMIC CONDITIONS, 1901-1941

Although the Comanches had gradually increased their agricultural activities prior to allotment, these activities declined soon after. In the five years after allotment, farming continued in much the same pattern as in the five years prior to it, with cultivated land fluctuating between 5,000 and 20,000 acres for all tribes in the reservation area (Stahl 1978:209). By 1910, however, only 15 percent of the Comanches were estimated to be farming their allotments.[3] While this number increased somewhat during the next decade as agricultural prices rose, by 1920 Comanche agricultural activity went into a permanent decline as commodity prices collapsed and farming became increasingly mechanized (Stahl 1978:232). After 1920, Comanches were unable to compete with Anglo farmers because they lacked the capital—or the ability to mortgage their allotments to obtain capital—to purchase mechanized agricultural equipment.

Just 500 Indian farmers were reported for the Kiowas, Comanches, and Kiowa-Apaches in 1925, and 559 in 1931 (out of total populations of 5,023 in 1925 and 5,500 in 1931),[4]and the average agricultural production, was estimated at no more than $250 per year. Most of those counted as farmers were raising gardens whose produce was not intended for commercial sale but for household consumption. The gardens were significant sources of food for Comanche families, particularly during the depression years of the 1930s.

The decline of the Comanches' cattle herds, one of their more successful economic activities during the reservation period, was even more precipitous. By 1910 only 2 percent of Kiowa, Comanche, and Apache (KCA) Indians were reported engaged in stockraising.[5] Anglo thieves, Anglo laws that held Comanches responsible for the damage their cattle did to crops, and the end of federal rations in 1901 all contributed to the exhaustion of Comanche base herds.[6] As with their gardens, the stock that Comanche households did raise was used almost exclusively for household consumption. In 1934, for instance, only 95 out of 805 KCA households had beef cattle, while 332 had milk cattle. Only 81 livestock sales were reported in that year, for a total gross of less than $2,000.[7]

In 1927 Superintendent Buntin closed the chapter on Comanche farmers: "There are only a few Indian farmers or stockmen of this reservation who are wholly self-supporting."[8] The continuing economic distress of the 1930s did not give Comanches any new access to agribusiness. In fact, most Comanches who still farmed cash crops quit at that time and leased their lands (Stahl 1978:276). In place of their own agricultural activities, Comanches obtained cash by leasing their allotments to Anglo farmers and ranchers. In the year immediately after allotment, 443 allotments totaling more than 3,700 acres were leased to Anglos by Kiowas, Comanches, Apaches and Wichitas.[9] In 1903, 1,200 allotments were leased,[10] and in 1905, 1,700.[11] The leasing trend continued to grow, with 2,000 allotments leased in 1906[12] and 2,600 in 1909.[13] By 1920, more than 4,000 allotments out of some 4,500 (including Wichita and Caddo allotments) were leased.[14]

With the agricultural depression that followed World War I, the value of those leases declined (Stahl 1978:232).[15] Not only were Comanches getting less money for their leases, they were also getting less money when they farmed their allotments. Leasing continued to be the choice of most allotment owners. By the time of the Great Depression, one-fifth of KCA lease payments were delinquent.[16] Also during this time, inheritance splintered the control of allotments, and many were simply sold outright. Although allotments were designed to be held in trust to prevent the alienation of

MAP 2. The Kiowa, Comanche, and Apache Reservation. The reservation was opened to Anglo homesteading in 1901. Anglo towns around which concentrations of rural Comanche allotments were located are marked here, as is the Big Pasture, which remained under KCA ownership until 1906, when it too was opened to homesteading. (Map by Christine Schultz)

Indian land, allotments that were inherited in part could be sold to non-Indians. Thus, between 1907 and 1920, 357 allotments totaling more than 80,000 acres were sold by Comanches, Kiowas, Apaches, and Wichitas (Stahl 1978:222–223).

The loss of the Comanches' land base was accelerated in the next decade. Between 1920 and 1934, the local agency actively promoted the sale of allotment lands, especially those inherited by Indians already possessing their own acreages. The superintendent then used these funds to build houses for Indian families, with the idea of breaking up extended families into nuclear family residence units.[17] Between 1922 and 1927, more than 450 homes were built in this manner through the sale of more than 250 allotments.[18] By 1930 more than 800 homes had been constructed for a KCA population of slightly more than 4,500 (that is, one home per 5.6 persons).[19] In effect, the local superintendent was persuading Comanches to exchange land that generated lease money for houses that generated no revenue. As Mah-sook-wah testi-

fied before a Senate investigating committee in 1930, "He [the superinten-
dent] has caused all these Indians to be broke. . . . He has gone on and has
built fine houses for them and when they got them built, why, they are
hungry and living in those good homes."[20]

Land sales decreased in frequency after 1934, when policies of the Roosevelt administration made the sale of allotment land more difficult (Jackson
and Galli 1977:99). By 1934, however, there were more KCA Indians without
land than with allotted land—only 1,836 out of 4,863 individuals were receiving income from leases.[21] This was due both to the alienation of allotted
land and a 43 percent population increase since allotment. By 1940, KCA
allotted lands had decreased to slightly more than 378,000 acres from an
original total of slightly more than 540,000 acres.[22]

The Comanches' other sources of income after allotment were per capita
payments from various funds, including the land settlement from the Jerome
Agreement. Comanches, Kiowas, and Apaches received grass payments on
the "Big Pasture" lands (480,000 acres along the Red River left under their
joint ownership) until that land was ordered allotted among KCA children
born after 1901, with the remaining land sold. The money from that sale was
added to the funds paid Comanches for their former reservation lands in
1901 and distributed in annual per capita payments.

To make use of these funds, Comanches, along with other Indian peoples
after allotment, had to go to local BIA officials to obtain allowances from
what was in reality their own money. Per capita payments were administered
by the Bureau of Indian Affairs, but a congressional appropriation was required each year. The BIA, which helped write the legislation, effectively
decided the annual amount. It also applied some of the appropriated funds
to administrative costs and capital improvements over which Comanches
had no control. While this arrangement was meant as a protection for Indian
funds, Anglo traders took advantage of it by allowing Comanches to obtain
goods on credit and then collecting from the agency on annuity and grass
payment days. In 1910 the superintendent reported that Comanches were
"much in debt" on account of this practice.[23]

When the funds were not used, or when the superintendent would not
allow disbursement, lease money, annuities and grass payments, and oil roy-
alties accumulated in Comanches' agency accounts. Between 1919 and 1927,
Comanches could, with the approval of the BIA, withdraw all the money in
their accounts, including their share of the 1900 and 1906 land settlements,
from which per capita payments had been made. More than half of the KCA
accounts were closed by 1926.[24] Those Comanches who were not considered

competent, however, continued to receive two fifty-dollar annuities per year, which exhausted the land settlement fund in 1928.[25]

In about 1919, the Comanches, along with the Kiowas and the Apaches, had realized that a new source for per capita payments was needed to replace the rapidly depleting annuity fund. By 1921 the Comanches had focused on the bed of the Red River, which flows along the border between Oklahoma and Texas and which the 1867 Medicine Lodge Treaty included in the reservation area. The Red River land was significant even though it was underwater most of the year because it was unallotted land, and oil had been discovered there.[26] Between 1921 and 1926, when the Red River case was won by the KCA business committee, political activity among and within the three tribes was centered around efforts to select lawyers, send delegations to Washington, and agree on the best negotiated settlement of the Red River claim.[27] The Red River annuity fund, however, provided per capita payments only from 1927 to 1934. Business committee and tribal council meetings between 1935 and 1944 were dominated by attempts to secure per capita payments and other sources of per capita funds to replace the Red River funds, but without success.[28]

Aside from per capita payments and lease money, Comanches obtained some cash from employment in the Anglo economy. At no time, though, between allotment in 1901 and World War II did Comanches or any other Indian people in western Oklahoma have significant access to the Anglo-dominated economy surrounding them. Out of 4,863 Kiowas, Comanches, and Apaches in 1934, only 15 had full-time jobs, with another 227 having part-time or seasonal jobs.[29] In that year, 1,220 KCA Indians received some form of government relief. A petition by the KCA business committee for per capita payments in 1929 described the economic situation that lasted from allotment to World War II: "We doubt if an Indian on this reservation can be found in our three tribes up to this time who has made enough money either by farming or otherwise to build himself a good home and improve his allotment. Very few, if any, have made enough money by farming or otherwise to make even a descent [sic] living and stay clear of debt."[30]

By 1941 the Comanches' economic position was, if anything, worse than in the years immediately after allotment. Per capita payments had ceased, leases were less profitable, and allotment land still was being alienated from Comanche ownership. As agriculture became increasingly mechanized, it came increasingly to be outside the Comanches' financial grasp. Comanches also experienced continuing prejudice in the Anglo community, which denied them access to most opportunities for everyday employment.

COMANCHE-ANGLO INTERACTION AFTER ALLOTMENT

The stereotype of an inferior "Indian" person already mentioned in previous chapters lay behind attitudes that caused Anglos to hold Comanches apart from their own newly established communities in southwestern Oklahoma. Robert Thomas, an Anglo who worked in various stores in southwestern Oklahoma that sold goods to Indians between 1901 and 1937, expressed several of the typical stereotypes about Comanches' character: "Most of the Indians had their money spent before they received their payments, and as a result most of them are today destitute. . . . They are a lazy tribe when it comes to farming. . . . The men are lazy workers. . . . When one has money, they all have money. They do not know how to save money and spend every cent they get and go in debt for every cent they can."[31] An official of the Chamber of Commerce of Lawton, the largest city to be established within the old reservation boundaries, gave the following summation of Comanche "progress" in 1938:

> For years past, it has been the hope and aim of the Indian Bureau of the United States Government to fit the Indian to take his place in the life of the American people. In some quarters in Congress the belief prevails that the point of development has finally been reached when this process of assimilation may be completed. Even some who have had an opportunity to live daily with the Indians are of the opinion that the time has come when he may be regarded as fit material for the cauldron which molds the average American citizen. But here in southwestern Oklahoma, in the heart of what was once called the Comanche country, the present day Indians, following the example of the illustrious Chief Quanah Parker, will be the last to lay aside the old.[32]

Thus Comanches found themselves marked as a separate category of people in their interactions with Anglos.[33] Their community gatherings, especially peyote meetings, became suspect soon after allotment, and it was necessary to fight a long political battle in Anglo contexts to maintain the legality of peyote possession and use (Stewart 1987:132–147). For the most part, Comanches responded to these conditions by staying off Anglo lands, out of Anglo towns, and as disengaged as possible from the Anglo-dominated economy.[34]

At the same time that they were essentially locked out of the Anglo economy, Comanches continued to be faced with various BIA policies that encouraged assimilation. Cultural activities such as traditional dances were discouraged, while Anglo-style clothing and "legal" marriage were promoted (Jackson and Galli 1977:91–92). The control that local superintendents held over Indian funds was a coercive force in implementing these and other policies (Hoxie 1984:153–155).[35] The files of the Kiowa Agency provide numerous examples of superintendents writing to individual Comanches, pointing out their reported deficiencies with respect to marital relations or dancing and hinting at the financial consequences of these lapses. Superintendents also sent out monthly letters of commendation to individuals and families recommended by district farmers and matrons as making special progress toward Anglo-style social life.[36]

One of the primary means designed to assimilate Indians to Anglo ways was the boarding school. Schools for Indian children had been established on the reservation as early as 1870, but Comanches had been more reluctant than Kiowas or Apaches to enroll their children.[37] After allotment, however, Comanche community leaders made the rounds of Comanche families, collecting school-age children in wagons and driving them off to attend these "Indian schools."[38] As was noted in the annual report for 1910, "There is some feeling against the full blood Indian attending the public schools."[39] The Indian schools, run by the BIA, were essentially vocational-technical academies with two objectives (McBeth 1983). The first was to equip Indian students with the skills needed for occupations that would further their assimilation into Anglo society. Boys were taught farming and ranching, smithing, and cobbling, among other skills, while girls were taught homemaking skills such as cooking and sewing. Some Comanches moved on within the Indian educational system to attend secondary and college-level institutions, but most counted their time in the local Indian boarding schools as an experience in Anglo socialization, applying the lessons they learned in later encounters with Anglos.[40]

The vocational objective of the Indian schools, however, was not generally fulfilled in the Anglo economy. As the agency superintendent noted in 1910, "The young people who return from school do not follow the trades they learn. They prefer to remain near their relatives and generally assist in working such part of the home allotment as is under cultivation."[41] One of those returning schoolboys, Tony Martinez, who came back to the local community in 1913 after being away at an Indian vocational school, explained in 1984 that Anglo prejudice against Indians was such that he could not find a job in the field in which he had been trained, repairing shoes. This situation continued through the 1920s, when district farmers and matrons commented almost monthly on the "laziness" of Indian school graduates.[42] The Great Depression, which hit an already weakened rural Oklahoma economy in 1929 and which effectively lasted until the beginning of World War II, did nothing to improve Indian school graduates' access to the Anglo job market.

The second objective of the schools was to teach Indian children English and, perhaps more important, to force them to use English as their primary, everyday language. To that end, students were prohibited from speaking their native languages under threat of corporal punishment (McBeth 1983:132–133). This process of compulsory language change was successful because students lived at the schools for long periods, and the schools had larger supervisory staffs than instructional staffs. Simply to get along in many everyday contexts, students were forced to resort to English.

In addition to learning about the Anglo world, the Indian school experience was one of Comanche-Comanche socialization. The boarding schools provided opportunities for the formation of generational peer groups and for the development of close friendships, both of which would have consequences for later choices in community participation.[43] The boarding schools also exposed Comanches to other Indian peoples on an everyday basis. In many respects, the boarding school experience may be seen as the foundation for the networks of cross-community Indian participation that developed after allotment (McBeth 1983:120–122). By 1931, though, a majority of KCA children were attending local public schools rather than Indian boarding schools.[44] This trend continued as the BIA attempted, unsuccessfully, to close the three KCA-area boarding schools during the administration of Indian commissioner John Collier from 1933 to 1944.[45] Comanche high school students preferred, however, to attend one of the Indian schools rather than a public high school even when all their previous education had been in public schools.[46] This may have been a result of continuing local prejudice against Indians or a desire to make wider acquaintances among other Comanches of their generation.

In representing their community to Anglos after allotment, Comanches pursued two contradictory lines. When attempting to obtain approval for economic actions from the BIA, such as annual per capita payments, they would cite progress toward the assimilationist objectives of the federal government. However, when arguing for such matters as the extension of the twenty-five-year trust period on Indian allotments, they would represent themselves as ignorant of Anglo ways. As late as 1944, Comanches were still making statements to officials in Washington such as this: "The average Indian today is incompetent to handle his own affairs without government supervision."[47]

The Comanches' objective in interactions with Anglo officials was to maintain the ability to continue to "be Comanche" by whatever economic and political means necessary. By replenishing per capita funds, extending the trust status of allotment land, and arguing against termination of the relationship between the federal government and Indian peoples (a proposal that was first seriously proposed in Congress in the 1940s) Comanches were preserving the economic and legal basis for their shared community. The transcript of a meeting between Assistant Indian Commissioner William Meritt and a delegation of Comanche leaders in 1917 provides some insight into the Comanches' conception of their relations with Anglos:

[Willie] Ahdosy: Well, we come down here to see you about our treaty with the government at the time our country opened for settlement.

Meritt: What do you know about the treaty?

Ahdosy: Well, it give us 25 years to act as Indians, and Indians be not like white men until the trust period [on allotments] expired.

Wo-ok-sook: The government gave us 25 years to act as Indians and we got several more years to go yet as Indians, and they [Comanches] do not understand why it is that the government is going to give some of our young generation their citizenship.[48]

The logic of this way of thinking about the Comanche-federal relationship was that being Indian depended on the economic means (allotment land to lease and per capita payments, for example) that allowed Comanches to maintain a social life distinct from that of the Anglo-Americans who surrounded them. When Comanches began to act in the same economic and political ways as Anglos, their community and identity were threatened. Thus in 1923 many Comanches had the idea that those who had voluntarily taken their allotments out of trust status and who had withdrawn their individual shares from the per capita fund had lost the legal right to be Indians.[49] This belief recognized that the maintenance of a Comanche identity required a different pattern of economic behavior from the Anglo-style ownership of land and use of capital. The function of Comanche-federal relations after allotment was to maintain that economic distinction.

COMANCHE-FEDERAL RELATIONS

After allotment, Comanche leaders were intermediaries who negotiated with Anglo officials for the annual per capita payments and later for funds to replenish the per capita pool. The comments of Willie Ahdosy, addressed to the local superintendent[50] at a Kiowa-Comanche-Apache Business Committee meeting in 1914, are a good example of this intermediary role:

If you help us to get this money, it will be a great help to us, in the future most of us be in better shape, there will be good feeling for that. I think that if we can get this money, we can improve ourselves, and in the future you will see us in better shape than we are now, and it will make you feel good, it will make everybody feel good, and we will be in a better shape than we have been in the past. When you report about what we have said here, and you help us so that we can get this money, we will all feel good for it.[51]

Tribal representatives, however, were much less important to the functioning of the local agency after allotment than they had been before. Indeed, one of the goals of allotment in severalty was to reduce the importance of the tribal community in the lives of individual Indians, thus encouraging assimilation (Hoxie 1984). This was stated explicitly in the 1921 annual report of the Kiowa Agency: "The affairs of these Indians are no longer tribal, but are purely individual. The Indians will for a long while try to hold together as a tribal unit, but this inclination on their part should always be combatted by representatives of the government."[52]

The emphasis was on the individual accumulation of property and capital. Collective economic entities were discouraged. As Assistant Commissioner Meritt put it in a meeting with Comanches in Washington in 1917, "We want the Indians to accumulate property and provide for themselves and their maintenance and not to give up their property promiscuously. Follow the example of the white man and try to work the same as the white man does and save the result of your labors and not give away property [to other Indians]."[53]

In Oklahoma, tribal peoples were left with few joint economic interests after allotment. Those that remained—mainly small acreages of land that had been abandoned by the federal government and so, by treaty, reverted to tribal ownership—were administered by the local superintendents in consultation with business committees representing the reservation areas. Because they lived within the same reservation area, Comanches, along with Kiowas and Kiowa-Apaches, were represented by elected members of a joint business committee who served at the pleasure of the local BIA superintendent. This committee was established soon after allotment, with committeemen chosen at separate tribal councils. By organizing the business committee in this fashion, the federal government could largely ignore tribal differences and focus mainly on the objective of merging a general "Indian" category into that of "American."

The tribal councils at which business committeemen were selected were moderated by the superintendent, or his representative, who largely set the agenda.[54] The superintendent would make some opening remarks that established the purpose of the council meeting and would often interrupt a discussion to steer the gathering back to the topics upon which he wanted to focus. KCA business committee meetings were managed by the superintendent in a similar fashion. Because of this topic management, it was quite clear that both tribal councils and business committee meetings were located primarily in the domain of Indian-Anglo interaction rather than Indian-Indian or Comanche-Comanche interaction.

Through his ties to the superintendents, Quanah Parker dominated the three Comanche committee members who served with him on the first KCA committees. For the most part, Quanah supported BIA policy. From the immediate postallotment period to World War II, the local superintendents tended to favor KCA business committee members such as Quanah who were supportive of their policies, encouraging their selection at tribal council meetings and consulting them outside the monthly business committee meetings. Opposing Quanah on the KCA committee were Eschiti and Mamsookawat—both of whom had also participated in residence-band life prior to the reservation period—and Millet, then in his forties and the only representative of the reservation-period generation.[55] An example of the official attitude toward committeemen who did not agree with BIA policy may be seen in a letter written in 1917 by Superintendent Stinchecum to the commissioner of Indian affairs:

> These members are elected by popular vote and it usually happens that the best members of the tribe fail to receive election. The Indians of the opposite class are inclined to use their position more for their personal aggrandizement than for the welfare of the tribe. They are prone to take the position that their influence with the Supt. is necessary before the requests of individual Indians can be complied with, and I am practically certain that in numerous instances the tribal committeemen when accompanying Indians to the agency, ostensibly to act as interpreters, have been drawing down not only traveling expenses but compensation for services which were not performed.[56]

The "best members of the tribe," of course, were those who went along with BIA policy. Otherwise, what Stinchecum has described are leaders acting as intermediaries between members of their community and Anglo officials. As noted in previous chapters, this was a type of leader found in the Comanche community since at least 1786, one whose authority rested primarily in the area of Comanche–Euro-American relations. These leaders depended for their authority on symbols of their influence with members of the Euro-American community. Otherwise they were of little use to members of the native community. Both those Comanches in favor of BIA policies and those opposed to them traded on their influence with local BIA officials, officials in Washington, and members of Congress for influence within the Comanche community.[57]

In 1911, soon after Quanah's death, Eschiti and Mamsookawat tried to convince the BIA to establish a Comanche tribal organization separate from the Kiowas and Kiowa-Apaches. This effort continued through at least 1917.[58] The goal was not to replace the KCA business committee but to supplement it. The superintendent at that time interpreted this as an effort by Eschiti and Mamsookawat to succeed Quanah as the Anglo-designated principal Comanche chief.[59] Rather than an attempt at succession, though, it may have been an effort by the Comanches, most of whom were still participants in peyote gatherings, to have a clear channel of communication with Anglo officials apart from Kiowas and Kiowa-Apaches. Superintendents during this period tended to choose Kiowa, rather than Comanche committeemen to represent the KCA in Washington because the Kiowa committeemen were primarily Christian church participants who supported BIA assimilationist policies, including bills against peyote use that were then before Congress.[60] By establishing a separate, federally recognized intermediary voice, the Comanches intended to deal with social issues such as peyote apart from the economic issues that were the domain of the KCA committee.

This difference between Comanches and Kiowas was also the basis for factions within the Comanche community. Postallotment Comanche politics was polarized over the issue of peyote use. As the annual report for 1916 noted, "In all reservation matters Peyote is the political rock upon which the Indians divide. If the leaders or the friends of Peyote approve or disapprove of a certain thing, we are absolutely assured that all the followers of Peyote will take the same view and those opposed to Peyote, the opposite view."[61]

In general, the opponents of peyote tended to be those who participated in Christian missions. Comanches began to convert to Christianity in significant numbers soon after allotment in 1901. By 1912, opposing "peyote" and "church" factions were noted by the local superintendent in Comanche tribal council meetings.[62] While members of these two factions cooperated at times, such as in the Red River claim, peyote participants continued to be the majority through at least 1929,[63] and this distinction remained a key to Comanche tribal politics until just before World War II, when a generational split within the community became more significant.

Members of the Comanche "church" faction and other opponents of peyote tended to be more willing to accommodate to BIA policies—promoting, for instance, a compromise position on the Red River claim.[64] A succession of superintendents consulted with and promoted members of the church faction for business committee positions.[65] Members of the "peyote" faction, in contrast, were mainly interested in maintaining the economic base for their way of life, and they were among the most vocal proponents of per capita payments and the renewal of per capita funds. Because peyote faction members were not interested in programs that promoted assimilation, they received little encouragement or cooperation from BIA personnel.[66]

With the election of Franklin D. Roosevelt as president and his appointment of John Collier as commissioner of Indian affairs, the attitude of the BIA toward Indians underwent considerable change. Traditional cultural practices, including the use of aboriginal languages, were encouraged, and the cruder coercive manipulations of bureau personnel began to be curtailed (Jackson and Galli 1977:99–102). Getting money on account from the local agency remained, however, a considerable bureaucratic undertaking. Collier's approach to Indian-federal relations resulted in the passage of the Indian Reorganization Act (IRA) of 1934, which provided a framework through which Indian peoples could organize, or reorganize, their means of self-government. The IRA also provided for Indian-run credit associations (essentially revolving loan funds), which were funded through Indian money that had previously gone to per capita payments.

Curiously, Indian peoples living in Oklahoma were specifically exempted from the IRA as the result of action by the Oklahoma congressional delegation. The delegation perceived the IRA as encouraging Indian peoples in the words of Senator Elmer Thomas of Oklahoma, to "return to their ancient customs and way of life."[67] Oklahoma Anglo politicians may have been concerned about the IRA's potential for creating self-supporting Indian political and economic entities, whereas before Indian peoples had been only loosely organized as weak business committees serving at the pleasure of the BIA and with few economic resources of their own. In any event, a watered-down version of the IRA was applied to Indian peoples in Oklahoma through the Oklahoma Indian Welfare Act (OIWA) of 1936.

What is doubly curious, however, is the antipathy shown by Comanches toward both the IRA and the OIWA. Shortly after Congress passed the OIWA, a field agent from the Washington office of the BIA came to Oklahoma to help Comanches write their own constitution and bylaws separately from the Kiowas and Apaches who were being encouraged to do the same. By a vote of 162–472 Comanches failed to adopt an OIWA constitution.[68] Kiowas and Apaches also rejected their constitutions, though by closer margins. Comanche opposition to what seems to have been a stronger form of political and economic organization can best be understood in the context of their economic relations with federal authorities. As already noted, until 1934 the Comanches had relied upon a series of grass payments, land sale annuities, and Red River annuities to maintain their economic well-being. While these sources rarely exceeded $200 per individual per year, when added together as residence units (many of which were extended rather than nuclear families) they comprised a significant proportion of household income.[69]

The year 1934 marked the last of the Red River annuity payments, and Comanches were once again looking for some source of per capita income.[70] By 1936 the KCA business committee was looking for a lawyer, as they had done in the Red River claim, to help promote what was called the "Jurisdictional Bill" in Congress. This bill allowed the KCA tribes to sue the federal government for land claims on the basis of the highly controversial Jerome Agreement of 1892. A settlement of that claim would more than replenish the per capita pool. The political and economic provisions of both the IRA and the OIWA ran counter to this effort because, first, they separated the interests of the Kiowa, Comanche, and Apache tribes, and second, they favored revolving credit funds and other collective economic ventures over per capita payments. The KCA peoples may well have perceived the OIWA and separate tribal constitutions as undercutting the basis for their postallotment economic survival.[71]

It was at this point that generational cooperation began to break down, as younger men of both factions found some of the economic provisions of the so-called Indian New Deal attractive, while older church members found common cause with older peyote members in opposing those programs. White Parker and Norton Tahqueshi, for instance, who were both prominent Comanche pastors, nevertheless opposed ratification of the OIWA constitution.[72] By 1942 the only Comanche member of the KCA business committee under forty, William Karty, who was also chairman of the committee, found himself opposed to the older Comanche members on the question of per capita payments.[73] Karty argued that use of those funds in OIWA-style credit association programs was more economically beneficial to the community. The older Comanche committeemen, however—most of whom were members of the church faction—were mainly concerned with the short-term economic benefit that per capita payments would provide. This generational split would widen after the war as returning Comanche servicemen experienced greatly increased access to the Anglo economy.

CULTURAL CHANGE AFTER ALLOTMENT

Because allotment and Anglo homesteading were such fundamental changes in the social conditions surrounding Comanche life, changes in the Comanches' cultural and social means for interacting with one another were inevitable. For instance, a good deal of lexical innovation occurred in the

Comanche language just after allotment as Comanches came into contact with many novel Anglo objects and ideas.[74] Later, as more Comanches attended Indian and public schools, there was a greater tendency to borrow English words and phrases in place of creating equivalents in Comanche (Casagrande 1955:10). Rather than extend the Comanche language to describe Anglo society and culture, Comanches who came of age after allotment categorized and interpreted Anglo social interaction and culture in Anglo terms. Because this younger generation did not use the Comanche language as the primary means of constructing impressions and expressions of an increasingly invasive Anglo society, it gradually became a secondary language. Casagrande described Comanche language use in 1940 as follows:

> The whole range of bilingualism is to be found among the 2,400 or so Comanche, and there is a complete inversion as one descends through the generations as to which is other and which mother tongue. Most old people over 60 speak little or no English, while most young people under 30 speak little or no Comanche. . . . Although most Comanche between the ages of 30 and 60 are bilingual, the number who are equally fluent in both English and Comanche is relatively small. They are mainly men and a few women between the ages of 40 and 55; the generation that stands midway between the old culture and the new. (Casagrande 1955:9–10)

Many Comanche families made a conscious decision to shift the everyday language of the home to English. These choices were made in explicit reference to succeeding in an Anglo-dominated economy.[75] By 1944, interpreters were no longer regularly employed in tribal council meetings. Decisions about language shift were similar to choices made by traditional medicine men about passing on their knowledge and powers:

> Grandfather called all his grandsons together one day. Had reached the age where he was to pass on his power and knowledge. He had joined the church, yet he still had this thing in him. Had talked to his minister, who didn't understand. Fasted for three days to find out what to do. Had to make a choice between missionary's church and his heritage. Did not receive a satisfactory answer. Within himself, he felt it all right to doctor on his immediate family, but not anyone else. He told us: "Because of this modern day that you live in, you're going to have to live like a white man. This power has certain taboos. A black eagle feather on a wall with a lot of restrictions. I'd hate to have you out working for a living and someone defile that thing and make you sick. I'd hate to see you lose that job. I've decided just to take this to the grave with me." After grandfather died, I saw a big ole tarantula crawl out of his grave. I just feel like that was grandfather's power.[76]

On the surface, changing Comanche attitudes toward the English language, Anglo-run schools, and traditional medical practices would seem to suggest movement toward assimilation. Certainly if one looked only at the cultural forms used by Comanches or failed to distinguish between Comanche-Anglo interaction and Comanche-Comanche interaction, such a conclusion would be unavoidable. As Casagrande noted,

> Another 50 to 75 years may see Comanche cease to function as a living language. The constant contact with Whites, the teaching of English in the schools and, due to the fact that the Comanche live on scattered allotments, the lack of an integrated community or tribal life comparable to that of the Pueblo or Reservation tribes, are all factors in the evanescence of the language. English is the language of the dominant culture, the language through which one gets on in the world by means of widening social, economic and political contacts. Though it is doomed, the language is far and away the most vitally functioning part of the old Comanche culture. (Casagrande 1955:12)

When the question is approached from the perspective of how these forms were used as means for participation in the Comanche community, however, it is possible to demonstrate that Comanches continued to go on "being Comanche" because of, rather than despite, the changes they consciously made in such cultural frameworks as language and belief.

COMANCHE SOCIAL UNITS AFTER ALLOTMENT

While Anglo settlement in 1901 did not increase the actual distances between Comanches, it did raise barriers to Comanche-Comanche interaction. The most immediate barrier was Anglo ownership of every square foot of surrounding land not in trust status for Indians. Along with that ownership came, under the Homestead Act, the requirement that settlers live continuously on the land they claimed. This meant that up to four Anglo families were present in every square mile of land. By the time of statehood in 1907, Anglo settlers in the former Kiowa-Comanche reservation outnumbered Indians by more than 33 to 1.[77] Quite simply, away from one's own allotment, the chance of Anglo presence was greater than that of Comanche presence.

Comanches could no longer rely on proximity in order to encounter other Comanches. By choosing their allotments along meandering streams and creeks, Comanches had unwittingly exposed their lines of communication to a pervasive Anglo presence. While this presence only rarely impinged directly on gatherings within the community, it nevertheless constrained the opportunities available to Comanches for participation in Comanche-Comanche encounters. No longer could drums call people to peyote meetings, nor could families encounter one another as nomads on an open plain. The landscape was now crowded with white faces, carefully protected by barbed wire fences and the insistent symmetry of section-line roads.[78] Indian people who wanted to travel to see one another were restricted to the gridwork of country roads, on which they were watched by Anglo eyes. Their traffic was submerged in the greater volume and faster pace of the Anglo world.

Because of their severe economic disadvantage, Comanches became dependent on the castoffs of Anglo consumers for transportation. Thus, as the Anglo market was shifting from horse-drawn conveyances to automobiles, Comanches were the market of last resort for increasingly obsolescent technology.[79] In 1984 George Watchetaker described the Comanche market for old horse-drawn carriages in the 1920s, just as the Model T and other automobiles were making motorized transportation available to larger numbers of Anglo-Americans: "Get one of those hacks [horse-drawn taxis] with celluloid windows, boy you were in style. Those old Indians shining those up, that white hack. They get their best clothes and they ride, boy. That was one of the luxuries to the Indians. If you could own one, you were in the upper crust."[80]

Comanches were consistently several steps behind their more mobile Anglo neighbors, but that did not mean that Comanches were standing still. Soon after the reservation was opened to homesteaders, Comanches began moving around the country more frequently than they had done in the decade just prior to allotment. As already noted, only 103 Comanche families were living on their allotments by 1904. The rest, in the words of a district matron in her monthly report for May 1905, were "constantly traveling and camping from place to place."[81] The semiannual grass payments were made at five locations throughout the former reservation and drew large encampments until 1910, when payments began to be made to individuals through the district farmers and matrons. Comanches also gathered in encampments for Christmas and New Year's from at least 1906 on, and they camped in large gatherings during the summer months as well.[82] Camps were located on subagency and issue station land and on allotments.

When not camping with a larger gathering, Comanches lived in extended families on a member's allotment. In a report for April 1904, the matron for the Cache area noted that twenty-eight families were in houses and eighty-seven in tents.[83] Houses, most built with assistance from the agency, did not catch up with tents until 1911, and tent life did not appreciably decline until 1915 (Stahl 1978:218). Prior to 1917, it was not unusual for a district matron to note that a residence group with a house on the allotment nevertheless preferred to live in tents. Residence groups were similar to those that had formed after the breakup of residence bands in the 1880s. They varied from extended families (two or more older men, usually brothers, their wives, children, children's spouses, and sometimes also grandchildren and grandparents) to nuclear families.[84] Given the frequency of movement during the immediate postallotment period, residence groups were probably quite fluid, depending on the changing economic circumstances of family members.

By 1926, though, nearly all Comanches lived in permanent houses in rural areas.[85] Often, more than one residence group was located on the same allotment.[86] By 1934, however, a majority of Comanches were landless, having sold their allotment interests or having been born after 1910, and the problem of how and where to house those persons had become a federal concern. The BIA interest was not purely altruistic. While most Comanches without land of their own had housing available with relatives or friends, the federal government discouraged multifamily households as impediments to assimilation.[87] Still, given the increase in landless Comanches and the economic collapse between 1926 and 1934, Comanche households probably increased in size during that period, and multifamily households probably became more common.[88]

Residence groups that were near one another in the postallotment period comprised local communities, much as had developed during the 1890s. Where the reservation communities had been constrained by agricultural and ranching activities, postallotment communities were constrained more by the limitations of the Anglo-dominated landscape. The local communities were comprised of Comanches who lived within five miles of one another, people who could potentially be present to each other on an everyday basis, given the limits of horse-powered transportation and Anglo fences and roads.[89] These local Comanche communities were made up primarily of rural residences in the vicinity of the Anglo towns of Cache, Indiahoma, Faxon, Porter Hill, Richard's Spur, Pumpkin Center, Hatchetville, Walters, Elgin, Fletcher, Cyril, and Apache, and in an area known as Pleasant Valley.[90] People called these communities "bunches," referring to "that Cache bunch" or "that Walters bunch."[91]

As Comanches obtained motorized transportation in increasing numbers in the late 1930s, the local communities began to break down,[92] and as distance became less of a barrier to public gatherings, the limitations of geography and distance were no longer as significant as they once had been in Comanche gatherings. The kinds of gatherings in which Comanches engaged between allotment and the 1930s, however, were set in the context of these local communities.

FORMS OF GATHERING IN THE POSTALLOTMENT COMMUNITY

After allotment, Comanches had to devise public gatherings that fit within new constraints on mutual presence and movement. In the process, they evolved a range of alternative public gatherings, participation in which tended to segment the community in contrast to the consensus around peyote gatherings that had evolved during the reservation period.

Peyote meetings continued to be held in much the same manner as before, though somewhat less conspicuously in deference to Anglo neighbors.[93] Immediately after allotment, peyote meetings were held nearly every weekend. These gatherings reflected the division of the larger community into local communities, creating distinctions that were noted by participants: "Songs. That's the only difference. They [different local communities] didn't sing each other's songs."[94]

Peyote use was recorded as being frequent among Comanches in the superintendent's annual report for 1910 and in matrons' reports for 1913.[95] In 1916 the political split over peyote use had grown prominent enough for the local agency to notice. Comanche peyote men participated in the legal establishment of the Native American Church in 1918 (Stewart 1987:224–225). A survey of American Indians published in 1923, based on information collected from local superintendents, reports that from 50 to 60 percent of Kiowas, Comanches, and Apaches attended peyote gatherings at that time (Lindquist 1923:187). A district matron observed in the same year that peyote was being sold among Comanches on the street in Cache. By the 1920s, though, superintendents reported that peyote use was in decline. In 1930 the superintendent stated that only "30–40% of older Indians use peyote."[96]

The decline in peyote participation was the result of a split between the reservation and postallotment generations in their choice of public gathering. Older Comanches who had grown up on the Plains or the reservation for the most part stayed with peyote, while younger Comanches increasingly chose to participate in Anglo-derived forms of gathering such as Christian church meetings.[97] This was in part the result of an emphasis on age as a qualification for full participation in peyote meetings. Men did not join peyote circles until their late twenties and were not considered, within the circle, to be full members until they were more experienced, in their late thirties or forties. As Tennyson Echawaudah observed, "The elders were really strict. A young person couldn't just go in there. They were serious about what they were doing."[98]

While peyote gatherings no longer drew the participation of almost all the Comanches, as had been the case at the end of the reservation period, these meetings had become occasions for the exercise of traditional curing practices (Jones 1968:38). Peyote curing was open to any Comanche, even a Christian church member, and was often resorted to when Anglo doctors had failed. This function, in addition to the religious beliefs of longtime participants, helped to maintain the frequency of peyote gatherings after allotment. Indeed, many of the younger Comanches who were recruited as participants after allotment had first attended meetings in order to be cured of some ailment.[99]

Still, although the peyote faction had an advantage in numbers during the first thirty years following allotment, recruitment did not keep pace with either the postallotment increase in population or the number of Comanches, young and old, who were converting to Christianity. Younger Comanches were more willing, and more motivated, than older Comanches to consider forms of community participation that provided greater opportunities in the Anglo world. As already noted, local BIA personnel favored members of the church faction, who were more likely to be agreeable to federal Indian policy.

Anglo Christian missionaries had been active among Comanches since 1889, but initially their success in making converts was minimal. During reservation times, Comanches were suspicious of representatives of Anglo religion. Robert Coffey, who later became the first Comanche pastor of the Deyo Baptist Church, described his family's early experience of Anglo missionaries around the time of allotment:

> Here's our two-room house on the plains. And here comes this missionary in his wagon. He ties up at the hitching post and walks up to our house. My father says, "Here comes that white man. We got our religion and he got his. I wonder what he wants." My mother says, "Let him come. He'll tell us what he wants." "He wants to cheat," my father says.

A list of converts at the Deyo Baptist Mission shows Comanches seldom turned to Christianity until after allotment but then did so in significant numbers.[100] Between 1892 and 1901, Rev. Deyo had only thirteen Comanche converts. Between 1902 and 1911, however, he had 150, with 36 in 1903 alone. Within a decade of allotment, at least six churches with predominantly Comanche memberships were attracting converts.[101] They corresponded to the local communities that had developed after allotment. Although they were led by Anglo pastors, their members were almost all Comanches, locating them well within the boundaries of the Comanche community as defined by Comanche-Comanche interaction. By 1920, thirteen Indian churches were active among KCA peoples, with memberships of 1,495 people out of a total population of 4,631 (1,635 of whom were Comanches).[102] In 1928 the superintendent expressed the opinion that the majority of KCA Indians had converted.[103] Most of these were younger people who had some economic motivation for doing so.

Prior to the reorganization of the Federal Indian Service under John Collier in 1933, local missionaries or their wives were often employed as district farmers and matrons. Of the four district matrons responsible for Comanches, for instance, three were wives of Anglo missionaries or were associated with Anglo missions between 1900 and 1926.[104] Because these matrons were the conduits for requests for funds, as well as sources of information about individual Comanches for the agency superintendent, their churches and they were important economic factors in the local communities. Often they were responsible for recommending younger Comanches for Indian educational opportunities beyond high school.[105] The approval of the local Anglo-run Comanche church was quite useful in obtaining economic and other support from the local agency, and arguably that approval was more useful to younger than to older Comanches.[106]

There was, of course, a price attached to the missionaries' assistance. To become members of a Christian church, Comanches were required by Anglo missionaries to renounce participation in peyote meetings, dancing, and other traditional activities.[107] This meant that Comanches who wanted to make use of church gatherings had to do so as an exclusive strategy. Given the barriers to younger peoples' participation in traditional activities such as peyote gatherings, Christian church participation was an attractive alternative for some. The missionaries' expectation, of course, was that this would force Comanches to become assimilated into Anglo society.

Being "Christian," however, did not prevent a Comanche from also being "Indian" in Anglo eyes. Thus, Comanche church people were subject to the same general social conditions and constraints as were other Comanches. Because they were prohibited from participation in other Comanche community gatherings and excluded from the Anglo community, church members were left with little choice but to make Christian church gatherings occasions for "being Comanche" as well as being Christian.

The isolation of church members from other, more traditional types of public gathering in the Comanche community resulted in a division of the community between "peyote people" and "church people." This began to take shape between allotment and World War I.[108] Interestingly, the factionalization of the community that resulted was restricted to public gatherings and had little effect on private encounters and relationships within families and between friends. Church people and peyote people continued to associate with one another on a private, personal basis, taking care to restrict their interactive differences with one another solely to public gatherings.[109] But while their public gatherings were separate, peyote and church gatherings were isomorphic in form. Peyote meetings were held mostly on Saturday nights, with informal social gatherings following on Sunday mornings, the same time that Comanche Christian churches were gathering. And both peyote people and church people gathered for winter holiday and summer encampments.[110] These encampments had begun shortly after allotment as continuations of reservation-period nomadic movements, taking advantage of annuity and lease money payments on January 1 and July 1. They were adapted to Christian occasions by church people as the community split.

The traditional, or peyote, faction winter encampments for the Christmas and New Year's holidays were usually gatherings of residence groups that lived in proximity to one another. Leonard Riddles recalled the annual Walters winter encampment in a 1984 interview:

> Comanches would camp out at Christmas east of Walters starting one or two weeks before. Kids would ride their horses through camp. They'd have their Christmas trees set up and had two tents set up together, full of people. They'd have a Christmas tree in the middle and all kinds of decorations. Lanterns hanging up there from the poles. They'd have presents hanging up in the tree. Sacks of Bull Durham in socks. Other presents under the tree. The women would be doing the cooking out in the open.
>
> They used to have that handgame, too, at nights. Maybe this bunch at Walters would take on another bunch. And, of course, they'd have poker going on in one tent. Men played monte, women coon-can. Dealers were usually white. Sometimes they'd bust him, but he'd bust a whole camp. Sometimes two or three different outfits would be playing in the same tent. They'd bet on the handgame. Most of 'em put up a kind of jackpot.

The winter encampments were occasions for both focused and unfocused interaction. In addition to the gaming and gambling,[111] they also featured dancing, but the gatherings were not structured around any single central activity. Winter encampments must have been much like prereservation divisional gatherings, as people who lived in the same geographic area throughout the year interacted with each other intensively for a brief period. The first report of a winter encampment after allotment, one outside Cache, appears in a district matron's report in January 1907. Thereafter they are

mentioned almost annually for each district, with the matrons giving particular attention to the gambling.[112] Andrew Perdasophy noted that at least
one of these encampments, south of Lawton, occurred in 1937, though the
practice was not as common as it had been in the past.[113] He also noted the
distinction between these encampments and those of Comanches belonging
to Christian churches. The church faction winter encampments were on the
church grounds, and they focused, of course, on the religious nature of the
Christmas holiday. They also may be interpreted as local community occasions, though without the gambling.

Summer was the time for the other annual encampment. Actually, the
traditional summer encampment was more like a series of gatherings. Many
Comanches left their allotments sometime in June and often did not return
until August or early September. In the course of their summer movements
from one camp to another, Comanches from different local communities
came into regular contact with one another. The sustained nature of summer encampments is first reported in 1906 as a feature distinct from the
more nomadic movements in which Comanches engaged in the years immediately after allotment.[114] By 1911, summer encampments had become
focused around traditional dances. Tennyson Echawaudah described these
early dances in 1984: "They'd camp different places. Mostly, just the elders
took part [that is, danced]. Just a few selected men, maybe five or six. They
respected what they did."[115]

The summer dances resulted from a move within the community to re-
vive traditional rituals that had been abandoned during the reservation
period. Their revival may have been inspired by local Anglo towns that
hired Comanches to dance at civic celebrations in the years immediately
after allotment. Surviving members of prereservation military societies subsequently were asked by their Comanche neighbors to perform the traditional dances in intracommunity contexts.[116] While the military societies had
ceased to function as social units, former members had not forgotten the
cultural forms they had used: "They'd go over the things they did before
reservation. It was just something they always had and it went pretty
strong."[117] Among the remaining societies were the Crow, Big Pony, Spear,
Shield, and Wolverine societies.[118] These societies had similar dances, but
each owned its own songs. Among the dances in the male Comanche repertoire were the buffalo dance, the victory dance, the horse-stealing dance, the
crow dance, the scalp dance, the spear dance, the eagle dance, and the snake
dance.[119] The gourd dance also was among the men's repertoire, though it is
not clear at what point it was taken up by Comanches (Howard 1976).
Children danced the rabbit dance, and women danced the round dance, but

these were not considered at the time as traditional dances in the same sense as were the men's dances.

While older members of the community kept younger Comanches from active participation in the traditional dances, the gatherings were focused occasions requiring the cooperative involvement of both participants and spectators, and attention to the maintenance of the social faces of all involved. Thus a sense of moral order was present at these gatherings, sanctioning appropriate community behavior: "They wouldn't let those young people come in, just those [older] people that were involved and their close relatives. Certain people felt, well, 'I'm not that close on it.' They sort of looked down on people who got in and didn't belong."[120] At some point, purely social dances were innovated to allow younger people a more active participation in the gatherings, but these dances, such as the "49," with their lessened concern for impression management, were not the central focus around which the gatherings were structured.[121]

More summer gatherings were held in 1912: "The Fourth of July marked the beginning of numerous picnics and dances."[122] In 1913, "unusual wanderings of the Indians" were reported as "picnics and dances took them from one place to another."[123] By this time, most of the local communities were involved. Leonard Riddles described this situation in 1984: "Each community began having its annual thing. Maybe two, three, four powwows a year, only summer." As Comanches were reported making more extensive plans for "old dances and old camps,"[124] the events of 1913 resulted in a 1914 circular from the Indian commissioner setting bureau policy against traditional gatherings and dances: "Both the Indians and the public should be made to realize that these old customs retard the march of civilization and that the government looks with disfavor on all appeals that mean perpetuating them."[125]

Also during the summer of 1913, a gift dance was held between Apaches and Comanches, the first report of a "giveaway," at which participants exchange presents. Giveaways were, and are, sponsored by families or groups wishing to honor the deeds or presence of particular participants. As such, they are occasions for the strategic management of private relationships in a public setting. Giveaways became a regular feature of Comanche dance gatherings and were used particularly to recognize the attendance of Comanches from outside the local community sponsoring the occasion.[126] Haddon Nauni, who grew up in the prewar community, put it this way in the fall of 1985: "People would gather things to give away and dance. That's still with us today, that desire to acknowledge things."

BIA officials were particularly concerned about the giveaway dances because they saw these as undercutting the Comanches' respect for private property. In a meeting with Assistant Commissioner Meritt in 1917, though, Willie Ahdosy explained the redistributive function of giveaways: "In these giveaway dances all the Indians do not give away property, only those who are able and have enough to give away."[127] Nearly every Comanche dance gathering featured some sort of gift giving. As Haddon Nauni observed, giving away and honoring was a way in which mutual respect for moral worth could be publicly marked. And as Willie Ahdosy noted, this was also a way in which those with economic surpluses could aid those in need. Nevertheless, in 1917 the superintendent withheld annuity payments from Comanches who had participated in traditional dances the previous year.[128] Despite this coercion, Comanches continued to gather during the summer for dances. After World War I, for instance, the older military society members used a traditional dance gathering to recognize returning Comanche veterans as warriors:

> They were given a reception, honored with a dance for them. My brother-in-law was a veteran and we went over to Indiahoma where they were going to have a dance on the bank of the creek right west there. I had a box Kodak and took some pictures. It was mostly those boys that live around Cache and Indiahoma there. We went on the buggy over there. They had a beef. Kind of a welcoming home. That was the biggest they had. Try to get all the Comanches over there, but the traveling distance was such that they couldn't get there.[129]

The local superintendents continued to complain of the "pernicious" influence of summer encampments and dances throughout the 1920s:

> We have always found it necessary to combat the natural tendencies of the Indians to hold prolonged camps. Such gatherings are almost always accompanied by prolonged periods of dancing. Prolonged camps encourage the mingling of the sexes; all restraints of home are cast aside. . . . The 49'er Dance is a pernicious form of enjoyment on the part of these Indians and needs to be curtailed. These camps encourage immoral practices and a goodly number of illegitimate children on this reservation have been traced directly to the prolonged camps.[130]

The winter and summer encampments continued, of course, but the participation of younger Comanches had begun to decline by 1922.[131] By 1928, as with peyote gatherings, younger community members were little involved in the summer dance gatherings. Instead they participated in other forms of gathering, notably summer Christian camps or retreats. "The younger people, as a rule," according to the annual report for 1928, "take very little part in the dances."[132] In 1931, though, the local superintendent was still frustrated with the dancing "problem":

In the past it has been customary to have agricultural rentals paid January 1 and July 1 of each year. The two periods in the year when dancing is done most are the Holiday period [Christmas and New Year's] and the period beginning about the Fourth of July. These are the two periods when lease money is paid to the Indians. A considerable part of these funds is doubtless used in paying necessary expenses to carry on dances and celebrations.[133]

Although the distribution of lease payments was moved to November 1 and April 1, the winter and summer encampments continued. As late as the summer of 1938, Comanches were petitioning the superintendent to move the date of a general KCA council meeting to accommodate several summer encampments scheduled for the same time.[134] By that time, though, the last members of the prereservation military society generation had passed on, and the character of and participants in the dances had begun to change, with a similar transition occurring in peyote gatherings. Both peyote and powwow gatherings were drawing new, younger members from church memberships.

Though carefully isolated from the traditional winter and summer encampments, Comanches who attended the corresponding church gatherings experienced much the same kind of focused and unfocused interaction as occurred at the traditional dance encampments. The summer church gatherings, for instance, were held at church-owned campgrounds and brought together congregations from different Comanche churches. The communal living arrangements allowed participants to interact with one another daily. They cooperated in focused activities such as prayer meetings, sermons, and testimonies at which a small number of those present actively performed and the majority passively supported the interaction with their attention. In this way, Comanches maintained a shared community through similar kinds of gatherings even though they did not agree on the cultural substance of those gatherings.

PEYOTE AND DANCING: GENERATIONAL TRANSITIONS, 1935-1941

Many of the older Comanches who had preserved dancing and peyote after allotment participated in both kinds of gatherings without conflict or contradiction.[135] Both had been elements of the same belief system in prereservation days. That belief system, however, died with the last of the prereservation generation. For the postreservation generations of Comanches, there was no common basis for integrating peyote beliefs with beliefs associated with traditional dances. In a 1985 interview, Leonard Riddles, who witnessed the generational transition, spoke of the younger Comanches who took over dancing and peyote in the 1930s: "Of course, they knew the old way, but others coming in, it's going to drift and change. So, they either have to drift and change with 'em or tell 'em about the old ways."

Because younger Comanches had been prohibited from leading dancing and peyote gatherings, their understanding of these occasions had not been subjected to public regulation. When they began to lead these gatherings in the 1930s, they naturally did so in their own way, innovating belief systems with which to interpret the events. Comanches speak of peyote and dancing becoming, at this time, two distinct "religions."[136] As Leonard Riddles described it, the "religious character of the powwows started up in the '30s. Maybe a lot of 'em wanted to keep up the traditions when a lot of the older people began to pass on. Honoring their dead. It sort of got into a religious thing."

The younger Comanches who took over dancing in the late 1930s were veterans of World War I, thus preserving the traditional connection between dancing and the military societies, and they had attended Indian schools. Many had participated in Christian church gatherings. Powwows provided these younger Comanches with their first opportunity to participate actively in a Comanche-derived, rather than an Anglo-derived, form of gathering. Consequently, they marked off the focused activity of the gathering— dancing—from the surrounding social occasion. Dance gatherings, which previously had had a carnival atmosphere, became more solemn occasions in the late 1930s. "It's a dance of respect for our elders who have gone before," Haddon Nauni said. "Even their spirits are there. In respect to them, we have to conduct ourselves in a dignified way."[137] The reservation-era generation had not needed to make explicit their claim to traditional authority. The generation that had grown up on allotments, though, emphasized the ritual of the gatherings as a way of claiming a tradition from which they had largely been excluded.

Peyote ritual, in contrast, was already well established, with clear links to Comanche tradition. The problem was not to assert a claim on tradition but rather to make the gatherings relevant to postallotment life. The younger Comanches who "took over" peyote in the 1930s incorporated Christian symbols and dogma into the ceremony (McAllester 1949:23). They went so far as to project the belief that peyote is a form of Christian sacrament into their accounts of the beliefs and actions of the older Comanches whom they succeeded: "Those older peoples were quoting the Bible," said Edward Wermy, "but they didn't know nothing about it."[138]

These innovations made peyote gatherings alternatives to Christian church gatherings for a generation that had grown up with the latter as their model for "religious" occasions. Peyote gatherings became places where Comanches could find help—that is, mental or physical curing—in times of crisis, a more specialized function than the gatherings had served for older Comanches. This function echoed the theology used by Anglo missionaries, who preached an evangelical gospel emphasizing the healing and restorative powers of Christianity. If peace of mind could not be found in the Anglo church, perhaps it could be found in the Comanche church.

The innovation in belief systems that occurred in the late 1930s made participation in dancing and peyote gatherings mutually exclusive. As Edward Wermy put it in 1985, "You didn't mix things." While peyote gatherings remained open to any Comanches who "needed help," those Comanches of the postallotment generation who chose to become strong peyote people did not actively participate in traditional dances. Similarly, their peers who chose to become strong powwow people did not actively participate in peyote gatherings.[139] Though some of the postallotment generation that took over peyote and powwow gatherings had grown up in traditional families, others had spent their youths and young adult lives as members of the church faction. Their move into more traditional activities was no doubt assisted in the 1930s by the increasing tolerance among BIA officials for traditional gatherings and beliefs. Still, by taking part in either peyote or dancing, they forfeited their status in Christian gatherings. Thus, by 1940 the Comanche community was divided into three segments: peyote people, powwow people, and church people.

COMMUNITY MAINTENANCE AFTER ALLOTMENT

As we have seen in this chapter, fragmented postallotment public gatherings still served a useful purpose within the Comanche community. Each form of public gathering brought together people whose interaction was unsupported by compelling personal relationships, requiring a mutual concern for the face of those present to support cooperative involvement in the social occasion. Thus church, peyote, and powwow gatherings were occasions in which personal relationships and individual behavior were made subject to community standards for social conduct, standards that might not have been enforced in private contexts. At the same time, a sufficient frequency of interaction was maintained through personal relationships in private contexts to keep the larger Comanche community from fragmenting into separate peyote, church, and powwow communities. Between 1910 and 1940 there were numerous examples of parents and children, of siblings, and of friends each pursuing different public alternatives (peyote, powwow, or church) without harming their personal relationships with one another.

The segmentation of Comanche participation in public gatherings reflected the differing economic conditions faced by the reservation and postallotment generations of Comanches. The older generation, most of whom had already raised families, and those Comanches who were, for one reason or another, economically self-sufficient used the economic resources available after allotment to maintain traditional gatherings. They lacked motivation to change interactional strategies and so simply adapted their reservation-era practices, such as peyote, to the postallotment world. This segment of the larger Comanche community used winter encampments to organize the local communities in which they resided. Dancing was revived as a focused activity for summer encampments, which were used to organize the older, traditional faction across local community boundaries.

The increasingly landless younger generation faced a somewhat different economic problem. To provide for growing families, they required some degree of access to the Anglo economy. This meant they needed the cooperation of agency personnel, who controlled both Indian funds and Indian educational opportunities. Thus, many younger Comanches chose to present the appearance of having become assimilated by, among other strategies, attending Christian churches and speaking English. This segment of the community used the same forms of winter and summer gatherings to organize its members as did the traditional faction.

Comanche politics also became fragmented after allotment as the intermediary function of Comanche leaders came to be discounted by Anglo officials. Economic and other rewards for accommodative behavior were less frequently bestowed by postallotment superintendents than by reservation and prereservation agents. Through their management of individual Comanches' accounts, BIA officials themselves took on many of the intermediary functions that Comanche leaders previously had carried out. Of course, Comanche leaders still carried out the important function of maintaining annuity funding, but now they did so as supplicants—alternately manipulating symbols of assimilation and savagery—rather than as negotiators with some economic and political capital of their own.

If, after allotment, Comanches had retained some freedom of action or ownership of resources (as they had previously in Euro-American eyes), their community would probably also have maintained a consensus form of public gathering to sanction the uses to which their leaders put these resources. Instead, choices in action and ownership, to the degree these were available, rested with individual Comanches, who, as we have seen, also made their own choices about participating in public gatherings.

Specifically, Comanche politics became polarized between peyote and church factions. The church and peyote factions each remained relatively solidary because of the summer encampments, where leaders from different local communities were exposed to public gatherings and where their internal competition for influence could be regulated. Though peyote and church factions tended to attract members of different generations, this should not be interpreted as generational conflict, because the two were not competing for the same economic resources. Generational differences became more important in Comanche politics when governmental resources began to be filtered more through tribal business committees after 1934. Intracommunity political leadership was given some authority over the distribution of economic resources. Generational disagreements over the provisions of the OIWA are typical of this change. The Comanche community was entering a period in which greater regulation of its leaders would be required, once again placing emphasis on a broadly shared form of public gathering. Peyote, powwow, and church gatherings were, in a sense, in competition for that community function.

Meanwhile, the Comanche community was becoming more mobile, which began to break up the local communities that had formed immediately after allotment, in the same way that residence bands had been broken up by the more intimate geographical confines of the reservation. Increasingly, all peyote, powwow, and church gatherings were accessible to all community members. The postallotment diversity of Comanche interaction would be sorted out into a more integrated pattern of public community participation in the context of the economic revolution brought about by World War II.

5

The Postwar Community, 1942-1990

There's so much difference in the way that white people view our culture and the way we view it. A Comanche isn't concerned with how others view our ceremonies, just as how he views it as a Comanche.

Haddon Nauni

Some use that powwow and some use that peyote. Others go to church. They're pretty strong in their religions. Leonard Riddles

As we have seen, the implementation of reservation and allotment policies had significant consequences for the ways in which Comanches organized their community. World War II had a similar impact on the Comanche community. The war and its aftermath changed the economic conditions that had supported gatherings within the Comanche community. Before the war, nearly all Comanches resided in southwestern Oklahoma. Since the war, one in two enrolled Comanches has left for employment elsewhere. Most of those Comanches, however, have not given up participation in their native community. The period since the war has seen the continuing innovation of ways for maintaining a community among an increasingly scattered membership.[1]

During this period, powwow gatherings have become the consensus form of public gathering Comanches have used to organize their community. Within the context of these occasions, social relationships and individual faces are subjected to public standards of conduct and concern for moral worth. Comanches who are geographically absent from everyday social life use powwows as a means of remaining in contact with their traditional community. Powwows also offer opportunities to channel economic resources from those Comanches who have entered into the Anglo economy to those who have remained as full-time facilitators of the traditional community. Finally, as others have observed (i.e., Powers 1980; Ashworth 1986), intra-community powwows allow Comanches to compare images of their traditional past with images of the Anglo world, while intertribal powwows provide Comanches with images of other Indian communities and of a general "Indian" identity.[2] In this way, Comanches are able to point to the distinctiveness of their community and thus to define what it is to "be Comanche" today.

ECONOMIC CONDITIONS, 1942-1990

The Comanches' increased economic and geographical mobility began with the war. Many Comanche men born between 1912 and 1926 saw military service, as did their Anglo contemporaries. Their duties forced them to live among Anglos and apart from their community for several years. For many, this was a social experience that had important consequences for their later lives.[3] While most Comanche servicemen returned to Oklahoma to live, their status as veterans made them more prominent within the Comanche community and more self-confident in interacting in the Anglo community. In addition, Comanches' military service provided them with educational and economic benefits, such as the GI Bill and federal job preference, of a kind that had never before been available to members of their community. Haddon Nauni, who served in World War II and who returned to find a job as a bookkeeper in Lawton, described the prewar economic situation in a 1984 interview: "Before that [World War II], very few Indians worked. People sat around the house, talked, played dominoes. There were very few jobs." For those Comanches who did not join the military, the war created other economic opportunities. Robert Coffey, who was too old for military service, described them in a 1985 interview: "Jobs was plentiful. A lot of non-veterans, didn't join or turned down, went out to work at a lot of places. Out to California. Found employment at a lot of places."

While the war did not eradicate Anglo prejudices against Indians, it did provide Comanches with their first substantial access to the Anglo economy. During and after the war, more Comanches, especially younger men, held everyday jobs than at any time before.[4] These began to be called "work-a-day people" within the community. The best jobs available to Comanches were with the federal government. The Fort Sill Military Reservation, in Comanche County, was and is the largest single employer in the region. Civilian positions at Fort Sill and with other federal agencies were better insulated from the interference of local prejudices, and Comanches who had served in the military were given the veterans' job preference. Comanches also benefited from new BIA policies that gave preference to Indians in hiring for jobs in the Federal Indian Service (Jackson and Galli 1977:100).

The BIA, which had engaged in few policy initiatives during and immediately after the war, instituted a program of vocational training and relocation to urban areas in 1952 (Jackson and Galli 1977:103, 123). Indians were taken from their local communities, given some training and orientation about life in Anglo cities, and placed in jobs the bureau found for them. According to some Comanches who participated in relocation, it was assumed that they could neither read nor speak English, so facilitators were hired to escort them to grocery stores and read the labels on packages and cans. Along with the general improvement in economic opportunities for Comanches after the war, the relocation program increased the number of Comanches who left southwestern Oklahoma. Prior to World War II, only a handful of enrolled Comanches lived outside the reservation area.[5] By 1980, though, only 4,244 of more than 8,000 enrolled Comanches remained in the reservation area. In 1988, 4,370 Comanches out of 8,317 enrolled still lived within the jurisdiction of the Anadarko Agency.[6]

Within the community, the BIA continued to exercise a paternalistic influence. As it still is today, the agency was responsible for negotiating leases, for handling funds derived from allotment lands, and for administering programs (like relocation) designed to improve the economic conditions of Indian people. Even after the war and the reforms of the Indian New Deal period, the Anadarko area office of the BIA refused to lease an allotment without a signed power of attorney executed by the Comanche owner in advance, essentially giving local BIA officials carte blanche in their administration of Comanche affairs.[7]

Still, despite the economic betterment of some Comanches after World War II, many remained only marginally employed or wholly unemployed for long periods. By 1970, 78 percent of those Comanches, Kiowas, Apaches, and Wichitas remaining in southwestern Oklahoma were living in rural locations, and only 22 percent in urban residences (Henderson and Bohland 1974:27).[8] These Indian peoples experienced nearly 50 percent unemployment and had an average income of $5,276 per year. Many of those who did have jobs were underemployed and had little opportunity for economic advancement. Thus, "Indians are forced to rely heavily on federal or state programs in order to obtain any semblance of an adequate standard of living" (Henderson and Bohland 1974:71–72). In 1970, fully 1,452 persons out of an Indian population of 8,483 in southwestern Oklahoma were on some form of government assistance (Henderson and Bohland 1974:74). Comanches who were successful in the Anglo economy were, for the most part, those who had moved away from the former reservation area to urban centers outside Oklahoma.

Families that owned allotments or interests in allotments had some income from leases. This income, however, became more fragmented with each generation through which the inheritance passed. And with each generation, more allotment land was alienated from Comanche ownership. By 1950 the Comanches, Kiowas, and Kiowa-Apaches had lost more than 50 percent of the land that had been allotted to them.[9] In 1960, though, the majority of Comanches were still deriving the bulk of their income from leases and seasonal agricultural employment.[10] By 1978 these tribes had lost 40 percent of the land remaining in their hands in 1950.[11] In the meantime, the population of all three tribes had more than tripled.[12]

Whatever their sources of income, those Comanches who had regular access to some amount of money tended to become the focal points for extended family households, because close relatives, their spouses, and their children would move in with or near them. Henderson and Bohland (1974:77) reported that in 1970 more than 30 percent of Comanche, Kiowa, Apache, and Wichita households were made up of extended families, as economic resources were shared among relatives and friends. The heads of extended families tended to be over sixty, while the heads of nuclear families tended to be between thirty and thirty-nine. For the most part, the older heads of extended families were those veterans who had used their military preference to get a federal job or older men and women who had, through inheritance, acquired allotment shares that gave them considerable annual lease income.

The economic situation of Comanches in 1980 was not much improved. The average income for Comanches had risen less than $400, to $5,667, which amounted to a loss of economic purchasing power, given the inflation of the 1970s.[13] A total of 38.3 percent of Comanche individuals and 34.6 percent of Comanche families were living below the poverty line. Fifty-seven percent of Comanches were reported as employed in 1980, with 27 percent unemployed and the remainder no longer in the work force.[14] Southwestern Oklahoma experienced an oil boom between 1978 and 1982. Some Comanches experienced sudden wealth as allotments were leased for exploration at relatively high prices, and oil and gas production, when a well was drilled and hit, brought in even more tax-free income. In many cases, however, this wealth was redistributed through personal networks, with little accumulated as savings or investments. While such redistributions had considerable impact in the Kiowa and Apache communities, most Comanches lived too far south in the KCA reservation area to be within the active fields and thus benefited from the boom only as lower-level employees in oil-related businesses. In the 1980s, the boom was followed by a bust that forced many local businesses and banks to close and tightened the local job market considerably.

The decline in energy and agricultural prices during the 1980s contributed to an economic depression in southwestern Oklahoma and has also caused a decline in the amount of lease payments.[15] At the same time, federal programs benefiting Indian peoples have been either cut back or terminated. Comanche Nation officials say that the rate of Comanche unemployment, especially among younger people, has increased since 1980. Those Comanches without jobs face the choice of remaining in the local area with few prospects for support except intracommunity networks or leaving for places where economic conditions are better. Comanches with job skills and a post-high-school education tend to choose the latter alternative, while Comanches without these credentials tend to remain in the local area. This pattern has created the most recent constraint on community organization: maintaining sufficient frequency of contact between members residing outside and within the reservation area.

COMANCHE-FEDERAL RELATIONS

The KCA business committee, which had evolved into a de facto OIWA-style tribal government by the end of John Collier's administration of the BIA, became a more powerful political force during and after World War II. As noted in the previous chapter, a revolving loan fund was established from KCA funds in 1934. This fund, totaling $50,000, was used to help Indian farmers compete with Anglo farmers, most of whom survived from year to year through crop loans. The fund was also used to assist Indians in improving their allotment lands, which allowed them to obtain higher lease payments.[16] In 1947 a similar loan fund was established for KCA servicemen under the provisions of the GI Bill.[17] Distribution of loan money from both these funds was controlled by KCA business committeemen. Indeed, an informal quota operated which divided up the available money among the three tribes.[18] Members of the business committee also had some influence over relief funds distributed through BIA social workers. Each committeeman represented a district with a per capita share of available relief funds. Committeemen played an intermediary role in securing relief funds and loans and in dealing with the Anadarko BIA office.[19]

Immediately after the war, the majority of Comanche members on the KCA business committee were church people, with some powwow people—members of the younger generation that had taken over dancing in the 1930s.[20] This was a function of a decline in peyote participation, the rise of dance gatherings, and a process in which a younger postwar generation took over leadership positions. Older church members and older peyote members still found common cause to oppose younger Comanches, particularly as those younger community members pushed to use KCA funds for longer-term projects rather than for short-term community subsistence.[21] Later, powwow people would rival and then outnumber church people in tribal politics, but by that time participation in the two kinds of gatherings had come to overlap.

By 1950, Comanche politics were focused on two issues that were to be the central points of political contention for the decade. The first of these was the land claim that the Kiowas, Comanches, and Apaches had initiated in 1934 over the Jerome Agreement. With the establishment of the federal Indian Claims Commission in 1947, the KCA claim moved toward resolution. In 1958 the three tribes were awarded $2 million as a partial settlement of their claims against the federal government.[22]

Anticipation of the land claim award created another problem: what to do with the money. On one side were those who wanted to disburse the award in one large per capita payment or in a series of annuity payments. On the other side were those who wanted to use the award to establish a more permanent tribal government structure, with economic development and educational funds. As Levy (1959:49–53) observed, the latter faction, sometimes labeled the "progressives" and backed by the BIA, was a minority in all three tribes. This faction was made up mostly of younger church members, though it also included older members and peyote and powwow people. In contrast, the faction favoring per capita payments had a larger proportion of peyote and powwow participants and older Indians.

This argument was set against the other "Indian" issue that dominated the 1950s: the federal policy of termination. Termination was an outgrowth of the 1943 attempt in Congress to end the treaty obligations of the federal government with Indian peoples unilaterally, abolish the BIA, and declare native peoples assimilated.[23] The faction that wanted to use the land claim money to set up a more permanent tribal structure did so in expectation of the inevitability of termination, though its members opposed the policy (Levy 1959:55). The faction favoring per capita payments wanted to dispose of the land claim money in part to avoid the appearance of having a self-sufficient tribal government.

The threat of termination receded with the end of the Eisenhower Administration in 1961, but the problem of the land claim settlement remained a defining issue in tribal politics. With the sword of termination removed from the equation, the argument for using the money to establish a tribal government gained momentum. The question then became what kind of tribal government there should be. The faction of Comanches then in control of their tribe's KCA business committee seats, most of whom had been members of the "progressive" faction in the 1950s, pushed for separating the three tribes and splitting the land claim settlement proportionately.[24] This issue occupied several years of debate and was not settled until a 1966 referendum, which approved the split.

The argument used by those Comanches who favored the split, now called the "yes" people, was that Kiowas and Kiowa-Apaches would outvote Comanches and so obtain a disproportionate share of the land claim money. In other words, the issue was presented as a short-term economic one, not as a long-term question of Comanche political organization.[25] Opponents of disaffiliation, the "anti-separationists" or "no" people, argued that the three tribes were politically stronger as a group than as separate entities, and they continued to press for per capita payment of the land claim funds.[26] In 1986, Robert Coffey described that period of Comanche politics:

> It always has been the Kiowas and Kiowa-Apaches against the Comanches. People came to me for about two years after I said to my Comanche men, "How about us withdrawing? We been getting left out. They been running over us. This ought to stop for us." Finally, it was given to us as a vote. The government conducted the election. The other two tribes began to holler. They argued [that we were] bound together by treaty. We argued that we're a separate tribe. Anyone can withdraw from membership from any society.

The "yes" faction succeeded because its leaders used a typical short-term economic argument that played on community solidarity instead of longer-term issues of Comanche-Anglo relations. The "no" faction failed because its major constituency, those Comanches who subsisted almost entirely from lease and per capita payments, had declined in number since the war. The separation of Comanches from the KCA was evidence that the younger postwar generation of Comanches who had more involvement with the Anglo economy was beginning to dominate Comanche politics. The KCA business committee had functioned mainly as a lobby for Indian interests with the federal government. In contrast, the Comanche Nation, which was set up in 1969, became an institutional means for Comanches to manage their own funds and programs, thus participating more actively in the politics of Indian affairs and in the Anglo economy.

The Comanches established a business committee composed of a chairman, a vice-chairman, a secretary-treasurer, and four other members.[27] It is both a legislative and an executive body that oversees a full-time staff under an appointed tribal director, who manages the daily operation of tribal programs. In 1970, soon after the Comanches set up their own business committee, the federal government mandated elected tribal self-government, giving native political entities a greater measure of political and economic power (Jackson and Galli 1977:133). Tribal governments were designated as administrators of the federal programs benefiting their members, giving them control over the local versions of the programs and revenue for administrative overhead. Programs such as those for federal educational grants, winter energy grants, job training, low-income housing, and many more were turned over to the tribe. Election to the business committee now had considerable importance for the distribution of federal funds and programs within the Comanche community.

In 1974 the Indian Claims Commission awarded the Comanche, Kiowa, and Apache tribes a $35 million settlement based on the questionable practices of the 1892 Jerome Commission, which initially negotiated allotment.[28] This settlement was divided among the three tribes according to their enrollments. The settlement initiated a turbulent period in Comanche politics. Once again, some favored using the land claim money for per capita payments, while others wanted to establish a permanent tribal complex and tribally sponsored economic and social programs. Elections for the business committee were hard fought, and those who were elected faced constant pressure from both their supporters and their opponents over the use of the land claim money. Tribal chairmen have been recalled from office before their terms ended, and at one point the tribal complex, financed by land claim money and completed in 1978, was taken over by opponents of the sitting business committee.

Ultimately, the land claim money was spent on permanent structures— including the tribal complex north of Lawton and a cultural center west of Cache—and on economic development projects, such as a meat processing plant, an oil exploration company, and other business enterprises that generally have not been successful. By 1984 most of the land claim funds had been exhausted, and tribal revenues depended primarily on administrative overhead from federal programs run by the tribe. This is supplemented by profits from tribal bingo games. Periodically, new economic projects are promoted by tribal officials, the latest being the purchase of the largest hotel in Lawton and the construction of a pari-mutuel racetrack and a living history Comanche village for tourists.

The main difficulty that Comanche economic projects have encountered, aside from adequate financing, has been in forming and maintaining a broad enough consensus to support long-term development. Comanche politics always have been more sensitive to economic concerns about everyday subsistence. Comanche politicians have been better able to provide help to individual community members as personal needs arise than they have been at

administering and expanding collective resources. This is in part the consequence of elective politics, but perhaps it is more fundamentally due to the
continuing difficulties that many Comanches experience in putting together
sufficient economic resources to maintain their everyday subsistence.

Though business committeemen often attempt to take refuge in their
traditional intermediary role, blaming the federal government for shortages
of funding and failed programs, they have also taken on the role of economic
providers. Increasingly, tribal government has come to be perceived as a
source of economic support. Thus, when Comanches are in financial difficulty, the tribe and tribal officials are now one of the first places, after family
and close friends, that people look for help. Many of the same kind of personal requests, petitions, complaints, and charges that were addressed to
federal officials during the first hundred years of reservation and postallotment social life now are addressed to tribal officials. The tribal government,
though, is constrained by the amount of federal funding it receives, and
despite the various economic development projects, it has no dependable
source of funds of its own. Thus tribal officials lack the financial resources to
redress fully the continuing economic needs of their community. At the
same time, federal officials have used the existence of an autonomous tribal
government and the issue of tribal sovereignty as excuses for not undertaking significant initiatives to relieve the situation.

COMANCHE-ANGLO INTERACTION

As Henderson and Bohland noted in 1974 and as can still be observed today,
Indian people in southwestern Oklahoma are not considered full members
of the Anglo-dominated community, even with the educational and employment opportunities that were opened up after World War II. Indeed they
are firmly excluded from participation in many significant economic and
political activities. Even today, few Comanches own retail businesses in Anglo towns in southwestern Oklahoma.

Though by no means ignorant of Anglo conventions and structures for
everyday social interaction,[29] Comanches have had little incentive to engage
in the elaborate work practiced in the Anglo community to present and
maintain particular forms of face. In fact, with little face at risk in Anglo
public situations, Comanches often opt to "play Indian"; that is, they refuse
to engage in any active management of the social encounter. In this, Comanches take advantage of Anglo expectations that Indians will do little of the
social work required to sustain face-to-face encounters. Comanches pursuing this strategy give an impression of taking little or no account of Anglo

interactive strategies and conventions. Their attention is fixed primarily on the outcome of the encounter, on the accomplishment of practical results. Comanches are less concerned about knowingly violating Anglo expectations and less motivated to repair any damage that might ensue.

An older Comanche woman at the checkout stand of a local supermarket, for instance, when asked to produce identification to confirm her check, may simply wait for her bag of groceries without replying. The store clerk asks her if she drives or has a credit card. He asks her if she has a "government card." He asks if she is deaf. Eventually, the line of Anglo shoppers becomes impatient, he rings up the check, and she takes the groceries.[30]

Anglos have taken this interactive strategy as reinforcement for their stereotypes of "uncivilized" and socially "incompetent" Indians. This, however, confuses a particular style of interaction (which, in fact, betrays considerable knowledge of Anglo ways) with an inherent inability to act in an appropriate fashion. Similarly, the economic and political disenfranchisement of Indian people, which has severely restricted their opportunities for participation in the prevailing "American" economic and political systems, also has been taken by their Anglo neighbors as a reflection of the inability of Indian people to act competently in the Anglo-dominated social world.

When an Anglo has background knowledge of the life history and personality of an Indian, however, he or she often exempts that person from the general Indian stereotype. Often Anglos in southwestern Oklahoma make reference to "good" Indians, as if the general category were inherently bad. Thus exemptions are made in implicit reference to the stereotype itself, showing it to be the basic preconception employed by Anglos for anyone who may be classed as an Indian. It is at this level that ethnicity and dependency theories are useful frameworks for understanding Comanches' relations with Anglos. Finding themselves identified with a general category of "Indians" in their encounters with most Anglo-Americans, Comanches use that ethnic identity as best they can to accomplish their short-term interactive goals. But this does not mean that Comanches carry this "Indian" ethnic identity over into their interactions with one another.

Finding themselves enmeshed in the Anglo-dominated political economy, Comanches take advantage of whatever federal and other resources are available to support the social life of their community. But that does not mean that their community gatherings are extensions of their encounters with the Anglo world. What is unique about the Comanche community is the way in which its internal social organization is constructed, a matter separate from its external ethnic and economic relations with Anglo-Americans.

COMANCHE-COMANCHE INTERACTION

Comanche strategies for interacting with Anglos are necessarily exercises in "playing Indian" and not in "being Comanche." While the former involves taking account of Anglo styles and models of interaction, the latter is in no way predicated upon those Anglo means. To "be Comanche" is to orient one's social participation with reference to the ongoing Comanche community and to invest one's social capital in the typically less economic outcomes of intracommunity gatherings. While "playing Indian" is a short-term interactive strategy, "being Comanche" results in social identities that last well beyond any discrete social encounter.

"Playing Indian" and "being Comanche" are linked in that both may be employed by the same person, but it would be inaccurate to say that the means and meanings of Comanche identities are defined by contexts and experiences of "Indian"-Anglo interaction. As we have seen, the social occasions, social identities, and strategies associated with participation in the Comanche community have been shaped primarily by Comanches' shared conventions and expectations for interacting with one another, not by their encounters with Anglos. As Haddon Nauni observed in 1985:

> There's so much difference in the way that white people view our culture and the way we view it. A Comanche isn't concerned with how others view our ceremonies, just as how he views it as a Comanche. Because these things [social occasions within the Comanche community] weren't dependent on monetary value, these things continue to exist today. The success of the gathering wasn't judged in monetary terms, but in relationship terms. A Comanche, everything he does, he doesn't do without basis or meaning. Whatever we do or are involved in has a purpose. If they can't do something that has meaning, then they just won't do it. He participates as one of us. He knows all the meanings. There's a purpose to everything. Respect the purpose by conducting yourself in a dignified manner. Your life was an open book to your people. You grew up in their sight. Your life is still an open book. It keeps you in line, if you care.

Mr. Nauni's explanation of Comanches' interactions with one another emphasizes the uses they have made of public social occasions and participants' concern for the images that others have of them in those contexts as means for community organization. The social dimensions of these public gatherings may be summarized as follows: (1) Comanche gatherings are organized to regulate interaction within the community they share, not as a consequence of their interactions with Anglos; (2) gatherings depend on long-term social relationships among participants, not anonymous, short-term social transactions; (3) participation has a strategic purpose within the community and is not an idle function or a surviving custom or tradition; and (4) gatherings expose Comanches to shared standards for appropriate conduct and concern for moral worth, which, if one cares about one's identity as a Comanche, serve to regulate the actions of individual members in the social unit of the larger cultural community.

After World War II the economic and geographical mobility of some Comanches and the continuing geographic concentration and economic disadvantage of others posed new problems for community maintenance. By the 1940s, personal relationships and encounters continued to provide the background for participation in the Comanche community, but kinship ties had become looser.[31] Leonard Riddles discussed this in 1986: "In the 1930s, that [kinship] began to weaken. They still thought of cousins as brothers, but not as strongly. These [families] getting to where they're not as close as they used to be. Some of 'em moving out to bigger jobs in bigger towns. They just break away."

Kinship obligations are no longer as compelling as they once were.[32] With respect to kin terms, for instance, most adult Comanches are aware of both "Indian" and "white" ways of reckoning kin. In formal public gatherings, Comanches may attend to appropriate traditional categories carefully, though they often use the English term rather than the Comanche to designate these. In more informal settings, however, younger Comanches tend to use standard Anglo-American reckoning of kin. Thus a Comanche man who publicly honors his mother's sister in the course of a powwow gathering will refer to the honoree as his mother, replicating traditional usage. If the man is over age sixty, he will likely use the Comanche term, /pi'a?/. If he is younger than sixty, he will likely use the English term.[33] In contrast, there is little use of traditional terms or categories in the everyday context of Comanche households. When a traditional term or category is used, it is often explicitly identified by the user as such (i.e., "She's my Comanche mother" in reference to one's father's sister) while use of the standard Anglo-American category is not identified as "my white" or "my Anglo" mother.

The practice of forming close institutionalized friendships also appears to have weakened among younger generations of Comanches.[34] No longer are kinship terms extended to the families of close friends who have grown up in the Comanche community.[35] Instead, Comanches have taken the term previously used for one's lifelong "close friend," /ha'ic/, and extended it to include real and classificatory siblings (parents' siblings' children, parents' parents' siblings' children's children, etc.) as well as co-participants (of the same sex and generation) in a public gathering (Hoebel 1939; Gladwin 1948).[36]

In addition, a practice of adoption or "taking someone as kin" has developed between some senior and junior co-participants in public gatherings.[37] The initiation of the adoptive relationships and the degree to which they are continued depend mainly on the senior person involved.[38] A younger Comanche cannot "take" an older woman as his "mother," for instance, though he may behave toward her as a son would, sitting with her at powwows and bringing her food and drink, indicating that he would like to be thought of as such. Adoptive kin relationships, once formally established through a public announcement at a powwow or a peyote or church gathering, often are treated as being at least as binding as actual kin relationships designated by the same terms. As Haddon Codynah put it in the winter of 1985, "Some of these people treat their adopted kin better than their own." However, should either of the participants drop out of the shared activity on which the kin relationship is founded, mutual use of kin terms and kin behavior is dropped as well.

The extension of kin terms to co-participants in social gatherings and the weakening of kinship obligations reflect changing patterns of Comanche residence. Despite the persistence of extended families, the trend since the war has been the geographic scattering of family members. The sentiment of kinship has remained strong, but previously unquestioned obligations, as among classificatory siblings, have loosened. The extragenealogical extension of kin terms to co-participants in public gatherings has allowed Comanches to create effective social networks among those persons with whom they are most frequently in contact. This is a way of both honoring a fellow participant and establishing a relationship that obligates or compels future cooperation. Geographically absent relatives are replaced by persons with whom one is frequently face-to-face in an attempt to maintain the use of private relationships that obligate participants to overlook offenses that might otherwise lead to breakdowns in communication.

Adoptive kin relationships among co-participants, however, are not as well insulated against potential breakdowns in interaction as extensive (i.e., collateral) genealogical relationships once were and as most close (i.e., lineal) genealogical relationships are still. This is because the genealogical kin among whom interaction is supported tend to share the same residence units and many of the same economic interests, while co-participants in public gatherings lack most of these compelling reasons to ignore perceived challenges to one's face. Thus adoptive kin, though able to depend on some mutual interest in maintaining the personal relationship, nevertheless spend some greater effort in publicly affirming their obligations to one another through honorings and other means than do genealogical kin. This may be the reason that adoptive kin often are treated better than "real" kin.

At the same time that social relationships have changed, so have patterns of participation in community gatherings. In taking advantage of greater economic opportunities, Comanches have sacrificed some flexibility to participate in their own community. However, various strategies for maintaining participation in that community have been developed to compensate for the constraints on mutual presence resulting from Comanches' increasing participation in the Anglo economy. Since World War II, community gatherings have tended to be shorter in duration. For example, summer dance gatherings now last only two or three days, rather than a week or longer, and are held almost exclusively on weekends. Federal and state holidays, when most work-a-day people have a long weekend, also have become popular times at which to gather.

Comanches who have moved away from the community often use their vacations to attend one kind of gathering or another. When these people retire, they also tend to move back to southwestern Oklahoma and reenter regular community participation. Haddon Nauni, who left the community for eight years to work in a factory in Wichita, Kansas, in the 1960s, explained the tendency to return in a 1984 interview: "When you retire, you gonna come back. Comanches is deeper-rooted than anybody. They'd rather be home with their people." Wallace Coffey, speaking in 1967, described similar motivations: "More than likely the Indian will come back to Oklahoma. They love their home. They love their people. They can't stay away from the people. That's one thing that Indians really have but lack. In other words, they have the unity but they don't go about it."[39]

Meanwhile, those Comanches who do not have steady jobs and who have not left southwestern Oklahoma have become the active agents in arranging gatherings to which others may return. Although they may appear lazy and unambitious to Anglos, they invest considerable effort and commitment in intracommunity activities. They act as peyote road men, they are pastors and deacons of Comanche churches, and they are on the head staffs of powwows. In these positions, they receive some economic compensation for their efforts from those who take advantage of the gatherings as a means of remaining in contact with the traditional community. Money is redistributed in the context of these public gatherings, as well as through personal networks, from those who have Anglo-derived incomes to those who spend their time organizing gatherings such as powwows and peyote meetings.[40]

Prior to 1950, when few Comanches had well-paying jobs, patterns of assistance probably were more reciprocal, with fewer disparities in economic activity. In 1974, though, Henderson and Bohland discovered, contrary to their expectations, that assistance within Indian communities in south-western Oklahoma tended to be unidirectional. They identified one category of individuals who almost always were in the position of providing assistance and another category of individuals who almost always received that assistance (Henderson and Bohland 1974:81). What they discovered is a tacit economic relationship between those Comanches who have taken advantage of increased economic opportunity in the Anglo world and those who have maintained opportunities for participation in the traditional community. This economic relationship also would help to explain the changes that have occurred in Comanches' social relationships as they have become focused more on co-participation in gatherings rather than on genealogical kinship and co-residence.[41]

FORMS OF PUBLIC GATHERING

The younger generation of Comanches who had taken over dancing in the 1930s and who were veterans of World War I used powwows to honor Comanche servicemen soon after American involvement in World War II began.[42] This transformed both the form of the gatherings and their uses. Leonard Riddles, who served in the military at that time, described the changes in powwow gatherings: "With WWII, you got a change with these boys going and coming back from the services. Every week they'd have it [a powwow] somewhere, someone's relative coming in on a furlough or leaving, and they'd honor him."

Powwow people made use of the traditional connection between dancing and military societies to link dance gatherings to the impact of World War II on the Comanche community. By using this form of public gathering to honor Comanche servicemen, powwows came to reflect the comings and goings, or in more traditional terms, the comings-home and the goings-away, in the community occasioned by the war.[43] Powwows thus were transformed from annual gatherings into occasions as frequent as every weekend.[44] At the same time, local communities, around which the prewar annual dance gatherings had been oriented, had begun to blur as Comanches in larger numbers were able to acquire automobiles.[45] Proximity remained a factor in who attended a powwow, but the very nature of these affairs—focused as they were on specific individuals—shifted powwow participation from a background of local community networks to a background of kin and friendship networks. People participated in powwows according to who was being honored and, more specifically, according to their personal relationships with that person and the members of that person's close family.[46] These relations often cut across local community boundaries.

After the war, when the movements of servicemen ceased to provide frequent occasions for gatherings, the frequency of powwows continued.[47] Four types of powwows emerged: homecoming, descendant, honoring, and benefit.[48] Dance gatherings had begun before the war as social occasions focused on local communities. In several of these local communities, a large annual gathering still endures as a sort of homecoming.[49] These are occasions for Comanches who have moved out of the area to renew ties with relatives and friends, as well as with the larger Comanche community. Homecoming powwows are held in the summer and last from two to four days.

Another change from the prewar period was the transformation of dance gatherings into semireligious occasions for honoring the memories of elders of the prereservation and reservation generations. Descendants of some of these well-known Comanche leaders sponsor annual powwows in memory of their common ancestors. Some of these are continuations of prewar summer encampments, while others are postwar innovations. These occasions are associated with particular localities but depend in large part on networks of kin and friends. Over time, descendant powwows have become less focused on the memories of the specific ancestors for whom they are named and more generally centered on all the members of a particular family. Annual descendant powwows are held in the summer and last from two to four days.[50] Like homecoming powwows, these are gatherings that Comanches who live away from the community make an effort to attend.

A special type of descendant powwow is the memorial powwow. This is usually a one-day gathering held in honor of a deceased relative on the first anniversary of his or her death. A memorial gathering marks the re-entry of close relatives of the deceased into active powwow participation. The family "buys their way back in" to powwow activities by giving away presents to other family members and friends of the person for whom the memorial is held.[51] Increasingly, however, as powwows have become the central public gathering in the Comanche community, many Comanches are staying out only for a few weeks or months after the death of a close relative and then buying their way back in at one of the larger annual homecoming or descendant powwows. This latter practice also reflects the economic inability of some families to sponsor a separate memorial gathering.

Close relatives often sponsor powwows in order to honor a living family member on the occasion of an important transition in his or her life. Among these occasions are entry into powwow participation, graduation from school, engagement, recovery from a major illness, and retirement. Generally these are smaller gatherings limited to the personal networks of the honored individual and his or her family. Because they are not annual events, they tend to be more local in participation. "Honoring" powwows tend to be held mainly in the summer but may be held at any other time during the year when the occasion arises. It is unusual for an honoring powwow to last longer than one day.

The remaining type of powwow that developed after the war was the benefit, which is held to raise money for a person, family, organization, or purpose, including the funding of a larger annual or descendant powwow. A popular feature of a benefit powwow is the raffle, where chances are sold on a shawl, a bag of groceries, or some other prize. More than any of the other types of dance gathering, attendance at benefit powwows depends on who sponsors and co-sponsors them. Thus they rely on personal networks and obligations almost exclusively. Benefit powwows are held throughout the year but tend to be the primary form of dance gathering held during the fall, winter, and spring months, as families and organizations prepare for the more active summer powwow season. Benefit powwows usually last only one day.

Powwows of all four types described here are often sponsored or co-sponsored by Comanche powwow organizations. These are men's and women's dancing societies and the organizing committees for the various homecoming and descendant gatherings. The men's dancing societies became almost exclusively veterans organizations after World War II. Other powwow organizations, such as the Comanche War Mothers, also are associated with military service.

The more prominent Comanche organizations (also listed in Ashworth 1986:108) are Chief Wild Horse Descendants, Comanche Indian Veterans Association, Comanche War Dance Association, Little Ponies, Comanche War Mothers, Comanche Gourd Clan, Comanche Homecoming Pow-wow Club, Wahnee Descendants, and Yellowfish Descendants. Most of these societies are only informally organized, although in the last twenty years there has been a tendency to incorporate, with state charters and nonprofit status, largely for financial reasons. The status of these organizations as social units within the Comanche community more closely approximates that of peyote circles than it does lineages (in the case of descendants organizations) or voluntary corporate groups. These units have only minimal impact on Comanche political, economic, and social organization outside the context of powwow gatherings.

Another kind of Comanche organization associated with powwow gatherings is comprised of the various singing groups, called drums. Of the three popular Comanche drums in the 1980s, two are organized around a core of singers who are related to one another. Dancing societies are organized differently. Haddon Nauni and Leonard Riddles referred to a Comanche strategy of having at least one family member in each dancing society. This contrast may be explained by noting that singing organizations are, in essence, small businesses hired to provide a service, while dancing organizations are guilds for regulating and controlling participation in powwow gatherings. Drums perform best when there is a sense of solidarity among members, while dancing societies depend on the variety of personal networks among their members for invitations to co-sponsor or participate in powwow gatherings.

As with prewar dancing, whenever a local community, family, or descendants organization puts on a powwow, one or more of the dancing societies is asked to co-sponsor the gathering. Usually the society asked is one in which a prominent member of the organizing group is a member.[52] By involving other organizations as co-sponsors, a larger number of participants and spectators is ensured, as family and friends often accompany singers and dancers. The co-sponsoring organizations and their members, in return, are honored during the course of the gathering with presents or money.

Ashworth (1986) has surveyed powwows in Oklahoma for a two-year period, from 1978 to 1980.[53] During this period, according to Ashworth's data, sixty-seven powwows were held in locations where the majority of the Indian population is Comanche. Of these, the majority were held during the summer and were honoring or benefit gatherings. Ashworth (1986:63–64) observes that, in general, powwow activity in Oklahoma has increased dramatically since 1971. It was around that time that Comanche powwows experienced a difficult generational transition. While established dancers had recognized veterans of Korea as full participants by the late 1960s, they declined to recognize most veterans of Vietnam on the grounds that these men were too young.[54] Though younger men and nonveterans were able to be present as spectators and contestants in powwows, they were unable to participate fully in the organization and sponsorship of the occasions.[55] In the opinion of some Comanches, the older, established dancers, who constituted an informal guild, wanted to maintain their monopoly on powwow sponsorship, which provided them with both prestige and some economic benefits. The arguments that would-be dancers were too young or not warriors were traditional Comanche reasons for keeping younger generations from full participation in public gatherings of the community going back to prereservation days. In the early 1970s, though, after consulting with sympathetic older Comanches, younger men formed their own dancing society, the Little Ponies, and used this organization to enter into full participation in the round of powwow gatherings. This was a formally organized society with a charter, explicit qualifications for membership, and officers.[56] The Little Ponies used this more formal organization—along with carefully researched and stated claims of the group's continuity with prereservation Comanche tradition—as a means of competing with the more informal organization of older dancers.

Since that time, other Comanche dancing associations have become more formally organized, with memberships opened to younger Comanches.[57] In addition, as opportunities for military service decrease, nonveterans have gradually moved into fuller participation in dancing organizations and powwow gatherings. The successful organization of the Little Ponies society and the subsequent integration of nonveterans were crucial developments in the use of powwow gatherings in the Comanche community. Had older Comanches continued to exclude younger Comanches from full participation in powwows, the younger Comanches might have innovated a new form of gathering so that they could assert a social identity in the community. This would have segmented community participation in the same way that generational divisions segmented participation between allotment and World War II.

Three types of dances have become the focus of powwow gatherings since World War II: the round dance (for women), the gourd dance (for men), and the contest dances such as the war dance (for men) and the social dance (for women and men). Each has become a generic kind of dance found in powwows throughout the Plains area, and it is difficult to determine their respective origins. Of these, however, the round dance and the gourd dance hold the most significance for Comanche participants.[58] Both are considered dances that warrant displays of respect and dignity.

Contest dances are more significant within the context of intercommunity powwow participation. Especially among boys and young men, contest dances such as the war dance are highly competitive. In order to attract larger attendance and participation, many powwows sponsor dance contests with cash prizes. The standards and significance of such dancing, however, differ little from Comanches to Kiowas to Cheyennes, while the gourd dance and other "traditional" dances differ widely in what they are taken to mean (Howard 1976:253).[59] While Comanches generally are not jealous or critical of Kiowas who perform the war dance, they often are highly critical of what they interpret as Kiowa attempts to appropriate traditional Comanche dances and songs, including the gourd dance.

Powwow gatherings, as they were structured in the 1980s, are occasions for both focused and unfocused interaction. The central activity is dancing within a circular arena—outdoors during the spring and summer, and indoors during the fall and winter. A large drum, surrounded by a group of singers, rests in the center of the arena, and dancers sit on benches, often beneath arbors, around the edges. With each song, dancers move to the middle of the arena and dance counterclockwise around the drum. A good deal of social interaction occurs outside the arena among spectators and participants. Spectators sit outside the dancers' benches on folding chairs they bring. Here, they observe the activities occurring in the arena, but they also use the social situation to engage in focused encounters with one another. Outside the circle of spectators, dance organizations or individual entrepreneurs often set up concession stands, especially during the summer, and these become focal points for interaction. In the case of a homecoming or descendant powwow, many families camp at the powwow site for the two to four days of the event. This also results in a greater frequency of focused and unfocused interaction.

Most powwows begin in the late afternoon with men's gourd dancing, followed by a break for dinner (often provided by the sponsor through one of the women's dance organizations), and then dancing begins again in the evening. Evening dances may include gourd dancing, women's round dancing, and (especially where contest prizes are offered by the sponsor as a way of attracting attendance and participation) fancy dancing, straight dancing, grass dancing, war dancing, and other varieties of more elaborately costumed dancing.

The drum performs songs requested by sponsors, dancers, and spectators. Certain songs are considered the property of particular families and dance organizations and are reserved for their exclusive use. There is a continual coming and going of singers, dancers, and spectators. The activity within the arena is managed by an arena director,[60] who is responsible for attending to dancers' and singers' needs and maintaining order; and an emcee, who introduces songs and calls on dancers to participate, makes jokes, conducts the giveaway, and generally provides some explicit narrative continuity. Haddon Nauni put it this way in 1985: "That emcee, he sort of runs everything. He's got to sense the feeling of the people, feel the consensus, mood of the crowd. He's got to respect all elements: drummers, singers, dancers." An emcee usually is chosen for his ability to entertain, and there is the sense that the reputation of a good emcee will cause more people to attend a powwow (Ashworth 1986:74).

In addition to the sponsors, arena director, and emcee, other participants have designated roles. "Head dancers" for men, women, little girls, and little boys also are designated, as are "head singers." Head dancers usually are chosen from among the sponsoring families and organizations. These designations are ways of honoring individuals and may or may not have to do with their abilities as dancers. Especially in an honoring or benefit powwow, head dancers are chosen for their personal networks of family and friends in order to attract a wider participation (Ashworth 1986:165). The abilities of a head singer, however, are central to that designation because he must have a detailed knowledge of dance songs and the families, individuals, and organizations that are said to "own" each. This knowledge amounts to a catalog of Comanche powwow participants and organizations.

Throughout the evening portion of the gathering, the emcee repeatedly breaks into the singing and dancing to introduce one of the sponsors of the gathering, who will then call up a participant or spectator to honor or give away to that person. These breaks are often called "specials."[61] Honoring also may be done by a participant or spectator, but it is the responsibility of the primary sponsor and co-sponsors to recognize those who have assisted in the event.[62] Those who are "called up" receive either a material gift, such as a blanket, or money. When money is given, it is usually as recompense for the time taken and distance traveled to help organize the gathering or to be present at the powwow. This is one way in which those Comanches who have an outside income support those who are more involved in organizing gatherings. When a gift is given, it either is raffled off among the crowd for money (if the purpose of the gift is as recompense for services, such as when a dance shawl is given to the group of singers around the drum)[63] or it is taken by the recipient as a symbol of recognition and is subsequently given away to honor someone else later in the powwow or at another powwow.

While it is the primary responsibility of the sponsors of the powwow to honor selected participants, secondary honorings may be accomplished in a gathering by persons who are neither sponsors nor designated participants. As such, the powwow gathering is a public arena for the presentation of, and remedial work on, personal relationships. As Haddon Nauni described the idea behind this in 1984, "How many times do you actually have something to acknowledge that friendship? Here's something I'm going to give you. Teaches respect for one another. Strengthens that bond."

Honoring is a way of publicly recognizing and raising the moral worth of both the person being honored and the person doing the honoring. Comanches who are honored are presented to the gathering as exemplary participants in the community, the social occasion, and their family and friendship networks. Comanches who do the honorings present themselves as generous persons who recognize the value of what is shared by other members of the community and thereby mark their own membership and value. This is not solely an altruistic exercise. By honoring someone in a public context, private obligations such as economic or political assistance can later be claimed by both participants. Unlike genealogical kinship, however, the personal relationships that can be established by honoring are based on relations in public rather than in private. As suggested above, the popularity of honoring at powwows may be due to the geographical dispersal of the Comanche community since the war, which has lessened the accessibility of genealogical kin and decreased the significance of residence units in defining the community. Honoring creates a network of compelling personal relationships and obligations that support interaction within the community where these did not previously exist in private contexts. Indeed, some Comanches have observed that honoring, especially in the public context of powwows, reinforces obligations for future involvement and participation in community gatherings. An implicit but compelling standard of reciprocity makes it difficult for Comanches to disengage from powwow participation. Leonard Riddles used a metaphor that is common among Comanches to describe the mutual obligations that result from powwow participation: "It's just a mad, mad circle."

Honoring is also a way of redistributing economic resources within the community. Comanches who have good jobs or other economic resources, especially those who live outside the present reservation area, give "that handshake" (in which folded currency is passed from one palm to another) to Comanches who lack access to the Anglo economy and who have labored instead to maintain the traditional community by "putting on" the powwow. Finally, honoring is a means of social regulation. By "calling someone up" and giving that person a gift, he or she is publicly reminded of the interdependent nature of the Comanche community. Being placed at the center of focused involvement in the occasion emphasizes the accessibility of one's social face to others in both focused and unfocused interaction. Honoring may be used in this fashion to recall community standards for behavior to a relative or a friend whose face is at risk or to remind a prominent person, such as a member of the business committee, of his or her obligations to the community.

Honoring plays on Comanches' concern about the face they present to one another in public, but impression management is not restricted to the periodic honorings within the structure of the powwow gathering. Concern for face and acts of impression management may be found throughout the occasion. Haddon Nauni explained beliefs about powwow participation in some detail in 1986:

> This arena is our society. Because it's a society, then each family that's a member has to be represented. Usually one member of the family participates. Singers, drum-makers, dancers, all handed down through generations. Special drums [are] made for particular powwows and presented to [the] sponsor. The drum-maker doesn't work on the drum unless he feels good. Because good thoughts go into that drum and once he seals it, then all those good thoughts are enclosed in that drum. After a while, that good spirit in that drum radiates out to the singers, who are sort of captivated by it, and then to the dancers. It's a sort of thanksgiving. It's a time to be happy, a time to rejoice. Here you are with all your people, your family. You start to do the whoop, the highest point in your life. If you do it [the dance] in the right way, it'll be a blessing in your life. Not the place to show off, to use it as a challenge or for women. Our people never thought we were better than others. A lot of men get out there to show off, look for women. That's not the way. If you do it in the right way, for the right reason, then it's a blessing on you. There's a limit to how far you can go with things [power] in ceremonials and things. In dancing, it's easy to exceed that limit. There's a purpose to everything. Respect the purpose by conducting yourself in a dignified manner. Do something in a good sense, it's a blessing. That good feeling generates, expands, from the drum to the singers to the dancers to the people watching. You're doing what you're made to do.

In the Comanche belief system, powwow participation is firmly tied to ideas about appropriate social behavior. By acting in an appropriate or "right" way in a powwow gathering, one presents a carefully managed image of oneself and shows respect for the moral worth of others. Attention to the ritual within the arena indicates involvement in the occasion, a willingness to cooperate in maintaining public standards of conduct. Laughter, joking, and a certain boisterousness outside the dance arena are taken as signs of the good feelings that all participants should exhibit at powwows. In contrast, Comanches consider appearing drunk at a powwow gathering to be an egregious breach of social conduct, because intoxicated individuals are unable to maintain their own face, (indeed, they often degrade their social selves with acts such as public urination, staggering, and shouting obscenities) and by that inability also devalue the moral worth of everyone present.

Many emcees exhort those present to show respect for the gathering and to "keep away" from drinking while participating. The "49," though, is an entirely different matter. Perhaps as a release from the more formal standards of social conduct during the traditional dancing, the "49" is a much more informal social situation in which some drinking is allowed. Emcees always get a laugh when they jokingly refer to the licentious events of the previous night's "49." While less important for defining community membership than gourd dancing or even war dancing, the social dancing that occurs at "49s" does have significance as a means for bringing younger Comanches together. With only one federal Indian school still open in the area, younger generations of Comanches no longer have extensive opportunities to interact with one another, as they once did when most attended the same Indian school. Powwows fulfill an important function in providing opportunities for the formation of peer groups in a traditional community context. Reflecting this function, social dancing is not limited to children from "powwow" families, and indeed, many younger Comanches attend powwow gatherings mainly for the social dancing that follows.

Comanche beliefs about powwow gatherings reflect the importance that the gatherings have attained over the past fifty years. Powwows have become the central arena in which the Comanche community is maintained as a public social unit. In this they have become the equivalent of the divisional gatherings of the prereservation period and the peyote gatherings of the reservation period, and so have expanded to include the presence of both peyote people and church people.

OTHER FORMS OF GATHERING

One consequence of the transformation of powwows during the war and immediately after was an overlap in participation between powwows and peyote meetings. During this time, peyote meetings decreased in participation and frequency as powwows became more prominent.[64] There are several reasons for this change. First, the size of a peyote meeting is limited by the size of the tipi. Meetings require only seven participants and rarely exceeded thirty at the height of postallotment peyote gatherings in the 1930s.[65] Having too many participants present results in a confusion and disturbance of the good thoughts necessary for a meeting to be efficacious. Powwows, in contrast, often have several hundred people in attendance and are not disrupted by the constant physical movement and distractions found in large crowds. Second, peyote meetings are generally restricted to men, especially to older men with some special experience, while powwows involve both men and women, young and old. Thus powwows are more accessible to the entire community. Third, many Comanches have chosen to use Indian Health Service clinics and hospitals rather than peyote meetings for curing purposes.[66] This has led, in and of itself, to a decline in the number of peyote meetings. Except for special curing ceremonies, peyote meetings today are held sporadically, often around Mother's Day, Father's Day, and Labor Day. Peyote is often the last resort of those whom the Anglo health-care system has failed and those who, for one reason or another, cannot afford Anglo medical care.

At least two distinct peyote "circles" or networks have developed among Comanches since the war. One is dominated by older Comanches who have been strong peyote men since before World War II. These "old-time" peyotists stress the singular nature of peyote participation and the religious aspects of the ceremony. As noted in the previous chapter, many equate peyote beliefs with Christian beliefs. The other peyote circle is made up mostly of younger Comanches who mix peyote participation with church and powwow participation. They view peyote gatherings as one way among a whole range of ways of "being Comanche." Consequently, they are criticized by members of the older peyote circle for not taking the ceremony seriously and for not doing things in the right way. To many older peyotists, those who do not "live" the peyote way but engage in peyote use do so more as recreation than as a serious undertaking.[67] As Tennyson Echawaudah observed in the fall of 1985, "I've seen 'em have a powwow right the morning after a Native American Church ceremony [i.e., a peyote gathering]. Today, it's just more like a powwow. They [powwow people] treat it like a pleasure, a entertainment. It's changed so much. There's no church about it for me anymore. I can't go for this Indian way no more. It's lost out. It's gone."

As members of the older circle pass on, younger Comanches who pursue a mixed strategy with respect to public gatherings have increasingly come to dominate peyote gatherings. Indeed, in some respects, peyote meetings have become an adjunct to powwows over the past thirty years (Howard 1976:256).[68] It has not been unusual for peyote meetings to be scheduled in conjunction with powwows or for peyote leaders, once called road men and now called spiritual leaders, to be called upon to lend their presence to "strengthen" powwow gatherings. Indeed, peyote leaders often are asked to "say a few words" over the public address system at most of the larger annual powwows, though they do not actively dance or sing. In return, powwow people who have particular needs turn to peyote for help.

Peyote road men have been called upon to cure Comanches who have been made ill by witchcraft stemming from rivalries between dancing societies. As Leonard Riddles observed, "Somebody'd get sick, they'd ask a peyote man to get up a meeting for 'em."[69] The recent increase of witchcraft accusations among powwow participants may explain the overlap that has developed between powwow and peyote participation.[70] Another reason that cross-participation has become possible may be the Christian symbols and dogma that have come to pervade both. The Christian elements appropriated by both peyote and powwow people consist mainly of references to "the Good Lord" and Jesus and attempts to justify their respective gatherings as equivalents of Christian church services. This similarity in belief systems may be the rationale that allows many participants to switch between peyote meetings and powwows. For peyote people, as for powwow people, proper conduct consists of behavior that reflects good thoughts, both about oneself and about others. As Edward Wermy said in 1985, "If you're mad or thinking something bad about someone, don't go in there [the peyote tipi], get away. That's Comanches." This suggests that peyotism and dancing may once again be merging into the same belief system. Consequently, participation in peyote meetings tends to fluctuate. In a 1985 interview, Edward Wermy characterized peyote participation since World War II: "Lot of people moving in and out." The core of men knowledgeable in peyote belief and ritual, though, does not fluctuate. These specialists have continued to be committed to peyote meetings, and they hold themselves apart from active participation in other forms of community gathering. It is this very isolation that makes them appear to be strong, knowledgeable specialists to those powwow people who look to peyote as a way out of their troubles.

In some respects, though, peyote and powwow people disagree. Powwow people say that peyote people are "too particular," and peyote people say that powwow people are too interested in "showing off." These comments suggest different ideas about impression management. Within the smaller-scale peyote meetings, there is a greater concern for ritual detail and for the more detailed nuances of both focused and unfocused interaction. How, where, and when one stands and walks about in a peyote meeting, for instance, are strictly regulated. Facial expressions also are carefully scrutinized for what they may say about the attitude of a participant. Powwow gatherings, in contrast, are larger-scale occasions in which one's face expands to greater proportions, rather than detailed, to make it accessible to those present at the gathering. In a powwow, impressions are conveyed through louder words and actions that may be heard and seen above the constant activity of the gathering. Dancing, honoring, and singing all are outsize behaviors that are projected by means of colorful costumes and a public address system across the many different instances of focused and unfocused interaction going on at the same time. Thus, while both peyote and powwow participants manage the impressions they give other participants and try to project images of "good feelings" in doing so, the different scales of the two kinds of occasions require different interaction techniques.

Like peyote gatherings, participation in Comanche church gatherings also began to overlap with powwow participation after World War II. During the 1940s and 1950s, church participation remained fairly constant. There is no record of new churches being established during this period, nor of already established churches closing. The networks linking congregations were strengthened at this time, expanding into softball and basketball leagues and other like means of interaction between members without regard to denomination.[71]

Most national missionary organizations decided to withdraw their direct support for Comanche churches in the 1950s and 1960s, and during this period Comanche pastors took over from Anglo pastors. Though some Comanche pastors continue to hold themselves apart from powwow gatherings, as do some Comanche peyote leaders, they do not enforce the strict rule barring the attendance of church members that Anglo pastors had made the hallmark of the prewar church faction. In the 1960s, though, powwow participation began to cut into church attendance, just as it had peyote meetings.[72] One reason for the increased popularity of powwows at the expense of church participation may have been the heightened political consciousness among Indian people in Oklahoma throughout the 1960s and 1970s. This entailed an explicit rejection of many Anglo-derived forms of interaction and an emphasis on traditional forms.

In response, Comanche churches have emphasized the distinctly Comanche nature of their gatherings. Most maintain the use of the Comanche language in hymns and some ritual discourse even though many of their members are monolingual English speakers. Periodically, a Comanche church will initiate a Comanche language class, but such classes have had little success in teaching younger Comanches the native language without everyday opportunities to use it. Still, this is another way in which Christian churches can lay claim to representing a more traditional Comanche social life. Comanche churches have also taken some lessons from the organization of powwow gatherings. The Deyo Baptist Church, for instance, has had considerable success with an annual gathering at which old Comanche hymns are sung. This has become a popular social occasion for the community and is on the level of the homecoming powwows.

In addition, Comanche churches have devised their own form of honoring, as in powwows. Prayer meetings may be held "for" particular Comanches by the various Comanche churches. By "praying over" a specific person, church gatherings can be used as public occasions for impression management and social regulation. Thus the gathering may be used for public management of some personal relationship within the congregation (as in a family dispute) or social regulation (when a member has placed his or her face at public risk), or it may be used to place the person honored, who is not necessarily a member of the church, under some obligation to the congregation. This last is particularly true when the honoree is involved in tribal politics either as a candidate or an elected business committee member.

In these ways, Comanche Christian church services, like peyote meetings, continue to function as alternative public gatherings for some social work in the context of the larger community, though they have ceased to be a mutually exclusive alternative. And like the divisions that have developed between the older and younger peyote circles, there has been a weakening of the cooperative relationships among the Comanche congregations. The leagues and networks that were used to link the congregations into the church faction during the postallotment and immediate postwar periods have largely been abandoned, and congregations no longer close their own churches to attend another's revivals.[73]

There have also been changes in the form of church gatherings. While the denominations that missionized Comanches ranged from Mennonite to Methodist to Dutch Reformed, the style of church service that has developed among those congregations since they were turned over to Comanche pastors is remarkably uniform.[74] To outsiders, Comanche church gatherings appear to be much less structured than Anglo church gatherings. Songs, testimonies, and sermons are often initiated by members of the congregation as they feel the inspiration to get up and take part in the gathering. Leonard Riddles described this in 1986:

> Once in a while, one will get up and kind of bear a little testimony, and then he'll start singing and the rest will just join in and help him sing. The old people composed those hymns, and families still have a sense of ownership of those. All of these hymns are kept in peoples' memories. Wherever they're sitting, they all know just about where to come in with their singing, and then they all join in.

The gathering is led by the pastor as he reads the intentions and mood of the congregation. In fact, there is considerable structure, but it relies more on personal relationships among members of the congregation than on a formal public order of service. As Mr. Riddles went on to observe, "They just have their own way of carrying it out. It's in order. I mean, it's right. They just have their own way."[75] As in peyote meetings and powwow gath-

erings, Comanche church gatherings are occasions for the public presentation and management of personal experiences and relationships. Perhaps the
major difference is that church gatherings are more appropriate occasions
for the public expression of personal difficulties. Indeed, the social utility of
church gatherings for Comanches who also participate in powwows may be
the ability to unilaterally manage relationships and impressions in which
there is no direct interactive cooperation with another person, as in an honoring ceremony at a powwow. Instead, the presentation of self in church
gatherings does not require the presence of others involved in the relationship or social situation at issue, while there is no such thing as honoring
someone in absentia at a powwow.

Although church gatherings do not resolve the specific interpersonal conflict or trouble, they do repair the social face of the person who publicly
testifies about the difficulty. In this way an individual may restore the
damage done to his or her face by drunkenness, divorce, family arguments,
and other morally threatening situations without the risk of censure. A
church gathering is one public context in which one challenges one's own
face with the certain knowledge that others present will do any necessary
repair work to restore one's moral worth.

The most recently evolved forms of public gathering in the Comanche
community have developed as a result of the establishment of a separate
Comanche tribal government in 1966. Business committee meetings are held
one Saturday each month. Attendance varies according to community interest. The meetings are conducted by the elected officials of the tribe, but
audience participation is common. Through their attendance at committee
meetings, some Comanches have become known as "political." Generally,
these are people in their fifties or younger of both sexes.[76] When they speak
at meetings, they do so either in strong support of the tribal administration
or in strong opposition to it. Most speakers make reference to Comanche
"tradition" in supporting their arguments as to how things should be done.
Many issues and campaigns are argued on the basis of what the "Comanche
people" really want and who is truly representative of them. Candidates and
council members who are known to have some Kiowa or Anglo ancestors,
for instance, are criticized as not being "true Comanches" by their opponents, while nearly every person with a strong opinion on an issue claims to
speak not for himself or herself or for a particular faction but for the whole
community.

In response to especially contentious issues, and always in connection with
elections for committee seats and the chairmanship, more informal political

meetings are held in homes and churches to rally Comanches behind a particular viewpoint or candidate. These gatherings depend on proximity and the hosts' kin and friendship networks for attendance. Attendance does not imply an endorsement of the opinion or candidate around which the gathering is focused.[77]

Increasingly, younger Comanches have been more successful candidates for the business committee than older candidates. The feeling in the community has been that the postwar generation is better trained to administer the federal programs that are the economic basis for the tribal government. This is similar to the way in which younger Comanches were put forward during the immediate postallotment period as intermediary leaders because they were better equipped to interact with Anglos. Of course, this does not stop Comanches disappointed in an elected official from blaming his or her failure to act in a "right" way on youth, which is taken to mean a lack of experience in the traditions of the community.

Tribal political gatherings, however, have not become integrated with other forms of gathering in the same way that participation in peyote meetings and church gatherings has become integrated with participation in powwows. Peyote meetings, church gatherings, and powwows all have been used, directly or indirectly, for tribal politics. But political work at these gatherings is opportunistic; it is not a sign of shared beliefs about appropriate interaction. Comanche politicians go where they know they will find a crowd, and Comanches generally find tribal politics to be, frankly, fascinating. Political alliances in Comanche politics tend to follow networks of kinship and friendship, but these relationships do not necessarily obligate political cooperation as they once did.[78] Whom one backs or what position one agrees with still depends in large part, though, on who happens to be a candidate or prominently promotes an issue. Consequently, coalitions are rarely the same from one campaign or controversy to the next. Moreover, there is considerable alienation among Comanches with respect to taking an active part in tribal government (as opposed to talking about tribal politics). Rumors of scandal and wrongdoing by tribal officials are common.[79] In a recent election for tribal chairman, less than one-fourth of the eligible Comanche voters cast ballots. This is a level of voter participation similar to that found in the 1950s (Levy 1959:52).

Voting and eligibility to vote, however, may not be useful guides to community membership and participation. Under the tribal constitution, all persons of one-quarter blood quantum or more are Comanche. This is a measure of social identity that is alien to considerations of communicative

competence. Indeed, this is part of the Comanche constitution mainly because blood quantum is mandated as an official measure of Indianness by
the Bureau of Indian Affairs.[80] While blood quantum is both a necessary
and sufficient criterion for membership in the Comanche tribe according to
Anglo-American law, it is only a necessary, not a sufficient, condition for
participation according to Comanches.[81] People desiring to "be Comanche"
with respect to other members of that community also must be able to participate as Comanches in community gatherings. This is written into the
Comanche constitution in a way that maintains Comanche traditions of
using public gatherings to organize their community. Any time 250 or more
Comanches are gathered in an officially called tribal meeting (such as that of
the business committee), they may vote to throw out an elected official and
begin the process of electing a replacement.[82] Similarly, the business committee is prevented from committing economic resources to long-term
projects without the approval of a tribal meeting in which 250 or more
Comanches are present. In effect, this gives control of the tribal government
to those Comanches who are able to be physically present to one another. An
important consequence of that control is that it subjects people who attend
political gatherings, including tribal officials, to public social regulation on a
regular basis.

As they did with warriors and medicine men in prereservation days,
Comanches continue to require that their leaders validate personal experiences and achievements in public contexts. The strategy of those who rise to
voice criticisms is to question the moral worth of the official, suggesting that
he or she is not "true to Comanche ways" because of a personal transgression
or a public action. Tribal officials may be criticized for their personal behavior, such as being seen drinking in a bar, as well as for their decisions in
tribal affairs, such as the distribution of federal housing loans.

Tribal officials must formulate explanations for their actions that restore
their moral worth and show their commitment to the Comanche community. An acceptable excuse for the failure of a tribal program, for instance, is that Anglos have in some way tricked or gotten the better of an
elected official. This plays on the sympathy of the audience, all of whom
have been taken advantage of in Comanche-Anglo interaction at some point.
Criticisms of personal behavior are usually answered by a supporter of a
tribal official or candidate, who speaks of the great works that the person in
question has done for the Comanche people. This is an attempt to direct the
focus from private to public contexts of interaction, drawing a boundary
between the two as Comanches of the prereservation period did.

COMMUNITY INTEGRATION

While Comanche political gatherings have not yet played the same role in community maintenance and organization that powwow, peyote, and church gatherings have, they nevertheless have the potential for supporting those functions and may do so one day. At present, powwows are the gatherings through which the larger community is integrated as a whole. Howard (1955, 1976) and Thomas (1970), among others, have claimed that powwows, like peyote gatherings, are a "pan-Indian" phenomenon, developing out of the northern Plains grass dance in the 1880s and spreading throughout the Plains as a consequence of reservation conditions.[83] They associate powwow gatherings with a unitary Indian ethnicity expressed in relation to Indian-Anglo interactions. As evidence for these claims, they refer to dances, songs, dress, and behaviors that are common to almost all modern powwows in Indian communities.[84] Powers (1980, 1990) argues against the indiscriminate use of pan-Indianism as an explanation for all aspects of contemporary American Indian communities but substitutes his own regional version. In discussing contemporary Plains dance, Powers (1980:224) uses a northern-southern dichotomy to characterize styles and trends. He also suggests that Oklahoma Indians were particularly vulnerable to syncretic cultural development among communities as a consequence of allotment in severalty (Powers 1980:220). While Powers does distinguish between tribal and intertribal styles of dancing, he concludes his analysis of traditional dancing on the Plains by describing powwows as significant interethnic markers between Indians and Anglos (Powers 1980:225).

While many of the cultural forms used in powwow gatherings are similar from one community to another, the social uses to which powwows are put may be quite different for each community. As may be seen for Comanches, and as Ashworth (1986) has argued on a comparative basis for Indian peoples in Oklahoma, powwow gatherings are primarily intracommunity social occasions. Most powwows held in Oklahoma are sponsored, staffed, and participated in mainly by members of the same community, not different communities. Comanche powwows, because they are organized and attended mostly by Comanches, have primary social consequences for the Comanche community.[85] When powwow or peyote gatherings are interpreted primarily as bundles of cultural traits or styles, it is inevitable that the common use of these traits and styles by a number of different communities will be classed together. When they are viewed as public events within the context of the social life of particular cultural communities, though, the similarities disappear, and our understanding of contemporary American Indian communities increases. For instance, while Southern Cheyennes[86] have recently engaged in more frequent powwows than Comanches, they have not used powwow gatherings as the primary means of regulating their shared community (Ashworth 1986:116). Instead, they have relied on annual performances of the Sun Dance as public occasions in which to organize and regulate community membership (Moore 1988:328–329).[87]

At present, powwows constitute the framework around which other forms of participation are oriented within the Comanche community. Strong powwow people have made their gatherings the primary link in maintaining lines of communication within an increasingly fragmented community, while other Comanches have devised ways of using powwows for the general purpose of public social interaction without necessarily subscribing to beliefs powwow people associate with the dancing. Comanches also have other forms of participation (church and peyote gatherings) through which they may take on other social identities and other kinds of power within the community. Consequently, Comanches who take part in powwows do so at different levels of involvement. Those who sponsor and arrange the gathering have the greatest involvement, while those who sing and dance also have an active part. The individuals in both these categories are properly called "powwow people" in the community and may be considered to be full participants in the gatherings. Many powwow people switch between periods of very active participation and less active periods as they first become "burned out" on the constant round of gatherings and then later want, as Haddon Nauni said, to "get back to my culture, my tradition."[88]

A more ambiguous category of involvement is represented by those Comanches who are present at a powwow but who do not actively sing, dance, or honor. These people have the option of either representing themselves as powwow people or of retaining a social identity associated with another form of community gathering. Peyote meetings and Christian church gatherings may be seen as adjuncts to powwows, focused around special functions and smaller, more restricted memberships. Especially as avenues for becoming leaders in the community, peyote and church participation are still viable strategies for "being Comanche."

Comanches who also participate in church and peyote gatherings or who do not wish to become more deeply involved in the powwow circle use powwows as occasions for focused and unfocused social interaction with people to whom they are not usually physically present. Thus a peyote road man or a Christian pastor can attend a powwow and take advantage of the opportunities it offers for social interaction without "participating" in it and thus risking a dilution of his reputation. In fact, strong peyote or church people can have considerable social status at a powwow. Because of their strong beliefs, they are taken to be knowledgeable and thus to have a type of power. At some point, most Comanche families have need of one kind of specialist or the other. Peyote men, for instance, are still called upon to conduct curing ceremonies. Indeed, the change in designation from "road man" to "spiritual leader" may be interpreted as a way of generalizing the strength or power that a ritual leader takes from peyote gatherings to other kinds of gatherings in the community, such as powwows. Many church leaders, on the other hand, have come to be known as people who can "get things done" in tribal government and federal Indian agencies, also a type of power useful to Comanche people.

An apt comparison with powwows in the contemporary community might be with divisional gatherings in prereservation times. These too were gatherings in which a variety of social business was transacted and according to which participation in other kinds of gatherings (such as Sun Dances, military societies, and residence bands) was oriented. Involvement in divisional gatherings must have occurred at different levels, as does involvement in powwows today. In a 1984 interview, Leonard Riddles explained the similarity between prereservation times and the contemporary Comanche community in this way:

> They believed in the Great Spirit, and that he's beyond the sun. They had their prayers. Then you had some people that didn't believe in anything. They had their warrior shields, and some believed that if you decorated it up and had a medicine man blow on it, it would protect you. Others just believed that a shield was a shield. It's just like today, there's some that believed and some that didn't. Some use that powwow and some use that peyote. Others go to church. They're pretty strong in their religions.

Describing Comanche choices in public gatherings as religions is a particularly apt characterization of the moral force of those occasions. Community maintenance requires that members treat the conventions they use for interacting with one another as sacred rituals. Without a belief in the sacredness of their relations with one another, communities fly apart into smaller social units wherein face or moral worth is respected. "Being Comanche" has always been more of an expression of co-belief in a shared moral community than an act of co-membership in a unified political or economic unit. Ultimately, "being Comanche" is an act of faith that cannot wholly be reduced to an instrumental analysis of political or economic benefit. It is a commitment to the evidence of history, which shows that Comanches as a community have survived a remarkable series of changes in their social and physical world, with no suggestion that they will not as a community survive other changes to come.

6

The Consequences
of Social Life

Societies everywhere, if they are to be societies, must mobilize their members as self-regulating participants in social encounters. One way of mobilizing the individual for this purpose is through ritual; he is taught to be perceptive, to have feelings attached to self and a self expressed through face, to have pride, honor, and dignity, to have considerateness, to have tact and a certain amount of poise. These are some of the elements of behavior which must be built into the person if practical use is to be made of him as an interactant, and it is these elements that are referred to in part when one speaks of universal human nature.

Erving Goffman, 1967

Any good thing you say to me shall not be forgotten. I shall carry it as near to my heart as my children, and it shall be as often on my tongue as the name of the Great Spirit. I want no blood upon my land to stain the grass. I want it all clear and pure, and I wish it so, that all who go through among my people may find peace when they come in, and leave it when they go out.

Ten Bears, 1867

Ten Bears' sentiments are echoed in other Comanches' representations of their community before and after 1867. Comanches have always lived in a peaceable community. There were and are rules for properly entering it and for appropriate behavior in its confines. Once inside, however, one is surrounded by social arrangements that are calculated to enhance both the face of the individual and the solidarity of the collective social unit. Finding themselves among "hostile" Comanches in prereservation times, Euro-Americans were often surprised at the respect with which they were treated when visiting a Comanche camp. By the same token, Euro-Americans have frequently been just as surprised to find their activities taken as challenges by Comanches because of their consequences—unforeseen by outsiders—for the Comanches' ability to be present to one another. Comanche actions in both circumstances have been the result of moral choices in accord with the way in which they have constructed and maintained their community.

Because of the images we have attached to the name we have used for them, it is difficult for Euro-Americans to think of Comanches as living in a moral community regulated by a regard for mutual esteem. For this reason, explanations of Comanche social organization have ranged from ecology to economy to ethnicity, attempting to find some external cause for the cohesiveness of their relations with one another. It has even been asserted that their community ceased to exist once the landscape in which we first encountered them was remade in a European image.

As we have seen, though, Comanches have organized their community primarily through rules for public commingling and have maintained it from its protohistoric origins to the present by changing their units and strategies for public gatherings to conform to economic constraints on mutual presence. Public gatherings have proved useful for community organization because they expose members to standards of mutual conduct that emphasize moral worth. These standards help maintain the larger community by regulating the interaction of people who are otherwise divided by compelling personal ties and factional interests. Concern for face orients one to the larger public arena and away from smaller pockets of private selfishness. The innovations in Comanche forms of public gathering have included (1) divisional gatherings of contiguous nomadic residence groups; (2) peyote gatherings among increasingly localized reservation families; (3) Christian church meetings and traditional summer and winter encampments, which serve as gatherings of Comanches scattered by allotment among an Anglo population; and (4) powwow gatherings that accommodate Comanches absent from everyday reservation-area social life. Each of these innovations has provided an occasion for community members to keep open lines of communication. At the same time, these occasions have made individual members accessible to the social regulation of others. In this way Comanches have used public gatherings as the intersection of social life and social structure. Both Comanches and the constituent social units of their community have been organized through the different social situations they have devised to be present to one another.

A VOCABULARY FOR DESCRIBING COMMUNITY MAINTENANCE

Both integrative and segmenting functions may be seen in the various combinations of social units Comanches have used to organize their community.

In most periods of their history, Comanches have used units of social structure (groups and enduring relationships) to segment their community, and have used units of social life (situations and gatherings) to integrate it. Where there is segmentation (primarily for economic purposes) there must also be some counterbalancing means of integration to maintain the community as a whole.

During the prereservation, reservation, and postwar periods, the Comanche community was segmented among, respectively, nomadic residence bands, extended families living in local reservation communities, and Comanches living in the reservation area and those living outside that area. In response to segmentation in their social structure, Comanches have integrated their community by using social situations (public gatherings) to bring constituent residence units together. The gatherings that have served this function have been divisional gatherings during the prereservation period, peyote meetings during the reservation period, and powwows in the postwar period. In the immediate postallotment period, when their community was segmented among different kinds of public gatherings, Comanches integrated it through the enduring relationships formed through networks of kin and friends.

Segmentation has thus allowed Comanches to (1) use a nomadic subsistence strategy to exploit the Plains environment; (2) support themselves in part by farming and stock raising during the reservation period; (3) pursue differing strategies with respect to Anglo society immediately after allotment; and (4) take part in the Anglo economy after World War II.

At the same time, integration has allowed Comanches to (1) regulate residence bands, focused-activity groups, and popular leaders during the prereservation period; (2) maintain traditional beliefs and regulate intermediary leaders during the reservation period; (3) maintain communication among church, peyote, and powwow people after allotment; and (4) maintain communication and a certain degree of interdependence between Comanches participating in the Anglo economy and those remaining within the traditional community in the postwar period.

The glue that has bound Comanches to these various units of social life and social structure is of two kinds: compelling personal ties that have mitigated breakdowns in communication, and concern for one's social face in public gatherings unsupported by personal ties. Personal ties and concern for one's social face in public often pull in opposite directions, making them useful counterweights for such contrasting purposes as segmentation and integration.

Unlike much of contemporary Anglo-American social life, members of the Comanche community rarely are strangers to one another. This means that personal ties are almost always in play in Comanche-Comanche relations. Personal ties that have compelled Comanches to ignore potential breakdowns in interaction held together residence bands on the nomadic Plains; provided the basis for continued communication between church, peyote, and powwow people after allotment; and, to some extent, created obligations among co-participants with adopted or extended kin relationships in powwows.[1]

In contrast, the concern for face in public gatherings has, in every period of Comanche history, compelled self-interested individuals and groups to conform to community standards of appropriate conduct or to risk calling into question their own, and others', moral worth. To "be Comanche" has not been simply to be a member of a residence band or to have the necessary blood quantum to be listed on the Comanche tribal roll. Instead, it has entailed a more profound willingness to subject one's social self to public sanction in gatherings with other Comanches and to accept the conventions and values of that shared community. In the postwar period, both personal ties and concern for face have had integrative functions (through adoptive kinship and powwow gatherings, respectively), while the community has been segmented largely by external economic conditions that have caused some Comanches to leave the reservation area.

As a result of their continuing contacts with Anglos, Comanches have innovated both traditional and Anglo-derived forms of social interaction as ways of "being Comanche." Traditional forms, like peyote meetings and powwows, were logical extensions of pre-existing beliefs and practices. Peyote beliefs, for instance, were derived from prereservation beliefs as a way of adapting to the increasing Anglo presence during the reservation period. Anglo-derived forms, such as Christian church gatherings, appear to conform to aspects of the Anglo-dominated social landscape but are still means for Comanche-Comanche interaction. Thus Comanches who became Christians did so in their own church gatherings, not as members of Anglo churches, and have developed a distinctively Comanche order of service regardless of differences in denomination. In this way, a traditional community, facing pressure to assimilate with the dominant society, has been maintained under the appearance of acculturation. Most recently, traditional forms have been favored in the community as a way of representing Comanches' shared historical charter, an integrative function. Thus Comanche church gatherings have emphasized traditional forms such as Comanche hymns as a way of claiming participation in that historical charter.

With allotment, the Comanche community was segmented not only by participation in different forms of gathering but also by differences between the generations. Younger Comanches, who were excluded from full participation in peyote and dancing activities, tended to use Anglo-derived gatherings as a means of gaining access to economic resources such as education and agency-controlled funds, while older Comanches maintained peyote gatherings and revived dance gatherings. The exclusion of younger generations from these traditional forms of gathering probably contributed to the later segmentation of peyote and powwow gatherings as younger Comanches came to take over those occasions without being acculturated into the belief system used by older Comanches to integrate the two activities. At the same time, Comanche politics after 1932 was increasingly segmented by generation as the economic interests of younger and older members diverged.[2] A later generational split was avoided when younger Comanches were admitted to active powwow participation through the Little Ponies dancing society. Had the Little Ponies been kept out of powwows, they likely would have sought some other form of community gathering, once again segmenting Comanche social life. Instead, a generational transition was effected, with the result that powwow beliefs innovated in the late 1930s continue to be used to integrate the community today.

In all the changes that Comanches have made in their social relations with one another from 1700 on, two themes have been central: community and economy. The two themes are interdependent: in most periods of Comanche history, community has compelled integration, and economy has required segmentation. The Comanche community has been integrated primarily by public gatherings. Comanche economic units, on the other hand, have tended to be segmented by personal ties into private regions of interaction. For the most part, changes in the units of Comanche social structure have been responses to changes in economic circumstance. The transformation from residence bands on the open plains to extended families on the reservation to nuclear families living outside the postallotment region is a function of the changing sources of economic support available to Comanches. Comanches have deployed members of their community in different social groups to maintain the economic basis for everyday life. At the same time, though, the Comanche community is itself a unit of social structure that requires some public means of keeping members of its constituent social units in communication with one another and for regulating their behavior. While individual Comanches require economic sustenance, the Comanche community requires communicative sustenance, mainly through face-to-face encounters.

As Comanches have innovated and articulated their units of social structure and social life in each historical period, they have balanced the imperative of economic survival with the necessity of continued communication. What is remarkable is that they have always found a solution that accommodates these often-conflicting requirements.

A COMPARATIVE PERSPECTIVE

Many of the observations made here about Comanches and their community can also be made about other American Indian communities. In each instance, the details of community organization and maintenance differ, just as external social conditions and intracommunity innovations have differed. In general, however, the distinction between intracommunity and intercommunity relations and the interplay of social life and social structure will be the same. Some initial resemblances may be found in Fowler's studies of the Northern Arapahoe (1982) and Gros Ventre (1987) communities, in Moore's (1988) study of the Cheyenne community, and in Levy's (1959) study of the Kiowa community.

In contrast to the Comanches, each of these communities developed some form of central, formal social structure with which to connect constituent social units.[3] Their experiences of Anglo contact, however, were similar to those of Comanches. Each profited from raiding activities and Anglo trade, and each was forced onto a reservation as a result of largely economic constraints. In response to Euro-American economic relations, each developed a class of intermediary leaders who depended on Euro-American symbols of authority for their influence.[4] Once on the reservation, the Arapahoes and Gros Ventres, like the Comanches, represented their communities as progressing toward acculturation as a way of dealing with Anglo officials.[5] In contrast, prominent Cheyennes and Kiowas were often somewhat more resistant to Anglo policies.[6]

Like Comanches, Arapahoes reorganized their traditional beliefs and ceremonies to conform to changed social conditions.[7] Gros Ventres, however, abandoned their traditional ceremonies, and many joined Christian churches.[8] Kiowas joined Christian churches during the reservation period in larger numbers than did Comanches and were more active after allotment, especially in the Methodist church.[9] Other Kiowas maintained their traditional bundle ceremonies. Cheyennes have continued to hold their annual Sun Dance gathering to the present day.[10]

Peyote has been important since the late nineteenth century among Comanches, Kiowas, Cheyennes, and Arapahoes.[11] Consonant with the Gros Ventres' representations of acculturation and their rejection of traditional notions of power and medicine, however, peyote has not caught on among them.[12] Dance gatherings were revived in all communities after the turn of the century. Arapahoes, like Comanches, were careful not to mix dancing with other forms of public gathering, finding strength in segmentation.[13] Cheyennes and Kiowas, however, integrated dancing with other traditional forms of gathering in belief systems that emphasized how participation in one form made one stronger in another.[14] Arapahoes, Gros Ventres, and Comanches all experienced generational divisions after 1900. The Arapahoes found means to reintegrate younger generations into traditional community gatherings, while the Comanches and Gros Ventres experienced more turbulent generational transitions.[15]

Like the Comanche community, the other four communities use public honorings or giveaways to subject individuals, relationships, memberships, and social units to higher standards of social conduct and mutual concern for face. For Kiowas and Comanches, these have become consensus forms of public gathering. Among Cheyennes and Arapahoes, though, dance gatherings are secondary in importance to the annual Sun Dance.[16] For Gros Ventres, powwows have become one of several forms of public gathering segmenting their community.[17]

Other similarities and contrasts exist among these five communities, but the intention here is not to construct a set of diagnostics that will allow us to categorize Indian communities since Euro-American contact. Categorization tends to draw our attention toward the categories themselves and away from the individual communities that we place within them.[18] Instead, comparisons like the one briefly sketched above show how important a focus on community organization and historical context can be for understanding the continuity of American Indian identities. Even though most Plains peoples have been subject to many of the same social conditions, each has adapted by innovating interactive means that make sense in the context of their own community and history.

Just as American Indian communities are more than simply the sum of their relations with Anglos, they are also more than just combinations of means for social organization. Those means and their combinations change from one historical period to another; what has remained constant has been the frequency of interaction. The pattern of repeated interaction constitutes the tradition in each community. The modes of subsistence, the social units, the cultural frameworks, even the languages used in any one period are instrumental rather than fundamental to the pattern that is the tradition.[19]

THE IMPORTANCE OF BEING COMANCHE

Having considered how Comanches have organized and maintained their community, two questions remain: What has motivated people to continue to be Comanche, and will those motivations be sufficient to maintain the Comanche community in the future? We should note first that these are questions an Anglo would ask, not a Comanche. In all the changes their social life has undergone since their first contacts with Europeans, there is no evidence that Comanches have ever considered giving up their community. At each turn in the historical process, Comanches have found ways to go on being Comanche, making new economic arrangements and devising new means for publicly expressing that distinctive identity.[20]

Despite the images of defeat, alienation, and acculturation that Anglos have used to depict Comanches during and after the reservation period, the remarkable continuity of the Comanche community suggests that there is a utility to being Comanche that most Anglo images of Indians miss entirely. As shown in the preceding chapters, being Comanche has been and is a successful strategy, even with the relatively impoverished economic conditions in which most Comanches have lived. The Comanche community is well organized, regulated, and maintained. It provides opportunities for social interaction, economic support for social units, and identification with a continuous historical tradition. Further, unlike most of the cultural traditions brought to North America by European immigrants, the tradition of being Comanche has proved to be innovative and adaptive. Long after such traditions as "being Irish-American" or "being Italian-American" have melted into the Anglo-American mainstream, Comanches continue to construct their community apart from the dominant Anglo community.

Quite simply, people continue to be Comanche because being Comanche works. This holds true for most contemporary American Indian identities. The basis for a separate Comanche community likely will continue to exist as long as its members maintain a sufficient frequency of interaction to allow them to regulate individual and group behavior in public gatherings. This depends, of course, on their having sufficient economic support for those public gatherings of community members.

Ultimately, though, the motivation for continuing the community must come from each generation. Since the mid nineteenth century, Comanche elders have been pessimistic about the continuing utility of being Comanche for younger members of their community and have thought themselves the last of the "old time" Comanches. In his speech at the Medicine Lodge council of 1867, Ten Bears put this pessimism eloquently:

I was born on the prairie where the wind blew free, and there was nothing to break the light of the sun. I was born where there were no enclosures, and where everything drew a free breath. I want to die there, and not within walls. I know every stream and wood between the Rio Grande and the Arkansas. I have hunted and lived over that country. I lived like my fathers before me, and like them, I lived happily.

When I was at Washington, the Great Father told me that all the Comanche land was ours, and that no one should hinder us in living upon it. So why do you ask us to leave the rivers, and the sun, and the wind, and live in houses? Do not ask us to give up the buffalo for the sheep. The young men have heard talk of this, and it has made them sad and angry. Do not speak of it more. I love to carry out the talk I get from the Great Father. When I get goods and presents, I and my people feel glad since it shows that he holds us in his eye. If the Texans had kept out of my country, there might have been peace. But that which you now say we must live on is too small.

The Texans have taken away the places where the grass grew the thickest and the timber was the best. Had we kept that, we might have done the thing you ask. But it is too late. The white man has the country which we loved and we only wish to wander on the prairie until we die.[21]

For its members, the changing Comanche community is a continual source of both pessimism and hope. Over the past three centuries, the social world that each generation of the Comanches elders has known has been lost, and the social lives of younger generations have been rapidly changing. But like the grass of the Plains, the Comanches have bent before, but have not been uprooted by, the winds blowing across their land. Comanches have taken the initiative and have made the necessary changes in their relations with one another, orienting them to the organization of their shared community. In this way—their own way—Comanches have become an enduring feature of the North American social landscape.

Notes

CHAPTER 1. COMANCHES AND INDIANS

1. See Simmons (1988:4–5) for additional examples of anthropological images of "last" Indians.

2. In Pichardo (1931–46, 3:328–329).

3. Padilla (1919:53–56).

4. Bonnell (1838:130).

5. Agent Hunt, Annual Report for 1885, Kiowa Agency Records, Oklahoma Historical Society.

6. This is not to say, however, that the Indian and Anglo worlds are portrayed as existing independently of each other. The Scollons refer to "convergence" in speaking of the effects of Anglo literacy on Indian "orality." By this they mean a model in which Athabascan linguistic structures and interactional strategies have come, in part, to resemble Anglo structures and strategies. Convergence depends on interethnic contexts of interaction and is the gradual process by which native communicative means come to resemble Anglo communicative means. This is what Linton and Spicer referred to as "fusion," and it is the logical outcome of an acculturation theory that looks for ways in which native peoples come to resemble the dominant culture that surrounds them.

7. Whereas ethnicity theory focuses on the use of symbols by minority populations to represent themselves to dominant populations, dependency theory focuses on the economic bases of dominance-dependence relationships. A considerable literature has developed around the use of dependency theory to describe Native American populations (e.g., Jorgenson 1978; Anders 1980; Albers 1982; Bee 1982; White 1983). The advantage of dependency theory is that it isolates the economic component in Indian-Anglo relations. The disadvantage is that most proponents of it assume, without much examination of the actual case, that economic dependency results in a more general social and cultural dependency.

8. This process is the basis of the "primordialist" approach (e.g., Geertz 1963; Isaacs 1975), which holds that people rely on their affective attachments to key primordial symbols to form themselves into distinctive ethnic groups in the face of changing economic and political conditions (Bentley 1987:26).

9. Theories of ethnicity based on processes of this kind have been described by others (Despres 1982; Bentley 1987) as comprising the "instrumentalist" view of ethnicity (e.g., Despres 1967; A. Cohen 1969).

10. Wilmoth (1987) attempts to apply the concept of ethnicity to distinctions made between different categories of people within the Blackfeet community. In doing so, he also assumes that the categories used by an Indian people to conceptualize membership in their native community will be influenced by their interactions with Anglos.

11. Grobsmith's (1981) study of the contemporary Lakota community is another example of an approach that emphasizes the determinative effect of Anglo society on a native community's definition of "Indianness."

12. See, for example, Darnell and Foster 1988.

13. Miller (1987) demonstrates a similar process by which reinterpretations of Assiniboine history are used by a small group of tribal members to construct symbols useful in maintaining their shared community. Unlike Fowler, however, Miller embraces the acculturation framework devised by Spicer, specifically Spicer's notion of persistent identity systems. Thus Miller's interpretation of Assiniboine identity maintenance depends more on the status of their community as an enclave within Anglo-American society than upon its status as an ongoing unit of social interaction.

14. A good example of the approach Fowler argues against here is that of Holt (1987) in a study of the Utah Paiutes using dependency theory.

15. Golla (1987) argues for a similar form of cultural continuity through change among the Indians of western Vancouver Island. Golla, though, locates the mechanism for continuity in a vaguely defined notion of cultural structure rather than in the dynamics of the community as a social unit: "My ultimate concern is with the maintenance of identity in a changing world, and identity, though it is certainly acted out, and in large measure *created* through action, is in the end an affair of the mind, and heart" (Golla 1987:199). By concentrating on bringing into focus a hidden conceptual structure, Golla misses the more important sociological fact of the continuity of the communities she has studied.

16. Mexican and Canadian policies toward native peoples have differed somewhat from U.S. policies but have not been any more sensitive to differences among communities.

17. It is increasingly possible for Indian people to view this situation as a conscious choice between remaining within the traditional community and moving out into the Anglo community. Often, where a choice such as this is possible, it is also possible to alternate between the two courses.

18. The ideology of ethnicity theory is that ethnic identity is based on individual choice and self-interest. What many ethnicity theorists miss, though, is that choice and self-interest are always keyed, at least in interethnic encounters, to collective

those who choose to be ethnic. Ethnicity, in this view, is always a response to collective social forces. Ethnicity, then, is a macrosociological concept.

19. While I have avoided relying on these two terms, I do make use of the terms *social* and *cultural* to denote different kinds of phenomena. *Social* refers to human action and interaction, and *cultural* refers to human conceptions and conceptual frameworks.

20. Gumperz 1982a:26.

21. Participation in a community also entails what Gumperz (1982a:2–3) has called "involvement" and "cooperation" in face-to-face encounters. These are not just matters of motivation; they also depend on the shared linguistic and sociocultural knowledge upon which assumptions about context, interactive goals, and interpersonal relations are based, all facilitating the interpretation of what is going on.

22. To this extent, ethnicity theory accounts for much of the interaction between Comanches and Anglos. Where that theory is wanting is in accounting for much of the interaction among Comanches.

23. Doris Duke Oral History Collection, T-40:2.

24. The term *social life* is more mine than Goffman's. Though Goffman used it in places to contrast with social structure and individual experience, he did not do so consistently. Another term he used in this sense is *public life*. Of course, the category of social interaction as distinct from social structure is more important than the term used to designate it, and I have settled on *social life* merely as a matter of convenience.

25. Goffman, however, was little concerned with the analysis of social structure, except as it impinges on the organization of social gatherings (see Goffman 1971:x).

26. It should also be noted that the structuring of social relationships differs from the structuring of social groups. This seems an obvious point, yet the confusion of these two has led to a great deal of analytic imprecision in the study of kinship, descent, and descent groups in traditional societies.

27. Using these conventional means, participants in social encounters structure their interaction with reference to shared expectations (Goffman 1961, 1963a, 1971), engage in impression management (Goffman 1967) and topic management (Goffman 1981), and interpret what is going on, and has gone on, in the course of an encounter (Goffman 1974).

CHAPTER 2. THE NOMADIC COMMUNITY, 1706-1875

1. See Barnard 1941 and Buller 1977 for English translations of Comanche accounts of their separation from other Shoshonean peoples.

2. Hugh Scott ledger book, vol. 2, p. 166, Fort Sill Archives. If we assume that each "generation of old men" is a period of fifty to seventy years, six of these generations would date Comanche entry onto the southern Plains between 1647 and 1697.

3. This is found in Hackett 1923–27, 3:381.

4. In this list, Vargas (in Hackett 1923–27, 2:395) includes the Come Cíbola (the Buffalo Eaters), which is a term later used in the eighteenth century to refer to a Comanche division. It was also used by the Eastern Shoshone as a band name (Thomas 1940:201; Shimkin 1986). Pichardo (1931–46, 1:524) suggests that Comanches participated in the Pueblo Revolt of 1680, but this was probably due to a retrospective confusion of Comanches with Utes.

5. Opler suggests that this was a term generically applied by the Utes to peoples, such as the Cheyenne and Kiowa, with whom they found themselves in conflict. The Utes, however, did not come into conflict with these two peoples for nearly a century after the Spanish fixed the term on Comanche peoples. It is unclear why the Utes would have referred to Comanche peoples as longstanding enemies at a time when they were allies. It may have been a more general comment on the tenacity of Comanche warriors.

6. This is essentially the academic problem of the Apaches and the Sioux.

7. References are found, for instance, for Comanche use of cattle for meat in place of bison in 1749 and of Comanches trading horses for agricultural products in 1761 at the Taos fair and in 1769 from village peoples (Thomas 1940:121; Kenner 1969:37; Bolton 1970:156). By the nineteenth century, Comanches were trading for processed food, such as flour and bread (Kavanagh 1986:250).

8. An example of this seemingly contradictory policy is found in 1774, when Comanches were allowed to participate in a Pueblo trade fair during a period in which Comanche-Spanish hostilities were particularly sharp (Thomas 1940:44, 172). The consistent willingness of Spanish authorities to engage in trade with Comanches suggests a compelling economic motivation that overrode even the most serious Comanche "depredations" of Spanish settlements.

9. The Spanish prohibition against trade in firearms was not always successfully enforced (Thomas 1940). One suspects that Spanish firearms and ammunition were more readily available for Indian trade than the archival accounts suggest.

10. I am indebted to Martha McCullough for this observation.

11. It was even charged in 1774 that the Spanish governor of Texas, Ripperada, had an interest in Louisiana trading companies that were engaged in trade with Comanches and that this caused him to overlook orders to isolate the Comanches from European markets (Bolton 1970:117).

12. Thurman (1980) has taken these references as the basis for his claim that the Comanches constituted two suprabands during the late eighteenth and early nineteenth centuries.

13. Because Comanches worked through individual traders in gaining access to eastern markets, they did not have to maintain the same careful relations with Euro-Americans on the eastern margin of their range that they were forced to maintain with the Spanish in New Mexico.

14. Special Agent Neighbors in a letter to the Indian commissioner, 1847 (*Annual Report for 1847*, 743–744). From the evidence of their reports from 1847 to 1859,

federal Indian agents spent much of their time mediating between Texans and Comanches. The actions of Texas officials often reflected popular political sentiment, and this led to needless provocation of Comanche bands (Wallace and Hoebel 1952:293, 302, 303).

15. Correspondence files of the Upper Platte Agency and the Upper Arkansas Agency for the years in question reflect these movements.

16. Neighbors, in his annual reports to the Indian commissioner for 1848 (p. 592) and 1856 (p. 175) noted the role of Anglo traders in supporting Comanche raiding activities. References to "illegal" Comanche-Anglo trade may be found in the annual reports of Indian agents right up to 1875, when the problem of reservation trade took on a different dimension. The only Euro-American government that succeeded in restricting Indian-Anglo trade, and thereby using it as a means of regulating Comanche actions, was the Spanish administration in the eighteenth century.

17. The reports of Special Agent Neighbors (see Neighbor's Annual Report for 1847:904) offer many examples of Texas settlers and militias attacking Comanche bands simply because they were categorized as Comanche. This made the job of the federal Indian agent all the more difficult in attempting to persuade Comanches of Anglo-American reliability in agreements to regularize Comanche-Anglo interaction.

18. Neighbors in Annual Report for 1856, p. 175.

19. This popular image is perhaps best represented in the accounts written by Anglo captives of Comanches (see Eastman 1976; Harris 1977; Plummer 1977). Many of these accounts were embroidered or were complete fantasies (e.g., Lee 1957). See also Bollaert 1956 for Texans' impressions of Comanches gathered by an Englishman during a trip through the southern Plains from 1842 to 1844.

20. Other Plains peoples, such as the Caddo and Wichita, who were not as integrally involved in the trade for horses and cattle, were forced to accept federal reservations in Indian Territory at this time because they could not maintain traditional subsistence economies in the face of changes in the Plains environment.

21. There is some evidence that this scarcity had been developing for some time. Burnett, for instance, noted a marked failure of bison herds in 1818 (Wallace 1954:136).

22. *Annual Report for 1847,* 904; see also p. 896.

23. Prior to 1836, Comanches were little mentioned in the reports of Indian agents to the War Department and later the Indian commissioner. The estimates of their numbers are low (only 7,000 in 1835), and they are assigned to the general category of "wild Indians" beyond the western boundary of Anglo-American interests. After 1836, however, there is increased attention to Comanches' "hostile acts" (*Annual Report of the Indian Commissioner,* 1836, 567), and estimates of Comanche numbers suddenly inflate (more than 19,000 Comanches are counted in the *Annual Report* for 1837).

24. Reference was also sometimes made to the "middle" Comanches, but these

were simply the southernmost of the bands who resided north of the Texas frontier and who did not act in ways that distinguished them substantially from the more northerly bands.

25. The federal Indian administration was divided into superintendencies, agencies, and subagencies, each responsible for a certain territory rather than for specific Indian peoples. The Texas agency reported to the Southern Superintendency, and the Upper Platte and Upper Arkansas agencies reported to the Central Superintendency. After the Civil War, responsibility for relations with all Comanche bands was concentrated in the Central Superintendency. Due to the interval of time required for reports to be sent by an agent to his superintendent and then from the superintendent to Washington, and for instructions to come back down the line of command, agents had considerable freedom of action as long as they remained within their budgets. Easily 70 percent of the correspondence files between Indian agents and the Indian commissioner for the pre–Civil War period is concerned with budgetary matters rather than with Indian policy or events in Indian country.

26. U.S. Comm. of Ind. Aff., *Annual Report for 1858.*

27. U.S. Comm. of Ind. Aff., *Annual Report for 1855,* 180.

28. Letter of Nov. 21, 1853, from Agent Neighbors to the Indian commissioner, in Texas Agency correspondence files, M234, 859:303–304.

29. U.S. Comm. of Ind. Aff., *Annual Report for 1858,* 173.

30. Report from Neighbors to the Indian commissioner, Texas Agency correspondence files, M234, 861:252–253.

31. Some Comanche leaders may have attempted to play off Confederate and Union agents against one another, but neither side possessed sufficient resources to retain the attention of Comanche bands.

32. It is likely that some of the proceeds of this trade, particularly horses and cattle, found their way into Union and Confederate hands.

33. Significantly, one treaty was made with all the southern Plains peoples (Comanches, Kiowas, Apaches, Cheyennes, and Arapahoes), reflecting the federal perception of a single "Indian problem" with a single solution. While the signatories of the Medicine Lodge Treaty were not empowered to represent the whole of any of the peoples involved, the federal government, in ratifying and implementing the treaty, treated it as an agreement with sovereign nations. In establishing and populating the reservations in Oklahoma over the next ten years, the United States succeeded in approximating that interpretation in fact.

34. U.S. Comm. of Ind. Aff., *Annual Report for 1871,* 503; Tatum to Walker, May 1, 1872, Central Superintendency files, roll 41, pp. 590, 839–40.

35. Other participants in the 1933 Santa Fe Laboratory of Anthropology expedition were Waldo Wedel, Gustav Carlson, J. Nixon Hadley, and Claiborne Lockett. The 1933 field season occupied a summer, in which Linton and his students, as a group, interviewed the same informants. In 1940 a group of students from Columbia University under the direction of George Herzog made another summer field expedition to work with Comanches. Among those students were Joseph Casagrande,

Thomas Gladwin, and David MacAllester. While Mooney made some observations about Comanches during the course of his work with Kiowas at the turn of the century, the only other early fieldwork was done by Lowie during a very brief visit in 1912. Linton 1935; Hoebel 1940; Carlson and Jones 1940; McAllester 1949; Gladwin 1948; Casagrande 1955.

36. Ernest Wallace was a historian whose contribution to *The Comanches: Lords of the Southern Plains* (Wallace and Hoebel 1952) has been somewhat controversial. The folklore surrounding the publication of the book suggests that Hoebel was hired by the University of Oklahoma Press to rewrite a manuscript on Comanches submitted by Wallace. It is likely that Hoebel simply left the historical narrative intact, adding to it the ethnographic information Linton and he had collected in 1933, much of which Hoebel had already published in his 1940 monograph on Comanche law. Much of the historical narrative in the book is simply a paraphrase of passages from Rupert Richardson's *The Comanche Barrier to Southern Plains Settlement* (1933). The friendship between Wallace and Richardson prevented this questionable borrowing from becoming an issue. See Thurman 1982 for a discussion of the historical accuracy of Wallace and Hoebel 1952.

37. Twentieth-century academic images of a Comanche problem, exception, or anomaly have a curious resonance with nineteenth-century Anglo images of a Comanche threat, menace, or problem.

38. When he does treat social organization, Gelo follows Hoebel's sociological analysis of Comanche society quite closely. Gelo (1987, 1988) has emerged as Hoebel's defender in response to critiques by Thurman (1982) and Kavanagh (1986, 1989).

39. Such a claim, however, follows logically from the view that what was distinctive about "being Comanche" was the means used to participate in the community (the language, the activities, the social groups and categories) rather than the act of sharing a community.

40. This claim, though, follows logically from the view that Indian-Anglo interaction came to dictate the social identities that Indians presented to one another, and thus also Indian-Indian interaction.

41. Where anthropologists have been unable to identify these social structures and formal statuses and roles, they have typically characterized the people in question as loosely organized, individualistic, or even anarchical, or they have discovered a hidden structure not immediately visible to earlier scholars.

42. In their descriptions of the various Comanche bands, Wallace and Hoebel (1952:23) are unclear as to how often a particular named band constituted an actual social group. The band lists presented by Neighbors (U.S. Comm. of Ind. Aff., *Annual Report for 1853*), Mooney (1907), Hoebel (1940), and Wallace and Hoebel (1952) include both smaller groups that obviously were residence bands and larger divisions not oriented around some principle of filiation. There also is considerable confusion in historical accounts of Comanche leaders with respect to divisional and residence band identities (see Kavanagh 1986 for a detailed consideration of this

documentary problem). Often these two are confused, so that a "chief" is referred to as a leader of the Yamparika division when in fact he may only have been a leader of a residence band (focused on his personal reputation) that happened to participate in Yamparika divisional gatherings. This sort of confusion has contributed to the reification of divisions as synonymous with the actual groups in which Comanche people lived on an everyday basis.

43. Confirmation of this may be found in comments made to Hugh Scott by Comanches in the 1890s; Hugh Scott ledger book, vol. 1, p. 19, Fort Sill Archives.

44. Most of what we know of this period of Comanche history is, unfortunately, male oriented. When women are mentioned, their identity and status is almost always tied to that of their kin or spouse.

45. The gossip, of course, was comprised of challenges to the face of those who deserted, a potential threat to their reputations once the war party had returned to the public social arena of a Comanche gathering.

46. In his diary entry for July 13, 1789, Pedro Vial reports meeting such a band of seventeen young Comanches "without a chief, who were going on a campaign against the Lipan Apaches"; cited in Loomis and Nasatir 1967:363.

47. As, for instance, Neighbors' description of upper Comanche leaders recruiting lower Comanche warriors for raids on Texans and Mexicans.

48. Comanches did have military or shield societies of some sort, according to both ethnohistorical sources and contemporary consultants, but little is known about how these were organized or functioned. Lowie (1915) collected some very minimal information in 1912 but worded his report in an ambiguous fashion, perhaps purposely, so that it is difficult to discern whether he was told that these sodalities were organized within each division or across divisions. My Comanche consultants suggest that membership did indeed cut across divisional or supraband boundaries (Haddon Nauni, Leonard Riddles, and Haddon Codynah). Comanches today speak of a traditional strategy in which a family has at least one member in each dance society. This would serve to confirm a more restricted interpretation of divisional functions.

49. Hugh Scott ledger book, vol. 2, p. 3. This was confirmed in Scott's interview with Quanah.

50. It is important to point out that the level of political organization and social sanction addressed by Hoebel and his informants is clearly that of the everyday residence band. The issues and case examples taken up in Hoebel 1940 (leadership, adultery, homicide, and sorcery) primarily arise from the circumstance of living together day and day out. Very few of the examples cited involve Comanches who are members of different residence bands.

51. In case number 4, for instance, a husband is willing to overlook his wife's transgression until it is accidentally but repeatedly called to public attention by her lover's grandfather during a stick game. The husband then has no choice but to restore his face by killing the horses of both the grandfather and his wife's lover (Hoebel 1940:51). Not one but two challenges to face were involved here: first that of

the lover violating the possessional territory of the husband (i.e., his wife), and second, that of the lover's grandfather challenging the moral worth of the husband by publicly stating the fact of adultery. To restore his face, the husband has to punish not only the lover but also the lover's grandfather.

52. In case 5, for instance, a husband sends his wife to collect damages from her lover after cutting her hair and clothes to call public attention to her movements. She then "publicly" leads the horse carrying these damages through the camp to her husband (Hoebel 1940:52).

53. Brown Robe was nearly killed by his sons, who then ran off with two of his wives but later returned to their father and were forgiven (Hoebel 1940:71).

54. Other ceremonies around which divisional gatherings may have been focused were the Beaver Ceremony and the Eagle Dance (Wallace and Hoebel 1952:175; Thurman 1980:57). Little information has survived relating to either of these public social occasions. Councils of residence-band leaders, which probably cut across divisional lines, also were public social occasions that functioned in ways similar to divisional gatherings.

55. The territorial dimension of divisions caused Euro-Americans, including anthropologists and historians, to accord them political functions in organizing Comanche activities, including raiding and hunting, within those areas. These functions were vested, however, in activity groups organized around strong leaders, which may have ranged in size from a small residence band or extended family to a large gathering of warriors from a number of residence bands.

56. The geographical significance of Comanche divisional identities may be seen in the use of the term Quahada to designate those Comanches, regardless of their previous band identities, who remained on the Staked Plains after others had centered their movements around the Fort Sill agency (Hagan 1976:89). The significance of geography was also reflected in the meaning of the division name Noyeka, glossed as the Move-abouts and indicating a characteristic pattern of nomadic movement in contrast to other distinctive divisional patterns.

57. Although Wallace and Hoebel (1952:320) claimed that Comanches had not performed their own Sun Dance prior to 1874, Linton (1935) asserted that they had their own Sun Dance throughout most of the nineteenth century. Shimkin (1986:327) states that a Comanche shaman communicated the Sun Dance to the eastern Shoshone around 1800. According to information collected by Linton (1935:426), Sun Dances were opportunities for the maintenance and increase of power already received by individuals through personal visions. These gatherings also were opportunities for medicine men to enhance their professional reputations by directing the ceremony. In other words, Sun Dances were public social occasions in which the larger community could legitimate or sanction personal claims to power or medicine.

The pattern of individual achievement and public legitimation embedded in the Sun Dance may be seen as well in the authorization of warrior's deeds in the context of military society gatherings and in the authority of band leaders in the context of residence band and divisional gatherings. One could not become a respected warrior or leader whom others followed without the sanction of a public gathering of the community.

58. See Winfrey and Day 1966, 1:266–272, for an account of an 1843 council witnessed by an agent for the Texas Republic, one of the few eyewitness descriptions of the etiquette followed at such gatherings.

59. The classic anthropological notion of "participatory validation" as a condition for leadership is another way of expressing the constraint of physical presence on personal authority. Where the selection, powers, and rights and obligations of a leader are not formally established in an institutionalized status and role, the actions of both leaders and their followers are more open to negotiation. Thus membership in a social group or participation in a focused activity depends in large part on the agreement of members and participants to follow a specific leader, who has no term or right of office (indeed, not even a formal office) to fall back upon in establishing his authority.

60. U.S. Comm. of Ind. Aff., *Annual Report for 1847,* 743–744.

61. U.S. Comm. of Ind. Aff., *Annual Report for 1848,* 579.

62. Neighbors, annual report for 1857, p. 267.

63. Tatum in a letter to the superintendent of the Indian Office, Feb. 3, 1872, correspondence files of the Kiowa Agency, Oklahoma Historical Society.

64. Later, Ketumsee was able to achieve a higher status as a leader by accepting a reservation in Texas and thereby becoming an important broker of Comanche-Texan relations and trade (Kavanagh 1986:147–150).

65. Despite their ill feelings, Sanaco and Ketumsee did not violently oppose one another, and Sanaco later came in for a time to the Texas reservation dominated by Ketumsee (Kavanagh 1986:148).

66. Still, some of Toroblanco's former followers continued to oppose the treaty after 1786 by raiding Spanish settlements (Thomas 1932:335).

67. This constitutes yet another argument against the interpretation of Comanche divisions and "principal chiefs" as institutionalized means of social organization.

68. Thurman (1980, 1987), for instance, portrays divisions as the most important aspect of Comanche social structure and attempts to show that three and only three divisions existed from 1700 to 1875.

CHAPTER 3. THE RESERVATION COMMUNITY, 1875-1901

1. U.S. Comm. of Ind. Aff., *Annual Report for 1871,* 503. Tatum to Walker, May 1, 1872, Central Superintendency files, M856:41:590.

2. U.S. Comm. of Ind. Aff., *Annual Report for 1875,* 275.

3. U.S. Comm. of Ind. Aff., *Annual Report for 1901,* 320.

4. Actually, the Kiowa, Comanche, and Apache Reservation has never legally ceased to exist, nor have any of the reservations in the present state of Oklahoma

despite allotment in severalty and administrative denials of reservation status by BIA officials.

5. The name Eschiti is sometimes rendered as Ishatai. The name means, roughly, "coyote's anus," and it was given to him after the failure of the Adobe Walls campaign. Previously he was known as White Eagle.

6. Wallace and Hoebel's assertion that Comanches performed the Sun Dance only once, in 1874, is difficult to understand. Linton (1935:420) categorically states that Comanches had performed the Sun Dance periodically both before and after 1874: "From at least 1860 on it was held at irregular intervals, whenever some individual received the necessary supernatural sanction. . . . Participation seems normally to have been limited to the band of the supervising medicine man with a few others who were in close and friendly contact with it and who came by invitation." In addition, all older Comanches with whom I have spoken say that the Sun Dance was an important social occasion within each division during prereservation times. Linton and Hoebel conducted their fieldwork with Comanches jointly in 1933, and Hoebel (Wallace and Hoebel 1952:x) specifically thanks Linton for the use of the latter's field notes in the writing of the 1952 book. I can only assume that Wallace and Hoebel chose to ignore the available evidence for other Comanche performances of the Sun Dance in order to strengthen their arguments for what they describe as the catastrophic consequences of the 1874 performance for the Comanche community.

7. Haworth to Beede, Dec. 8, 1873, and Haworth to Delano, Dec. 15. 1873, Central Superintendency files, M856, 47:1062, 1080–1096.

8. March report, Haworth to Hoag, Central Superintendency files, M856, 55:596.

9. Haworth to Hoag, June 11, 1874, Central Superintendency files, M856, 55:631.

10. Agent Haworth's accounts of the deliberations at the medicine camp consistently discount the danger of Comanches raiding Anglos until early June. While Haworth may not have been told of earlier discussions of raids on Anglos, the larger point is the lack of a focused agenda among the participants.

11. Haworth to Smith, July 7, 1874, Central Superintendency files, M856, 55:700.

12. Haworth to Hoag, June 11, 1874, Central Superintendency files, M856, 55:631.

13. The Indian agents, at least, were sympathetic to Comanche complaints about the Anglo buffalo hunters, so there may have been some basis for such an assumption (Hagan 1976:106).

14. U.S. Comm. of Ind. Aff., *Annual Report for 1880*, 72.

15. U.S. Comm. of Ind. Aff., *Annual Report for 1890*, 186. Other than the main agency at Anadarko, subagencies and issue stations were located at Fort Sill, on West Cache Creek, at Rainy Mountain, and at Mount Scott. Comanches mainly patronized the first two of these.

16. U.S. Comm. of Ind. Aff., *Annual Report for 1879*, 65.

17. U.S. Comm. of Ind. Aff., *Annual Report for 1885*, 85. In this report Agent Hunt summarizes the previous ten years of reservation life.

18. U.S. Comm. of Ind. Aff., *Annual Report for 1896*, 253.

19. The Indian-Pioneer Papers contain numerous references to Comanche raids on Chickasaws in the 1890s (e.g., 44:113, 74:347). What the interviewees, who were residents of the Chickasaw reservation, left out, however, was that Comanche raids often were in response to raids on Comanche herds by Anglos living on the Chickasaw side of their common boundary. In fact, that part of the Chickasaw reservation was known locally as "Rustlers' Bend" (U.S. Comm. of Ind. Aff., *Annual Report for 1885*, 85).

20. U.S. Comm. of Ind. Aff., *Annual Report for 1885*, 85.

21. U.S. Comm. of Ind. Aff., *Annual Report for 1879*, 66.

22. U.S. Comm. of Ind. Aff., *Annual Report for 1879*, 67.

23. The Kiowa Agency files document more than twenty traders licensed to operate on the reservation from 1884 to 1901. These traders allowed Comanches to charge goods at their stores and then collected at each grass payment. The license was meant to allow Indian agents to control the prices that were charged and to allow the traders to have first priority in collecting debts.

24. U.S. Comm. of Ind. Aff., *Annual Report for 1882*, 69.

25. U.S. Comm. of Ind. Aff., *Annual Report for 1887*, 83.

26. U.S. Comm. of Ind. Aff., *Annual Report for 1890*, 186.

27. Rations were continued until allotment in 1901 even though annuity payments under the 1867 treaty ceased after 1898 (Hagan 1976:219). After July 1901, lease payments, continuing grass payments, and annuity payments from the sale of reservation lands for homesteading began to be doled out by the agency to support Comanche families.

28. In Indian Territory, promoters of land openings were called "Boomers" (among whom were some of the missionaries assigned to the Kiowa-Comanche reservation, who used their advance presence to argue for homesteading through letters to newspapers and pamphlets). Those would-be homesteaders who entered the territory before the legal opening to get a leg up on claims were called "Sooners."

29. Ultimately the questionable procedures surrounding the Jerome Agreement became the basis for a successful Comanche claim against the federal government in the 1950s and 1960s.

30. The Kiowa-Comanche reservation was the last to be opened for homesteading in what is today Oklahoma.

31. This is also evidenced in the Indian Councils file of the Kiowa Agency at the Oklahoma Historical Society, which contains transcripts of the various councils held on the reservation both during the Jerome Commission's visit in 1892 and after, as late as 1898.

32. Reports, Agents file, Kiowa Agency, Oklahoma Historical Society.

33. U.S. Comm. of Ind. Aff., *Annual Report for 1890*, 188.

34. W. T. White, Indian-Pioneer Papers, 97:298.

35. D. W. White, Indian-Pioneer Papers, 97:139.

36. J. C. Grimmitt, Indian-Pioneer Papers, 36:224.

37. Agent Hunt, annual report for 1885.

38. Lee Strode, Indian-Pioneer Papers, 88:86.

39. U.S. Comm. of Ind. Aff., *Annual Report for 1891,* 351.

40. In 1895 just 145 of the more than 3,000 Kiowas, Comanches, and Apaches were counted as church members in the agent's annual report (Reports, Agents file, Kiowa Agency, Oklahoma Historical Society).

41. U.S. Comm. of Ind. Aff., *Annual Report for 1881,* 78. This reluctance continued throughout the reservation period.

42. Lee Strode, who lived on the reservation during the 1880s, recalled Anglos taking advantage of Comanches when grass payments were issued at Fort Sill (Indian-Pioneer Papers, 88:84–85).

43. S. H. Orendorf, who lived on the reservation during the 1890s, recalled that Comanches drove hard bargains in exchanges with Anglos (Indian-Pioneer Papers, 68:251).

44. A rather extensive literature has developed around the myth of Quanah. Most works portray him as a leading prereservation warrior who became, with his surrender in 1875, the leading reservation spokesman for Comanches. However, as Hagan (1980) has pointed out, Quanah was too young a warrior to have been a war leader in the last prereservation skirmishes or to have been a major beef-band leader in the initial (1875–1880) reservation period. Instead, Quanah was among those younger intermediary leaders who benefited from the federal strategy of decreasing the prestige of prereservation residence-band leaders. Agents and other Anglos consistently promoted Quanah's prestige within the reservation community by using him as a middleman and recognizing him as the "Chief of all Comanches." The intracommunity validity of this title is still hotly debated among Comanches, with descendants of Quanah maintaining its legitimacy and most other Comanches denying it. A careful examination of transcripts of hearings and Indian councils held on the reservation in which Quanah and other prominent Comanches participated suggests that Quanah was not the paramount leader in the community, though he was one of the more successful intermediary leaders during the reservation period.

45. Indian Council file, Kiowa Agency, Oklahoma Historical Society.

46. U.S. Comm. of Ind. Aff., *Annual Report for 1885,* 89. In this report Agent Hunt summarized the previous ten years of reservation life.

47. Comm. of Ind. Aff., Letters Received, M234, 66:511; Kiowa Agency files, Oklahoma Historical Society, KA1:858, 872. The 1869–70 lists include two Quahada bands. In addition, during both 1869–70 and 1875, a band of Penetaka Comanche resided at the Wichita Agency. An 1874 list has twenty-nine residence bands, ranging from 37 to 200 members (KA1:874). There may have been a reduction in the number of bands due to the events of 1874–75, resulting in the existence of only twenty-four bands in late 1875.

48. U.S. Comm. of Ind. Aff., *Annual Report for 1879,* 66: "Except in the matter of

issuing beef and annuities the band is now scarcely recognized, and there is certainly a decline in the power and influence of the chief. . . . During the past year there has been shown a disposition to move off from the main camps and settle down elsewhere—some having already done so."

49. As Agent Hunt notes, this was done to "sever their connection with the bands, to make them independent, and rely upon themselves for support, and to think of becoming themselves the head of a family, instead of being the blind and idle followers of a chief, who cares nothing for him except that as his name counts for one in numbering his band, it brings him more glory and more beef" (U.S. Comm. of Ind. Aff., *Annual Report for 1879,* 66).

50. U.S. Comm. of Ind. Aff., *Annual Report for 1880,* 72–73.

51. Kiowa Agency files, Oklahoma Historical Society, KA1:942–966.

52. U.S. Comm. of Ind. Aff., *Annual Report for 1880,* 73.

53. Kiowa Agency files, Oklahoma Historical Society, KA1:769–792.

54. U.S. Comm. of Ind. Aff., *Annual Report for 1881,* 78.

55. Kiowa Agency files, Oklahoma Historical Society, KA2:65–93.

56. Kiowa Agency files, Oklahoma Historical Society, KA2:370–430.

57. U.S. Comm. of Ind. Aff., *Annual Report for 1885,* 84.

58. Indian-Pioneer Papers, 71:7.

59. Kiowa Agency files, Oklahoma Historical Society, KA2:607.

60. Doris Duke Oral History Project, T-27:8.

61. Robert Coffey and Haddon Nauni, interviews with author.

62. U.S. Comm. of Ind. Aff., *Annual Report for 1892,* 386.

63. Kiowa Agency files, Oklahoma Historical Society, KA87.

64. Indian Houses file, Kiowa Agency, Oklahoma Historical Society.

65. U.S. Comm. of Ind. Aff., *Annual Report for 1886,* 127.

66. Millet and Joe Harry, who later were members of the Kiowa-Comanche-Apache Business Committee just before and after allotment, also resided in this southern district.

67. Even Eschiti, the instigator of both the vision and the attack of 1874, remained a powerful, respected person in the Comanche community throughout the reservation period. His name appears, for instance, in the Indian Council file of the Kiowa Agency as a leading figure in Comanche negotiations about reservation conditions with various Indian agents.

68. U.S. Comm. of Ind. Aff., *Annual Report for 1885,* 84.

69. As, for example, a group from the district south of Quanah who tried to form a rival tribal council in 1897 to oppose the ratification of the Jerome Agreement (Kiowa Agency files, Oklahoma Historical Society, KA48:417).

70. One might argue that by 1870 there were in fact only two functional divisions, one comprised of Comanches operating on the Staked Plains and the other of Comanches residing on the reservation in Indian Territory.

71. Thomas Kavanagh, personal communication.

72. That a Sun Dance was in fact performed in 1878 is indirectly confirmed by

the annual report for that year, which was entitled "Pagan superstitions and ceremonies universal among the three tribes" (Reports, Agents files, Kiowa Agency, Oklahoma Historical Society). In 1885 the same agent could report that Comanches had held no dances during the year.

73. Albert Attocknie, Doris Duke Oral History Project, T-448:7–8.

74. Sarah Pohocsucat, Doris Duke Oral History Project, T-40:19.

75. Leonard Riddles, interview with author.

76. In 1985 Tennyson Echawaudah related the story of the Comanches' acquisition of peyote: "Chiricahuas and Mescaleros were first users of the peyote and Comanches were first users on the Plains. They had a different way of using it. A couple Comanche scouts ran on to these Apaches using this medicine. They was using it in another way. They'd have a ceremony to find out if their enemies were coming this way or not. Comanches used it in a worship way and doctored people who were sick." See Opler 1938 and Bittle 1954 for discussions of possible origins of the peyote ceremony used by Comanches.

77. Letter from E. L. Clark to Agent Hunt, Aug. 11, 1883, Kiowa Agency files, Oklahoma Historical Society.

78. U.S. Comm. of Ind. Aff., *Annual Report for 1888,* 98.

79. One consequence of this, however, was the appearance of all manner of misconceptions about the detrimental effects of peyote among Comanches (Stewart 1987:128), which contributed to Anglo efforts to suppress its use.

80. A peyote meeting was "put up" by a sponsor, as in the Sun Dance, who invited a peyote road man to run the meeting (Stewart 1987:76–77). The primary obligation of the sponsor was to provide a meal for participants on the morning after the ceremony (McAllester 1949:19).

81. Edward Wermy, interview with author. Mr. Wermy first participated in peyote meetings in the late 1920s and was instructed by older Comanches who had taken part in peyote ceremonies in the reservation period. In describing Comanche beliefs about the location of power, Mr. Wermy put it this way: "There's a hill up there. I'm looking to that hill to where that blessing comes from."

82. Quanah Parker and nearly all the prominent Comanche leaders of the reservation period named in the previous section, with the possible exception of Eschiti, were prominent peyote participants and leaders. Arguably, Eschiti did not need to participate in peyote meetings, as his claims to power were already validated by his status as a medicine man.

83. See Bee 1966, Lieber 1972, Siskin 1983, and Swan 1990 for other examples of peyotism as an arena for political competition.

84. U.S. Comm. of Ind. Aff., *Annual Report for 1887,* and *Annual Report for 1888.*

CHAPTER 4. THE POSTALLOTMENT COMMUNITY, 1901-1941

1. Robert Coffey, interview with author. Andrew Perdasophy, Indian-Pioneer Papers, 71:3. This is also reflected in the distribution of allotments, which were

almost all scattered along river- and creekbeds, the only places in the reservation that were heavily forested. See also Kavanagh 1989 for a discussion of the Comanches' allotment choices.

2. Doris Duke Oral History Project, T-40:1.

3. Reports, Agents file, Kiowa Agency, Oklahoma Historical Society.

4. Annual Statistical Reports of 1925 and 1931, Kiowa Agency Records, Annual Statistical Reports File, Fort Worth National Archives Center.

5. Annual Report for 1910, M1011, 70:821.

6. By 1925, 640 KCA Indians had some stock grazing on 8,515 acres, but only 12 were full-time cattlemen. Out of 1,899 households, 285 had milk cows. In 1931, 45 KCA Indians are listed as obtaining income through stock raising, with an average income from stock raising of $334 per year. Annual Statistical Reports of 1925 and 1931, Kiowa Agency Records, Annual Statistical Reports File, Fort Worth National Archives Center.

7. 1934 Social and Economic Survey, Intermarriage File, Kiowa Agency, Fort Worth National Archives Center.

8. Buntin to McKenzie, July 27, 1927, in report to Meriam Survey, Meriam Survey file, Kiowa Agency, Fort Worth National Archives Center.

9. *Annual Report for 1902,* 290. The figures available for the period after allotment are generally composites of the four tribes, all of which were under the jurisdiction of the Anadarko agency.

10. *Annual Report for 1903,* 263.

11. *Annual Report for 1905,* 301.

12. *Annual Report for 1906,* 309.

13. *Annual Report for 1909,* 95.

14. *Annual Report for 1920.* This total includes the leases of Wichita and Caddo Indians. The Anadarko superintendency was responsible for administering those tribes, along with the Kiowas, Comanches, and Apaches. Depending on the superintendent and the year, statistical reports sometimes lump all five tribes together and sometimes make a distinction between the KCA and the Wichita and Caddo. Only rarely are separate figures noted for Comanches alone.

15. Farmers files, Kiowa Agency, Oklahoma Historical Society.

16. Annual Report for 1932, M1011, 72:535.

17. Annual Report for 1926, M1011, 71:573.

18. Annual Report for 1927, M1011, 71:671.

19. Annual Report for 1930, M1011, 72:169.

20. *Survey of the Conditions of Indians in the United States,* U.S. Senate, 1937, p. 7449.

21. 1934 Social and Economic Survey, Intermarriage File, Kiowa Agency, Fort Worth National Archives Center. A total of 2,062 people were reported as having some interest in allotment land, while 2,801 were reported as having no interest.

22. 1940 annual statistical report, Kiowa Agency, Fort Worth National Archives Center.

23. Annual Report for 1910, M1011, 70:821.

24. Buntin in report to Meriam Survey, Meriam Survey file, Kiowa Agency, Fort Worth National Archives Center.

25. Ibid.

26. Minutes of Comanche tribal council, May 25, 1921, Tribal Council File, Kiowa Agency, Fort Worth National Archives Center.

27. In the end, the Red River case was settled by congressional action, with the KCA getting two-thirds of the revenues from the oil wells and the state of Oklahoma getting one-third.

28. The falling price of oil after 1927 was the reason given by federal officials for not expanding the Red River field. KCA committeemen, however, were suspicious of Anglo-owned wells on the right bank of the river, claiming these were drawing off reserves properly belonging to the KCA wells. Whatever the case may have been, BIA officials were consistently opposed to exploiting the Red River field as a way of financially empowering the KCA business committee. Tribal Council File, 1927–1944, Kiowa Agency, Fort Worth Federal Archives Center.

29. 1934 Social and Economic Survey, Intermarriage File, Kiowa Agency, Fort Worth National Archives Center.

30. Tribal Council file, Kiowa Agency, Fort Worth National Archives Center.

31. Indian-Pioneer Papers, 110:138–158.

32. Indian-Pioneer Papers, 88:99.

33. Luella Webster described encountering, sometime in the early 1920s, a young Comanche woman who had once worked for her (Indian-Pioneer Papers, 96:131): "She was glad to see us and talked lots, even though we did find her sitting among some other Indians on the street."

34. Robert Coffey, Haddon Nauni, Leonard Riddles, and Edward Wermy, interviews with author.

35. Ethel Howny, who attended Indian schools just after allotment, described the agency in 1967: "Because if you go to the Indian office and if you have money there, they ration you just so much what they think" (Doris Duke Oral History Project, T-78:8).

36. Relations, Family file; Farmers file; and Matrons file, Kiowa Agency, Oklahoma Historical Society.

37. Indian Schools file, Kiowa Agency, Oklahoma Historical Society.

38. Tony Martinez, interview with author. This event was also remembered by Sarah Pohocsucat in 1967 (Doris Duke Oral History Collection, T-40:14). The few children who were missed were marked in later life as monolingual Comanche speakers lacking Anglicized names. These mostly were women whose parents saw little purpose in exposing them to Anglo forms of social interaction (Leonard Riddles, interview with author).

39. M1011, 70:819.

40. Almost all Comanches over the age of fifty have had some experience of Indian schools. Many speak warmly of their experiences, proudly describing the

lessons they learned in Anglo etiquette: always using "sir" or "ma'am," respecting turn-taking in conversation, never using "cuss words." Comanches credit these and other lessons from their Indian school educations with enabling them to get along in the Anglo world in their later lives.

41. Reports, Agents file, Kiowa Agency, Oklahoma Historical Society.

42. Farmers and Matrons files, Kiowa Agency, Oklahoma Historical Society.

43. Tony Martinez, Robert Coffey, Haddon Nauni, and Leonard Riddles, interviews with author.

44. Annual superintendent's report for 1931, narrative section. A total of 699 KCA children attended Indian schools, and 884 attended public schools. Annual Reports file, Kiowa Agency, Fort Worth National Archives Center.

45. The threat of closing the boarding schools was a constant theme at KCA business committee meetings during this period. By 1942 the BIA was pursuing the indirect strategy of selling the land attached to the Fort Sill Indian School to the city of Lawton for use as an airport. Despite these attempts, though, all three schools remained in operation through the 1970s.

46. Leonard Riddles, Eva Riddles, and Haddon Nauni, interviews with author. This cannot be demonstrated statistically, as the necessary figures are not available. This was also a period in which there was a fairly high dropout rate before high school.

47. Comanche tribal council response to House Committee on Indian Affairs, June 10, 1944, Business Committee file, Kiowa Agency, Fort Worth National Archives Center.

48. Meetings of Jan. 8–9, 1917, Tribal Council file, Kiowa Agency, Fort Worth National Archives Center. At this time, Indians did not have the right to vote. Some younger Comanches, however, were being drafted for World War I. A similar question about the Comanches' relationship to the federal government occurred during World War II as well. KCA business committee meeting, Jan. 15, 1942, Business Committee file, Kiowa Agency, Fort Worth National Archives Center.

49. Attocknie to Commissioner, April 10, 1923, Business Committee file, Kiowa Agency, Fort Worth National Archives Center.

50. Prior to allotment, the local BIA official in charge of the Kiowa Reservation was called the agent. After allotment, the same official was called the superintendent.

51. Meeting of Nov. 14, 1914, Tribal Council file, 1900–1914, Kiowa Agency, Fort Worth National Archives Center.

52. M1011, 71:103.

53. Meetings of Jan. 8–9, 1917, Tribal Council file, Kiowa Agency, Fort Worth National Archives Center.

54. When a divisive issue faced the KCA peoples, separate tribal councils were often called, either by the superintendent or the business committee, as a way of reaching a consensus.

55. KCA business committee meeting minutes for 1909, Business Committee

file, Anadarko Agency, Fort Worth National Archives Center.

56. Supt. Stinchecum to Commissioner, Sept. 19, 1917, Business Committee file, Kiowa Agency,

57. The business committee file of the Anadarko superintendency contains copies of numerous letters written by leaders of different Comanche factions to the commissioner of Indian affairs and to Oklahoma senators and representatives, attempting to obtain personal responses on pressing issues that they then could show to other Comanches as evidence of their influence in the Anglo community.

58. Mamsookowat to Indian Commissioner, Feb. 8, 1915, and Supt. Stecker to Indian Commissioner, March 1, 1915, Business Committee file, Kiowa Agency, Fort Worth National Archives Center.

59. Ibid. The KCA business committee was subsequently suspended by the agent from 1917 to 1922, when it was reorganized at the direction of BIA officials in Washington.

60. On March 4, 1916, for instance, the superintendent telegraphed the commissioner to warn of two Comanche committeemen who were on their way to Washington to argue against a bill outlawing peyote use. In a subsequent letter of March 7, 1916, Supt. Stinchecum suggested that the two Comanches be discredited with members of Congress with whom they might meet. Subsequently the BIA refused to recognize the election of one of these Comanches, Wilbur Pewo, to the KCA business committee. Supt. Stecker to Pewo, May 10, 1916, Business Committee file, Kiowa Agency, Fort Worth National Archives Center.

61. M1011, 70:945.

62. Supt. Stecker to Commissioner, Jan. 31, 1912, Business Committee file, Kiowa Agency, Fort Worth National Archives Center.

63. At least, the peyote participants were in the majority with respect to business committee elections, where peyote men dominated the positions to 1929. As Albert Attocknie, who was opposed to peyote use, observed in 1925, "Sometimes I think peyote has been used more for business [committee] campaigns than it has been for any other purpose by those who could not get votes any other way." Dec. 16, 1925, Business Committee file, Kiowa Agency, Fort Worth National Archives Center.

64. Minutes of Comanche tribal council meeting, Jan. 2, 1926, Business Committee file, Kiowa Agency, Fort Worth National Archives Center.

65. For instance, as part of the BIA promotion of a constitution under the terms of the Oklahoma Indian Welfare Act of 1936, Comanches from the church faction were hired to travel around the reservation area and campaign for approval. Ben Dwight, memorandum of Jan. 27, 1938, Business Committee file, Kiowa Agency, Fort Worth National Archives Center.

66. There were, of course, some exceptions to this general pattern. Robert Coffey, for instance, who was a Christian church participant and a prominent younger man in Comanche politics from the 1920s on, was associated politically more with the peyote faction.

67. Sen. Thomas to Supt. McCown, Oct. 28, 1943, Tribal Council file, Kiowa

Agency, Fort Worth National Archives Center.

68. Ben Dwight, BIA organization field agent, memorandum of Jan. 27, 1938, Tribal Council file, Kiowa Agency, Fort Worth National Archives Center.

69. Washington BIA administrators and members of Congress never seemed to understand the significance of obtaining semiannual per capita payments of twenty or fifty dollars to KCA peoples, considering such sums too small to make any difference. KCA business committeemen, on the other hand, consistently pushed hard for these payments, understanding that even a twenty-dollar semiannual annuity meant, to a household with twelve members, $480 per year, a sum which, in the 1920s and 1930s, could provide a good measure of subsistence.

70. As evidence of this concern for per capita funding sources, see Attocknie and Komah to Supt. McCown, May 18, 1932, Tribal Council file, Kiowa Agency, Fort Worth National Archives Center.

71. In fact, with little KCA input, most of the remaining Red River funds were used to establish a $50,000 revolving loan fund by congressional appropriation in 1934. This effectively ended the possibility of per capita payments. W. V. Woehlica, District Director, memorandum of July 17, 1947, Business Committee file, Kiowa Agency, Fort Worth National Archives Center.

72. Ben Dwight, BIA organization field agent, memorandum of Jan. 27, 1938, Tribal Council file, Kiowa Agency, Fort Worth National Archives Center. A KCA constitution was approved in 1940, though it was not modeled on the OIWA.

73. KCA business committee minutes for 1942, Business Committee file, Kiowa Agency, Fort Worth National Archives Center.

74. Robert Thomas, a clerk at an Indian trading post between 1901 and 1909, observed the frequent coining of new Comanche words for Anglo-manufactured objects (Indian-Pioneer Papers, 110:136).

75. Eva Riddles and Haddon Nauni, interviews with author.

76. Haddon Nauni, interview with author. The events of which Mr. Nauni spoke occurred sometime in the 1930s.

77. This ratio is figured on the basis of a census taken at statehood for those counties in which Comanches owned allotments.

78. Richard O. Rathburn, one of the homesteaders, noted in 1937 that in just a short time after the land opening, land was fenced, cleared, and planted, and roads were built (Indian-Pioneer Papers, 74:279).

79. The reports of agency farmers frequently mention assisting Comanches in purchasing wagons and horses from local Anglo merchants (Kiowa Agency, Oklahoma Historical Society). Lillian Gassaway described Indian transportation from just after allotment to 1937: "Later there were wagons and two-seated hacks. Now [1937] most of the Indians have cars and you seldom see a hack, but there are a few wagons yet" (Indian-Pioneer Papers, 105:337).

80. Ruth Palmer also recalled Comanche purchases of used hacks (Doris Duke Oral History Collection, T-119:1).

81. Farmers and Matrons files, Kiowa Agency, Oklahoma Historical Society.

82. Ibid.

83. Ibid.

84. Dana Chibitty and Joe Attocknie both describe these extended families for the late reservation and postallotment periods (Doris Duke Oral History Collection, T-177:1, T-448). The Matrons files include references to both extended families of this sort and to smaller nuclear families (Kiowa Agency, Oklahoma Historical Society). All of my consultants who grew up in the period between 1900 and 1940 described households in which parents' parents, parents' siblings, and parents' siblings' children were present for extended periods.

85. Meriam Report, 1926, Meriam Report file, Kiowa Agency, Fort Worth National Archives Center.

86. Ibid.

87. 1934 Social and Economic Survey, Intermarriage File, Kiowa Agency, Fort Worth National Archives Center.

88. The 1926 Meriam Survey suggests an average household size of slightly less than three persons, while the 1934 Social and Economic Survey suggests an average household size of slightly more than six persons. The Meriam Survey figures, however, appear to be estimates rather than the results of an actual count, while the 1934 survey appears to have been based on a fairly systematic count of KCA households. The 1931 Annual Statistical Report shows an average of slightly less than 4.6 persons per household.

89. George Watchetaker, interview with author.

90. Ethel Howry, Doris Duke Oral History Collection, T-78:8. This is confirmed by Comanches with whom I have spoken.

91. Dana Chibitty, Doris Duke Oral History Collection, T-177:1–13.

92. George Watchetaker, Leonard Riddles, Robert Coffey, Edward Wermy, and Tennyson Echawaudah, interviews with author. By 1934, KCA members owned 350 automobiles and 375 wagons with 1,327 horses (1934 Social and Economic Survey, Intermarriage file, Kiowa Agency, Fort Worth National Archives Center).

93. Janie Elizabeth Ray noted that peyote meetings were held in Indiahoma in 1902 (Indian-Pioneer Papers, 76:173). Robert Owen observed that meetings were held in Cache every Saturday night in 1903 and 1904 (Indian-Pioneer Papers, 110:151). Mary Neido, however, began to find peyote doctoring in Indiahoma after 1945 to be "too noisy" (Doris Duke Oral History Collection, T-52:21). Peyote gatherings after allotment increasingly tended to be held on rural allotments, away from Anglos (Edward Wermy, interview with author).

94. Edward Wermy, interview with author. Each local community had its own peyote circle, a group of participants who lived within ready proximity to one another. There was also some cross-participation among the different local circles, especially by those persons who were considered to have special power in peyote rituals. Tennyson Echawaudah and Haddon Codynah, interviews with the author.

95. Kiowa Agency files, Oklahoma Historical Society.

96. Annual Report for 1930, M1011, 72:87.

97. Robert Coffey and Edward Wermy, interviews with author.

98. Tennyson Echawaudah, interview with author. This is confirmed by Edward Wermy. Both Mr. Echawaudah and Mr. Wermy began participating in peyote gatherings in the late 1920s as young men who attended to benefit from the medicinal curing. Both continued to participate—more fully as they grew older—for the next sixty years.

99. Tennyson Echawaudah, Edward Wermy, and Haddon Nauni, interviews with author.

100. In 1900 the agent's annual statistical report showed 434 church members among 3,733 Kiowas, Comanches, and Apaches. Most of these members were Kiowas, however, who had been exposed to Anglo missionaries more than members of either of the other two communities.

101. Robert Coffey, interview with author. These churches were the Deyo Baptist Mission near Cache, the Post Oak Mennonite Church near Cache, the Brown Church (Baptist) near Walters, the Cache Creek Presbyterian Church near Apache, the Yellow Mission (Methodist) near Lawton, and the Little Washita Methodist Church near Lawton. Each of the six churches named by Mr. Coffey is also listed in contemporaneous superintendents' reports. By 1905 the number of church members had risen to 760.

102. Annual Report for 1920, M1011, 70:1141.

103. Annual Report for 1928, M1011, 71:755.

104. Matrons files, Kiowa Agency, Oklahoma Historical Society.

105. Robert Coffey, interview with author. Mr. Coffey experienced this through his membership in the Deyo Baptist Mission in the late 1910s and early 1920s.

106. Leonard Riddles, Haddon Nauni, Tennyson Echawaudah, and Edward Wermy, interviews with author. Some older Comanches did choose to join Christian churches, and younger Comanches were present at traditional winter and summer encampments. The point is not that there was an absolute division between generations but that younger Comanches faced a different set of choices in community participation than that experienced by older Comanches.

107. Robert Coffey, Haddon Nauni, and Edward Wermy, interviews with author. This is also mentioned in a privately printed souvenir publication commemorating the seventy-fifth anniversary of the Deyo Mission.

108. Mary Neido, Doris Duke Oral History Collection, T-75:25. Reference to this division in the community is also found in the monthly matrons' reports for 1911 (Kiowa Agency, Oklahoma Historical Society).

109. Robert Coffey, Edward Wermy, Tennyson Echawaudah, and Haddon Codynah, interviews with author. All of these were young men in the 1920s, when the Comanche community was segmenting.

110. Because most of the district matrons were the wives of Anglo missionaries, their monthly accounts primarily reflect the mission-sponsored gatherings, which began in 1908.

111. The gaming aspects of winter encampments were simply a continuation of

Comanches' enjoyment of gambling from the prereservation and reservation periods. A certain carnival atmosphere had become attached to that segment of the encampments, with card games played in tents during the day.

112. A matron's report for January 1921 noted that the gambling at the Cache community encampment continued for several weeks beyond New Year's (Matrons files, Kiowa Agency, Oklahoma Historical Society).

113. Andrew Perdasophy, Indian-Pioneer Papers, 71:8.

114. Matron's report for Cache district, July 1906 (Kiowa Agency files, Oklahoma Historical Society).

115. Tennyson Echawaudah, interview with author.

116. Leonard Riddles and Haddon Nauni, interviews with author.

117. Leonard Riddles, interview with author.

118. These societies are among those that Thurman (1980:54) has identified as Comanche military organizations from various ethnohistorical sources.

119. Leonard Riddles, interview with author. Most of these dances are still performed from time to time at the larger Comanche powwows. All of them except the rabbit and spear dances are listed in Wallace and Hoebel 1952.

120. Leonard Riddles, interview with author.

121. Dancing at the winter encampments was probably of the social rather than the traditional or sacred kind.

122. District matron for the Cache area, July 1912, Matrons file, Kiowa Agency, Oklahoma Historical Society.

123. District matron for the Cache area, July 1913, Matrons file, Kiowa Agency, Oklahoma Historical Society.

124. District matron for the Lawton area, April 1913, Matrons files, Kiowa Agency, Oklahoma Historical Society.

125. Dances and Celebrations file, Kiowa Agency, Oklahoma Historical Society.

126. Leonard Riddles and Haddon Nauni, interviews with author.

127. Meeting of Jan. 8–9, 1917, Business Committee file, Kiowa Agency, Fort Worth National Archives Center.

128. Open letter of Jan. 12, 1917, to a number of Comanches, Business Committee file, Kiowa Agency, Fort Worth National Archives Center.

129. Robert Coffey, interview with author.

130. Letter of Dec. 20, 1921, Supt. Stinchecum to Commissioner of Indian Affairs, Dances and Celebrations file, Kiowa Agency, Oklahoma Historical Society.

131. Annual Report for 1922, M1011, 71:112.

132. Annual Report for 1928, M1011, 71:755.

133. Annual Narrative Report for 1931, Annual Report file, Kiowa Agency, Fort Worth National Archives Center.

134. Comanche petition of July 19, 1938, Business Committee file, Kiowa Agency, Fort Worth National Archives Center.

135. For example, Mumsekai, who is described as a prominent reservation peyote man by Wallace and Hoebel (1952:336), was also involved in the summer dance held

by the Walters community of Comanches (Leonard Riddles, interview with author).

136. Leonard Riddles, Haddon Nauni, Edward Wermy, and Robert Coffey, interviews with author.

137. Interview with author. Mr. Nauni was a high school student at the time dancing was undergoing a generational transition.

138. Interview with author. Mr. Wermy was one of the younger generation that took over peyote gatherings in the late 1930s. This retrospective view of peyote as Christian-oriented is almost universal among present-day practitioners. Mary Neido also described the influence that Christian beliefs had on peyote gatherings beginning in the late 1930s (Doris Duke Oral History Collection, T-52:22).

139. Certainly there was overlap in participation between peyote gatherings and dance gatherings during this period, but not among those Comanches who were known as leaders of the gatherings. Some church people engaged in casual rather than intensive participation in peyote meetings and powwows.

CHAPTER 5. THE POSTWAR COMMUNITY, 1942-1990

1. The observations in this chapter have been substantiated by speaking with Comanches who have been active in the community since World War II and by reference to the few published accounts of postwar economic and social conditions. Because some of the events described here are still issues in the community—specifically the discussions of Comanche witchcraft and politics—I have sometimes refrained from directly citing my sources. The descriptions of contemporary gatherings, where not otherwise credited, are based on my own experiences in the community between August 1984 and December 1990.

2. Comanches are quick to distinguish their dances, songs and traditions, from those of other Indian peoples, especially the Kiowas, and from generalized intertribal styles and forms.

3. My conversations with Comanche men between the ages of 58 and 75 almost always came around to the subject of their military experiences. They drew from these experiences to explain interactions with Anglos later in their lives and credited their service for providing them with knowledge and economic advantages they would not normally have acquired in the Comanche community of southwestern Oklahoma.

4. Leonard Riddles, Haddon Nauni, Robert Coffey, Haddon Codynah, and Edward Wermy, interviews with author. Mr. Riddles, Mr. Nauni, and Mr. Codynah all served in the military. Mr. Wermy and Mr. Coffey were too old for service. Mr. Nauni, Mr. Coffey, and Mr. Wermy each obtained employment in the Lawton area after the war in jobs that, as Comanches, they would not have had prior to 1942.

5. Annual Statistical Reports, Kiowa Agency, Fort Worth National Archives Center.

6. Not all of these necessarily lived within the present reservation boundaries. The first statistic is taken from a printout of 1980 U.S. Census information. The

1988 numbers are taken from the FY 1988 Anadarko Area Annual Report.

7. 1947 KCA Business Committee minutes, Business Committee file, Kiowa Agency, Fort Worth National Archives Center.

8. See also Tribble 1972 for general economic conditions of Indian households in Oklahoma.

9. U.S. Comm. of Ind. Aff., *Annual Report of the Commissioner of Indian Affairs for 1950*. Those people who are referred to in the anthropological and historical literature as the Kiowa-Apache have, since their separation from the Kiowa and Comanche in 1966, preferred to be known as the Plains Apaches of Oklahoma.

10. U.S. Public Health Service, *Indians on Federal Reservations in the United States* (Washington, D.C.: U.S. Government Printing Office: 1960).

11. U.S. Dept. of the Interior, *Annual Report of Indian Lands,* 1978.

12. In 1980, more than 12,000 Comanches, Kiowas, and Apaches lived in the five counties in which only slightly more than 3,600 of their ancestors had taken allotments in 1901 (Morris, Goins, and McReynolds 1986).

13. U.S. Census, American Indians, Eskimos and Aleuts on Identified Reservations and in the Historic Areas of Oklahoma (Excluding Urbanized Areas), January 1986, p. 1,051. Unfortunately, the city of Lawton, which lies right in the middle of Comanche country, is excluded from the 1980 census statistics as an urban area. Those separate statistics tend to be less detailed but do show that Comanches living in Lawton have a slightly higher average income of $7,490 per year, with 17.4 percent of all families living below the poverty level. The aggregate statistics for all persons identifying themselves as Comanche were released in 1990 and portrayed much higher levels of family income. Arguably, these later figures were skewed by individuals who falsely self-identified themselves as Comanche and by those Comanches who have moved away from the reservation-area community precisely for economic reasons.

14. U.S. Census, *American Indians, Eskimos and Aleuts on Identified Reservations and in the Historic Areas of Oklahoma (Excluding Urbanized Areas)* (Washington, D.C.: U.S. Government Printing Office, 1986).

15. Leonard Riddles, Robert Coffey, and Haddon Nauni, interviews with author.

16. KCA Business Committee meetings 1942–44, Business Committee file, Kiowa Agency, Fort Worth National Archives Center.

17. 1947 KCA Business Committee meetings, Business Committee file, Kiowa Agency, Fort Worth National Archives Center.

18. 1947 KCA Business Committee meetings, Business Committee file, Kiowa Agency, Fort Worth National Archives Center.

19. KCA Social Worker's quarterly report, Oct.–Dec. 1947, Social Relations file, Kiowa Agency, Fort Worth National Archives Center.

20. 1947 KCA Business Committee meetings, Business Committee file, Kiowa Agency, Fort Worth National Archives Center.

21. See Kowena to Supt. McCown, Dec. 5, 1944, Business Committee file, Kiowa

Agency, Fort Worth National Archives Center.

22. U.S. Indian Claims Commission, *Final Report, 1978*, p. 54.

23. See Fixico 1986 for a more detailed treatment of the termination policy.

24. A revised KCA constitution was defeated by voters in 1962. The KCA business committee voted to dissolve in 1963. *Lawton Constitution,* June 7, 1962, and January 20, 1963.

25. A similar effort at separation had failed in the 1950s; *Lawton Constitution,* December 1, 1958.

26. Mary Neido, Doris Duke Oral History Collection, T-89:29.

27. The KCA business committee has continued to operate in addition to the separate tribal governments. The three tribes continue to have joint ownership of several thousand acres of land in the former reservation area, most of which had been abandoned by the federal government and thus had been returned, by treaty, to KCA ownership. During the late 1970s and early 1980s, KCA lands were the focus of a promotion—headed by some prominent members of each tribe and called "Kiomanche"—which planned to build a horse racing track at a time when pari-mutuel wagering was illegal in both Oklahoma and Texas. The trust status of KCA land and the access of the KCA tribal entity to federal economic development loans were key points in the promotion. The proposal was a prominent issue in elections in each tribe, and it became a special target of those Comanches who were "strong" church people. Ultimately, the Kiomanche project failed to attract the necessary support from all three tribes. Most recently, the KCA business committee has begun to compete with the three tribal governments for economic development funds and for recognition as the primary representative of Indian interests in the reservation area. This has strained relations between the KCA business committee and the tribal governments.

28. U.S. Indian Claims Commission, *Final Report, 1978*, p. 54.

29. While Comanches and Anglos interact with one another every day, they do not necessarily share the same communicative competence. Although Comanches may learn an Anglo-American competence and thus participate in some activities of the Anglo community, they are not often considered full members of that community. Rarely do Anglos acquire a Comanche competence and participate in the Comanche community.

30. I observed this in a supermarket in Anadarko in the summer of 1985.

31. Robert Coffey and Haddon Nauni, interviews with author.

32. See Gladwin 1948 for a description of traditional Comanche kinship terms and behavior collected in 1940, just before the war. Kavanagh 1980 also describes postwar changes in traditional kin term usage.

33. It is my experience that most Comanches born after 1926 have little control of the Comanche language. These tended to be the children of the first generations of Indian school graduates, who had themselves been forced to learn and use English to the exclusion of Comanche. Those Comanches born after 1926 who do speak the native language tend to have been raised by their grandparents rather than by their

parents. In addition, those Comanches born since 1926 came of age in the community at the end of World War II and after, by which time control of community gatherings had shifted from preallotment to postallotment generations. These younger Comanches have few, if any, direct memories of what are called "old-timey" ways, referring to the practices of Comanche elders who had become adults during the reservation period.

34. The practice of taking a "close" friend of the same sex while a child and maintaining a special relationship with that individual as long as both lived was one of the bases for the formation of residence bands and focused-activity groups during the prereservation period (Gladwin 1948).

35. Leonard Riddles, Haddon Codynah, Robert Coffey, and Haddon Nauni, interviews with author.

36. Robert Coffey and Haddon Nauni, interviews with author. I have seen this in practice at powwow gatherings. Before, Comanches had made distinctions between one's younger brother and older brother and between one's younger sister and older sister (all extended to consanguineals of the same generation).

37. This is frequently witnessed at powwow gatherings, where adoptive relationships are "honored" by public gift-giving, usually from the person taken as kin to the senior member of the relationship.

38. Haddon Codynah and Leonard Riddles, interviews with author.

39. Doris Duke Oral History Collection, T-484:15–16. What Wallace Coffey refers to at the end of his comment is the lack of formal organization of a shared "Indian" or "Comanche" identity.

40. Ashworth (1986:143–144) interprets this economic dimension of powwow gatherings as a reflection of Indian-Anglo economic conflicts. He argues that conspicuous generosity in powwow giveaways is an expression of "Indian" values of sharing and generosity in explicit contrast to Anglo values of accumulation and greed. It seems to me, however, that if this contrast is recognized by Comanches at all, it is only as an epiphenomenon of the more fundamental economic transactions that occur in powwow contexts. That is, the redistribution of resources between those who have participated successfully in the Anglo economy and those who have concentrated instead on maintaining community occasions.

41. Comanche residence units were more significant for purposes of community organization when, as in prereservation and the immediate postallotment periods, Comanche participation in public gatherings was limited by geography and distance. During those periods, where and with whom one lived made a great deal of difference in determining which public gatherings one would be able, and obligated, to attend. Once Comanches obtained automobiles, however, residence ceased to be as significant a factor in constraining the possibility of mutual presence.

42. Leonard Riddles, Haddon Nauni, and Haddon Codynah, interviews with author. All three saw military service during World War II.

43. Leonard Riddles made this observation to me in 1985.

44. Leonard Riddles, Haddon Nauni, Haddon Codynah, Robert Coffey, and

Edward Wermy, interviews with author.

45. As noted in the previous chapter, Comanches were reported to have shifted from wagons to automobiles by 1937.

46. Leonard Riddles and Haddon Nauni, interviews with author.

47. Howard (1976) suggests that traditional dance gatherings among southern Plains peoples died out in the late 1920s and were revived only in the 1950s, while intertribal fancy and war dance competitions bridged the two eras. The material presented in this chapter and the previous chapter would argue against that interpretation, at least for Comanches.

48. See Corrigan 1970 and Ashworth 1986 for alternative categorizations.

49. The annual Walters Homecoming Powwow is the largest and best-known of these. Annual powwows are also held in the Paradise Valley and Elgin communities.

50. Among these occasions are the Chief Wild Horse, Yellowfish, and Wahnee descendants powwows. The Chief Wild Horse powwow may also serve as a homecoming powwow for Comanches from the Cache area.

51. Beginning with Radcliffe-Brown, anthropologists have described funeral ceremonies as ways of marking the social death of community members. The Comanche practice of "buying back in" to powwow participation is, in essence, a way of marking the social rebirth of community members. Indeed, some Comanches have described it as a "reinitiation" into dancing. By giving away goods after the death of close relatives, Comanches announce that they are once again socially active in the community and immediately establish a set of obligations for future interaction among those to whom they give the goods.

52. Haddon Nauni and Leonard Riddles, interviews with author.

53. Ashworth's descriptions of powwow types and structures agrees fairly closely with those presented here. Where I disagree with Ashworth is in his attempt to explain the phenomenon of powwowing by reference to Indian-Anglo economic relations. While I agree that those relations establish the conditions to which powwows are adapted, I find that the specific social functions of powwows as public gatherings in each native community provide a fuller explanation for participation in them.

54. This was not dissimilar to what happened in dancing and peyote participation immediately after allotment.

55. Leonard Riddles and Haddon Nauni, interviews with author. Mr. Riddles and Mr. Nauni, both members of the Comanche Business Committee during this controversy, were among those older Comanches consulted at the time to resolve the generational conflict.

56. See Kavanagh 1980 for an account of the formation of the Little Pony dancing society.

57. Leonard Riddles and Haddon Nauni, interviews with author.

58. The male dancing societies are organized mainly around performances of the gourd dance.

59. Powers (1980, 1990) focuses much of his discussion of contemporary Plains dance on "war" or "fancy" dancing. While this is certainly the most colorful of contemporary Plains dances, I would argue that it is also the least significant for intracommunity purposes. Many younger Comanche men and boys do participate in fancy dancing, as well as northern Plains style "straight" dancing, but only for purposes of competing in dance contests sponsored at powwows across the Plains. For purposes of community participation, gourd dancing is the more significant form, while some other traditional Comanche dances, such as the buffalo, scalp, and crow dances, are occasionally revived as expressions of traditional Comanche identity.

60. Called the "whip man" before World War II because he carried a whip, which he used to encourage dancers to participate.

61. A "special" refers specifically to honoring an individual while dancing. The emcee announces the special, asking the drum for an appropriate song, usually one "owned" by the family of the honoree. Supporters then dance behind the person being honored and place shawls around the honoree's shoulders or put money in a hat carried by a relative or friend immediately behind the honoree. There has been a recent tendency to use the term "special" to refer to any honoring in the course of a powwow.

62. Often a participant who is honored feels an obligation to call up someone else in the course of the same powwow but not necessarily the individual who honored him or her in the first place.

63. Raffles and auctions within the powwow occasion take the place of paid attendance, allowing those with money to contribute to the support of the gathering while not embarrassing or locking out those without money.

64. Edward Wermy, Tennyson Echawaudah, Leonard Riddles, Haddon Nauni, and George Watchetaker, interviews with author.

65. Edward Wermy and Tennyson Echawaudah, interviews with author.

66. Leonard Riddles, Edward Wermy, Robert Coffey, and Haddon Nauni, interviews with author. Mr. Nauni was both an occasional participant in peyote gatherings and an employee of the local Indian Health Service hospital in Lawton.

67. Edward Wermy and Tennyson Echawaudah, interviews with author.

68. Leonard Riddles, Haddon Nauni, and George Watchetaker, interviews with author.

69. Leonard Riddles, interview with author.

70. Jones (1968), in his study of Sanapia, a Comanche eagle doctor, concluded that witchcraft accusation was then decreasing among Comanches. If so, then the last twenty years have seen a resurgence.

71. Robert Coffey, interview with author. At the time, Mr. Coffey was a deacon of the Deyo Baptist Church.

72. Leonard Riddles, Haddon Nauni, and Robert Coffey, interviews with author.

73. Robert Coffey, interview with author.

74. Robert Coffey, Leonard Riddles, and Haddon Nauni, interviews with au-

thor. This point also is supported by personal observation.

75. Leonard Riddles, interview with author.

76. Leonard Riddles and Haddon Nauni, interviews with author. Both Mr. Riddles and Mr. Nauni are former Comanche Business Committee members.

77. Elections for committee members and the chairman occurred during the time I was in the community. These descriptions are based on my observations and the comments of people with whom I visited. Tribal politics was a popular topic of conversation.

78. Whether or not it was the case, many Comanches believe that it was not proper to go against family in political campaigns or disputes "in the old days."

79. The Comanche Business Committee is not the primary means by which the Comanche community is organized, though the memberships of the Comanche Nation and community are largely overlapping. At most, the business committee regulates some aspects of Comanche-Anglo economic relations. The Comanche Nation derives a significant percentage of its operating budget from a bingo operation that depends on Anglo players. With respect to Comanche-Comanche interaction, however, the committee has little control, mainly because allotments are scattered and do not make up a single territory. If anything, elected tribal officials are intermediary leaders whose influence within the community depends on their ability to channel Anglo economic resources to members of the tribe.

80. While Comanches wrote their own tribal constitution, they were assisted by a BIA department that does nothing but write such documents. The constitution as written was then subject to the approval of the secretary of the interior. Robert Coffey, interview with author.

81. Recently some Comanches have spoken about the possibility of lowering the blood quantum for tribal membership below one-fourth. With intermarriage, the average degree of Comanche ancestry gradually is declining. Ultimately, the tribal government will lower the quantum, placing increased emphasis on interactional standards to define what it is to "be Comanche."

82. This provision has been used once, during what Comanches still refer to as their Civil War, in the late 1970s, and was much discussed but never invoked during a later political controversy. Interestingly, the provision empowering an official political gathering to remove a tribal official was carried over from the 1937 Comanche constitution written under the Oklahoma Indian Welfare Act. See Fay 1970 for a copy of the Comanche tribal constitution.

83. Powers (1980, 1990) makes a similar case for the spread of the modern powwow from the northern to the southern Plains, though he does allow for some variation between cultural communities.

84. These arguments are similar to those made for peyote gatherings as a "pan-Indian" phenomenon.

85. Kavanagh (1980) also makes this point.

86. In discussing contemporary dances, Powers groups the Southern Cheyennes

with Comanches, Kiowas, and Arapahoes.

87. I would speculate that Cheyenne powwow gatherings are used mainly to regulate personal relationships and local residential communities.

88. Haddon Nauni, interview with author.

CHAPTER 6. THE CONSEQUENCES OF SOCIAL LIFE

1. Such as different social identities acquired through participation in different forms of public gathering or borrowing, and not returning, money from a fellow dancing society member.

2. One also might argue that, in the pre-reservation period, the interests of younger leaders of focused-activity groups and older leaders of residence bands often were at odds, especially as the older residence band leaders increasingly took on intermediary functions in Comanche–Euro-American relations.

3. Though these connecting structures have, I believe, been overstated in classic anthropological accounts, especially in the case of the Cheyenne. Moore's (1974, 1988) interpretations of Cheyenne social organization suggest a much more dynamic situation in which social life is instrumental in regulating Cheyenne leaders and social groups.

4. Fowler 1982:54–55, Fowler 1987:38–40; Moore 1988:192–193.

5. Fowler 1982:136–138, 1987:72–74.

6. John Moore, personal communication; Reports, Agents files, Kiowa Agency, Oklahoma Historical Society.

7. Fowler 1982:118–122.

8. Fowler 1987:134–135.

9. Reports, Agents files, Kiowa Agency, Oklahoma Historical Society.

10. Moore 1988:328–337.

11. Stewart 1987.

12. Fowler 1987:155.

13. Fowler 1982:219.

14. John Moore, personal communication; Indian Dances and Celebrations file, Kiowa Agency, Oklahoma Historical Society. Many Kiowas who were prominent in peyote were also prominent in dance gatherings and, later, powwows.

15. I have no information on Kiowas and Cheyennes in this respect. Fowler 1982:168, 1987:142–145.

16. Fowler 1982:262–265; Moore 1988:328.

17. Fowler 1987:171–173.

18. As an example, the recent exchange between Gelo (1987) and Thurman (1987) over the nature of Comanche social organization is, essentially, an argument about the definition of various features of the "classic" Plains model, and only secondarily is it an argument about whether Comanches fit that model or not.

19. This notion of tradition is taken from Shils (1981).

20. The ways in which Comanches changed public gatherings after World War II to accommodate community members involved in the Anglo economy show a desire—even on the part of those who have succeeded in the outside economy—to continue to participate in the native community.

21. In Vanderwerth (1971).

Bibliography

MANUSCRIPT SOURCES

Fort Sill Archives
  Hugh Scott Ledgerbook
Kiowa Agency Records, Fort Worth National Archives Center
  Annual Statistical Reports file
  Business Committee file
  Intermarriage file
  Meriam Survey file
  Social Relations file
  Tribal Council file
Kiowa Agency Records, Oklahoma Historical Society
  Census file
  Dances and Celebrations file
  Farmers file
  Indian Council file
  Indian Houses file
  Indian Schools file
  Letterbook
  Licensed Traders file
  Matrons file
  Relations, Family file
  Reports, Agents file
Letters Received, Office of Indian Affairs, National Archives (M234)
  Texas Agency Correspondence Files
Records of the Central Superintendency of Indian Affairs, National Archives (M856)
  Kiowa Agency Correspondence Files
  Upper Arkansas Agency Correspondence Files
  Upper Platte Agency Correspondence Files

Records of the Southern Superintendency of Indian Affairs, National Archives
(M640)
    Texas Agency Correspondence Files
U.S. Bureau of Indian Affairs, Annual Narrative and Statistical Reports, National
Archives (M1011)
    Kiowa Agency
Western History Collection, University of Oklahoma
    Doris Duke Oral History Collection
    Indian-Pioneer Papers

PUBLISHED WORKS

Aberle, David
    1982   *The Peyote Religion Among the Navajo.* 2d ed. Chicago: University of
            Chicago Press.
Albers, Patricia
    1982   Sioux Kinship in a Colonial Setting. *Dialectical Anthropology* 6:253–269.
Anders, Gary
    1980   Theories of Underdevelopment and the American Indian. *Journal of Eco-
            nomic Issues* 14:681–701.
Ashworth, Kenneth A.
    1986   The Contemporary Oklahoma Pow-wow. Ph.D. diss., University of
            Oklahoma, Norman.
Bamforth, Douglas
    1988   *Ecology and Human Organization on the Great Plains.* New York: Plenum
            Press.
Bannon, John Francis
    1970   *The Spanish Borderlands Frontier, 1513–1821.* New York: Holt, Rinehart
            and Winston.
Barnard, Herwanna Becker
    1941   The Comanche and His Literature, with an Anthology of His Myths,
            Legends, Folktales, Oratory, Poetry and Songs. M.A. thesis, University of
            Oklahoma, Norman.
Barth, Frederick, ed.
    1969   *Ethnic Groups and Boundaries: The Social Organization of Cultural Differ-
            ence.* London: Allen and Unwin.
Bee, Robert
    1982   *The Politics of American Indian Policy.* Cambridge, Mass.: Schenkman Pub-
            lishing.
Bentley, G. Carter
    1987   Ethnicity and Practice. *Comparative Studies in History and Society* 29 (1):
            24–55.

Berkhofer, Robert F., Jr.
  1978   *The White Man's Indian: Images of the American Indian from Columbus to the Present.* New York: Alfred A. Knopf.

Bittle, William E.
  1954   The Peyote Ritual: Kiowa-Apache. *Bulletin of the Oklahoma Anthropological Society* 2:69–78.

Blu, Karen I.
  1980   *The Lumbee Problem: The Making of an American Indian People.* Cambridge and New York: Cambridge University Press.

Bollaert, William
  1956   *William Bollaert's Texas.* W. Eugene Hollon and Ruth Lapham Butler, eds. Norman: University of Oklahoma Press.

Bolton, Herbert Eugene
  1914   *Athanase de Mezieres and the Louisiana-Texas Frontier, 1768–1780.* 2 vols. Cleveland: Arthur H. Clark Co.

  1964   *Bolton and the Spanish Borderlands.* J. F. Bolton, ed. Norman: University of Oklahoma Press.

  1970   *Texas in the Middle Eighteenth Century: Studies in Spanish Colonial History and Administration.* Austin: University of Texas Press.

Bonnell, George William
  1838   *Report of G. W. Bonnell, Commissioner of Indian Affairs.* Third Congress, First Session, Republic of Texas.

Braroe, Neils Winter
  1975   *Indian and White: Self-Image and Interaction in a Canadian Plains Community.* Palo Alto, Calif.: Stanford University Press.

Bruner, Edward
  1957   Differential Culture Change. *Items* (Social Science Research Council) 2 (1).

Buller, Galen
  1977   Comanche Oral Narratives. Ph.D. diss. University of Nebraska, Lincoln.

Canonge, Elliot
  1958   *Comanche Texts.* Norman, Okla.: Summer Institute of Linguistics, University of Oklahoma.

Carlson, G. G., and V. H. Jones
  1940   Some Notes on the Uses of Plants by the Comanche Indians. *Papers of the Michigan Academy of Science, Arts and Letters* 25:517–542.

Casagrande, Joseph
  1955   Comanche Linguistic Acculturation, III. *International Journal of American Linguistics* 21:8–25.

Castile, G. P.
  1981a Issues in the Analysis of Enduring Cultural Systems. In *Persistent Peoples: Cultural Enclaves in Perspective,* G. P. Castile and G. Kushner, eds. Tucson: University of Arizona Press.

1981b On the Tarascanness of the Tarascans and the Indianness of Indians. In *Persistent Peoples: Cultural Enclaves in Perspective,* G. P. Castile and G. Kushner, eds. Tucson: University of Arizona Press.

Chappell, Phillip E.
1906 A History of the Mississippi River. *Kansas Historical Collections,* vol. 4.

Clifton, James A., ed.
1990 *The Invented Indian: Cultural Fictions and Government Policies.* New Brunswick, N.J., and London: Transaction Publishers.

Cohen, Abner
1969 *Custom and Politics in Urban Africa: Hausa Migrants in Yoruba Towns.* Berkeley: University of California Press.

Cohen, Ronald
1978 Ethnicity. In *Annual Review of Anthropology,* 7:379–404. Palo Alto, Calif: Annual Reviews, Inc.

Colson, Elizabeth
1954 Review of Earnest Wallace and E. Adamson Hoebel, *The Comanches: Lords of the Southern Plains. Man,* 1st ser., 54:13–14.

Corrigan, Samuel W.
1970 The Plains Indian Powwow: Cultural Interaction in Manitoba and Saskatchewan. *Anthropologica* 12 (2): 253–277.

Darnell, Regna, and Michael K. Foster, eds.
1988 *Native North American Interaction Patterns.* Canadian Ethnology Service, Mercury Series, vol. 112.

DeMallie, Raymond J.
1977 *Comanche Treaties: Historical Background.* Washington, D.C.: Institute for the Development of Indian Law.

Despres, Leo A.
1967 *Cultural Pluralism and Nationalist Politics in British Guiana.* Chicago: Rand-McNally.
1982 Review of *Ethnic Change,* edited by Charles F. Keyes. *American Ethnologist* 9:603–604.

Dorsey, J. O.
1884 Omaha Sociology. *Bureau of American Ethnology Annual Report,* vol. 3. Washington, D.C.: U.S. Government Printing Office.

Drinnon, Richard
1980 *Facing West: The Metaphysics of Indian-Hating and Empire Building.* Minneapolis: University of Minnesota Press.

Driver, Harold
1969 *Indians of North America.* Rev. ed. Chicago: University of Chicago Press.

Eastman, Edwin
1976 *Seven and Nine Years Among the Comanches and Apaches.* New York: Garland Press.

Edgerton, Robert B.
  1985 *Rules, Exceptions, and Social Order*. Berkeley: University of California Press.
Eggan, Fred
  1955 *Social Anthropology of North American Tribes*. Chicago: University of Chicago Press.
  1966 *The American Indian: Perspectives for the Study of Social Change*. Chicago: Aldine.
Espinosa, J. Manuel
  1936 Governor Vargas in Colorado. *New Mexico Historical Review* 11:179–187.
  1939 Journal of the Vargas Expedition into Colorado, 1694. *Colorado Magazine* 16 (3): 81–90.
Ewers, John C.
  1955 *The Horse in Blackfoot Indian Culture, with Comparative Material for Other Western Tribes*. Washington, D.C.: U.S. Government Printing Office.
  1973 The Influence of Epidemics on the Indian Populations and Cultures of Texas. *Plains Anthropologist* 18:104–115.
Faulk, Odie B.
  1961 A Description of the Comanche Indians in 1786 by the Governor of Texas. *West Texas Historical Association Year Book* 37:177–182.
Fay, George E.
  1970 *Charters, Constitutions, and By-Laws of the Indian Tribes of North America*. Greeley, Colo.: Museum of Anthropology.
Fehrenbach, T. R.
  1974 *The Comanches: The Destruction of a People*. New York: Alfred A. Knopf.
Fixico, Donald
  1986 *Termination and Relocation*. Albuquerque: University of New Mexico Press.
Fletcher, A. C., and F. LaFlesche
  1911 The Omaha Tribe. *Bureau of American Ethnology Annual Report,* vol. 27. Washington: U.S. Government Printing Office.
Flores, Dan L.
  1985 *Journal of an Indian Trader: Anthony Glass and the Texas Trading Frontier, 1790–1810*. College Station: Texas A&M University Press.
Folmer, Henri
  1937 De Bourgmont's Expedition to the Padoucas in 1724: The First French Approach to Colorado. *Colorado Magazine* 14:121–128.
  1939 The Mallet Expedition of 1739 thorugh Nebraska, Kansas and Colorado to Santa Fe. *Colorado Magazine* 16 (5): 161–173.
Fortune, Reo
  1932 *Omaha Secret Societies*. New York: Columbia University Press.
Fowler, Loretta
  1982 *Arapahoe Politics, 1851–1978: Symbols in Crises of Authority*. Lincoln: University of Nebraska Press.

1987   *Shared Symbols, Contested Meanings: Gros Ventre Culture and History, 1778–1984.* Ithaca, N.Y.: Cornell University Press.

Geertz, Clifford

1963   The Integrative Revolution: Primordial Sentiments and Civil Politics in the New States. In *Old Societies and New States,* Clifford Geertz, ed. New York: Free Press.

Gelo, Daniel

1986   Comanche Belief and Ritual. Ph.D. diss., Rutgers University, New Brunswick, N.J.

1987   On a New Interpretation of Comanche Social Organization. *Current Anthropology* 28:551–556.

1988   Review of Wallace and Hoebel, *The Comanches: Lords of the Southern Plains. Plains Anthropologist* 33:539–541.

Gladwin, Thomas

1948   Comanche Kin Behavior. *American Anthropologist* 50:73–94.

Goffman, Erving

1959   *The Presentation of Self in Everyday Life.* Garden City, N.Y.: Doubleday.

1961   *Encounters; Two Studies in the Sociology of Interaction.* Indianapolis: Bobbs-Merrill.

1963a   *Behavior in Public Places: Notes on the Social Organization of Gatherings.* New York: Free Press.

1963b   *Stigma: Notes on the Management of Spoiled Identity.* Englewood Cliffs, N.J.: Prentice-Hall.

1967   *Interaction Ritual: Essays on Face-to-face Behavior.* Garden City, N.Y.: Anchor Books.

1969   *Strategic Interaction.* Philadelphia: University of Pennsylvania Press.

1971   *Relations in Public: Microstudies of the Public Order.* New York: Basic Books.

1974   *Frame Analysis: An Essay on the Organization of Experience.* New York: Harper and Row.

1981   *Forms of Talk.* Philadelphia: University of Pennsylvania Press.

Golla, Susan M.

1987   He Has a Name: History and Social Structure Among the Indians of Western Vancouver Island. Ph.D. diss., Columbia University, New York.

Grinnell, George B.

1920   Who Were the Padouca? *American Anthropologist* 22:248–260.

Grobsmith, Elizabeth

1981   *Lakota of the Rosebud: A Contemporary Ethnography.* New York: Holt, Rinehart and Winston.

Gumperz, John

1972   Introduction. In *Directions in Sociolinguistics,* J. Gumperz and D. Hymes, eds. New York: Holt, Rinehart and Winston.

1982a *Discourse Strategies*. London and New York: Cambridge University Press.

1982b *Language and Social Identity*. London and New York: Cambridge University Press.

Hackett, Charles Wilson, ed.

1923– *Historical Documents Relating to New Mexico, Nueva Vizcaya and Ap-*
1937   *proaches Thereto, to 1773*. Collected by Adolph F. A. Bandelier and Fanny R. Bandelier. 3 vols. Washington, D.C.: Carnegie Institution.

Hagan, William T.

1971   Kiowas, Comanches, and Cattlemen, 1867–1906: A Case Study of the Failure of U.S. Reservation Policy. *Pacific Historical Review* 40:333–355.

1976   *United States–Comanche Relations: The Reservation Years*. New Haven: Yale University Press.

1980   Quanah Parker. In *American Indian Leaders: Studies in Diversity*, R. David Edmunds, ed. Lincoln: University of Nebraska Press.

Haines, Francis

1938   The Northward Spread of Horses Among Plains Indians. *American Anthropologist* 40:429–437.

Hanson, Jeffrey R.

1988   Age-set Theory and Plains Indian Age-grading: A Critical Review and Revision. *American Ethnologist* 15:349–364.

Harris, Caroline

1977   *History of the Captivity of Caroline Harris, 1838*. New York: Garland Press.

Henderson, Arn, and James Bohland

1974   *Housing and Community Alternatives for American Indians*. Final Report to the National Science Foundation. Norman, Okla.

Herskovits, Melville J.

1958   *Acculturation: The Study of Culture Contact*. Gloucester, Mass.: Peter Smith Publishing.

Hildreth, James

1836   *Dragoon Campaigns to the Rocky Mountains*. New York: Wiley and Long.

Hoebel, E. Adamson

1939   Comanche and Hekandika Shoshone Relationship Systems. *American Anthropologist* 41:440–457.

1940   *The Political Organization and Law-Ways of the Comanche Indians*. American Anthropological Association, Memoir 54.

1941   The Comanche Sun Dance and the Messianic Outbreak of 1873. *American Anthropologist* 43:301–303.

1954   *The Law of Primitive Man: A Study in Comparative Legal Dynamics*. Cambridge, Mass.: Harvard University Press.

1960   *The Cheyennes: Indians of the Great Plains*. New York: Holt.

1977   *The Plains Indians: A Critical Bibliography*. Bloomington: Indiana University Press.

Holder, Preston

　1970　*The Hoe and the Horse on the Plains*. Lincoln: University of Nebraska Press.

Holt, Ronald L.

　1987　Beneath These Red Cliffs: The Utah Paiutes and Paternalistic Dependency. Ph.D. diss., University of Utah, Salt Lake City.

Howard, James

　1955　Pan-Indian Culture of Oklahoma. *Scientific Monthly* 81 (5): 212–220.

　1976　The Plains Gourd Dance as a Revitalization Movement. *American Ethnologist* 3:243–259.

　1983　Pan-Indianism in North American Music and Dance. *Ethnomusicology* 27 (1): 71–82.

Hoxie, Fred

　1984　*A Final Promise: The Campaign to Assimilate the Indians, 1880–1920*. Lincoln: University of Nebraska Press.

Hyde, George E.

　1959　*Indians of the High Plains*. Norman: University of Oklahoma Press.

Hymes, Dell

　1962　The Ethnography of Speaking. In T. Gladwin and W. C. Sturtevant, eds., *Anthropology and Human Behavior*. Washington, D.C.: Anthropological Society of Washington.

　1964　Introduction: Toward Ethnographies of Communication. In *The Ethnography of Communication*, J. J. Gumperz and D. Hymes, eds. *American Anthropologist* 66 (Memoir 2): 1–34.

　1974　*Foundations in Sociolinguistics*. Philadelphia: University of Pennsylvania Press.

Isaacs, Harold P.

　1975　*Idols of the Tribe: Group Identity and Political Change*. New York: Harper and Row.

Jackson, Curtis E., and Marcia J. Galli

　1977　*A History of the Bureau of Indian Affairs and Its Activities Among Indians*. San Francisco: R&E Publishers.

Jennings, Francis

　1975　*The Invasion of America: Indians, Colonialism, and the Cant of Conquest*. Chapel Hill: University of North Carolina Press.

John, Elizabeth A. H.

　1975　*Storms Brewed in Other Men's Worlds*. College Station: Texas A&M University Press.

　1984　Nurturing the Peace: Spanish-Comanche Cooperation in the Early Nineteenth Century. *New Mexico Historical Review* 59:345–369.

Jones, David E.

　1968　Sanapia: Comanche Medicine Woman. M.A. thesis, University of Oklahoma, Norman.

1972   *Sanapia: Comanche Medicine Woman*. New York: Holt, Rinehart and Winston.

Jorgenson, Joseph
1978   A Century of Political Economic Effects on American Indian Society, 1880–1980. *Journal of Ethnic Studies* 6 (3): 1–82.

Kardiner, Abraham
1949   *The Psychological Frontiers of Society*. New York: Columbia University Press.

Kavanagh, Thomas W.
1980   Recent Socio-Cultural Evolution of the Comanche Indians: A Model for Transformation and Articulation in Social Change. M.A. thesis, George Washington University, Washington, D.C.

1986   Political Power and Political Organization: Comanche Politics 1786–1875. Ph.D. diss., University of New Mexico, Albuquerque.

1989   Comanche Population Organization and Reorganization, 1869–1901: A Test of the Continuity Hypothesis. In *Plains Indian Historical Demography and Health*, G. R. Campbell, ed. *Plains Anthropologist* Memoir 23.

Kenner, C. L.
1969   *A History of New Mexican–Plains Indian Relations*. Norman: University of Oklahoma Press.

Kroeber, Alfred L.
1939   *Cultural and Natural Areas of Native North America*. Berkeley: University of California Press.

La Barre, Weston
1975   *The Peyote Cult*. 4th ed. New York: Schocken Books.

Lamb, Sidney
1958   Linguistic Prehistory in the Great Basin. *International Journal of American Linguistics* 24:95–100.

Lee, Nelson
1957   *Three Years Among the Comanches*. Norman: University of Oklahoma Press.

Levy, Jerrold
1959   After Custer: Kiowa Political and Social Organization from the Reservation Period to the Present. Ph.D. diss. Chicago: University of Chicago.

Lindquist, G. E.
1923   *The Red Man in the United States, an Intimate Study of the Social, Economic, and Religious Life of the American Indian*. New York: George H. Doran Co.

Linton, Ralph
1935   The Comanche Sun Dance. *American Anthropologist* 37:420–428.

1936   *The Study of Man*. New York: Appleton-Century.

1940   *Acculturation in Seven American Indian Tribes*. New York: Appleton-Century.

1949   "The Comanche." In *The Psychological Frontiers of Society,* A. Kardiner, ed. New York: Columbia University Press.

1955   *The Tree of Culture.* New York: Knopf.

Lithman, Yngve

1984   *The Community Apart: A Case Study of a Canadian Indian Reserve Community.* Winnepeg: University of Manitoba Press.

Llewellyn, K. N., and E. A. Hoebel

1941   *The Cheyenne Way: Conflict and Case Law in Primitive Jurisprudence.* Norman: University of Oklahoma Press.

Loomis, Noel M., and Abraham P. Nasatir

1967   *Pedro Vial and the Roads to Santa Fe.* Norman: University of Oklahoma Press.

Lowie, Robert

1909   Northern Shoshone. *Anthropological Papers of the American Museum of Natural History* 2:165–306

1915   Dances and Societies of the Plains Shoshone. *Anthropological Papers of the American Museum of Natural History* 11:803–835.

1920   *Primitive Society.* New York: Liveright.

1924   Notes on Shoshonean Ethnography. *Anthropological Papers of the American Museum of Natural History* 20 (3): 185–314.

1927   *Origin of the State.* New York: Harcourt Brace.

1948   *Social Organization.* New York: Rinehart.

1954   *Indians of the Plains.* New York: McGraw-Hill.

McAllester, David P.

1949   *Peyote Music.* Viking Fund Publications in Anthropology 13. New York: Viking Fund.

McBeth, Sally J.

1983   *Ethnic Identity and the Boarding School Experience: West-Central Oklahoma American Indians.* Lanham, Md.: University Press of America.

McMurtry, Larry

1968   *In a Narrow Grave: Essays on Texas.* Albuquerque: University of New Mexico Press.

Marcy, Randolph

1866   *Thirty Years of Army Life on the Border.* New York: Harper and Brothers.

Martin, Calvin

1987   *The American Indian and the Problem of History.* Oxford: Oxford University Press.

Mead, Margaret

1932   *The Changing Culture of an Indian Tribe.* New York: Columbia University Press.

Miller, David R.

1987   Montana Assiniboine Identity: A Cultural Account of an American Indian Ethnicity. Ph.D. diss., Indiana University.

Miller, Wick

1970 Western Shoshoni Dialects. In *Languages and Cultures of Western North America: Essays in Honor of Sven Liljeblad,* E. H. Swanson, ed. Pocatello: Idaho State University Press.

Mooney, J.

1907 Comanche. In *Handbook of American Indians,* F. Hodge, ed. Bureau of American Ethnology Bulletin 30:1.

1910 Peyote. In *Handbook of American Indians,* F. Hodge, ed. Bureau of American Ethnology Bulletin 30:2.

Moore, John H.

1974 Cheyenne Political History, 1820–1894. *Ethnohistory* 21:329–359.

1988 *The Cheyenne Nation: A Social and Demographic History.* Lincoln: University of Nebraska Press.

Morgan, Lewis Henry

1877 *Ancient Society.* New York: H. Holt.

Morris, John W., C. R. Goins, and E. C. McReynolds

1986 *Historical Atlas of Oklahoma.* 3d ed. Norman: University of Oklahoma Press.

Neighbors, Robert S.

1853 The Nauni or Comanches of Texas. In *Information Respecting the History, Condition, and Prospects of the Indian Tribes of the United States,* H. R. Schoolcraft, ed. Philadelphia.

Neighbours, Kenneth Franklin

1975 *Robert Simpson Neighbors and the Texas Frontier, 1836–1859.* Waco, Tex.: Texian Press.

Oliver, Symmes C.

1962 Ecology and Cultural Continuity as Contributing Factors in the Social Organization of Plains Indians. *University of California Publications in American Archaeology and Ethnology* 48 (1): 1–90.

Opler, Marvin K.

1943 The Origins of Comanche and Ute. *American Anthropologist* 45:155–158.

Opler, Morris E.

1938 The Use of Peyote by the Carrizo and Lipan Apache Tribes. *American Anthropologist* 40:271–285.

Osborn, Alan J.

1983 Ecological Aspects of Equestrian Adaptations in Aboriginal North America. *American Anthropologist* 85:563–591.

Padilla, Juan Antonio

1919 Texas in 1820: Report on the Barbarous Indians of the Province of Texas. Mattie Austin Hatcher, trans. *Southwestern Historical Quarterly* 23:47–68.

Parsons, Elsie Clews

1941 *Notes on the Caddo.* Memoirs of the American Anthropological Association, no. 57. Menasha, Wis.: American Anthropological Association.

Pearce, R. H.

   1965   *Savagism and Civilization: A Study of the Indian and the American Mind.*
           Baltimore: Johns Hopkins University Press.

Philips, Susan U.

   1983   *The Invisible Culture: Communication in Classroom and Community on the
           Warm Springs Indian Reservation.* New York and London: Longman.

Pichardo, Jose Antonio

   1931–   *Pichardo's Treatise on the Limits of Louisiana and Texas.* 4 vols. Charles
   1946   Wilson Hackett and Charmion Clair Shelby, eds. and trans. Austin: Uni-
           versity of Texas Press.

Plummer, Clarissa

   1977   *Narrative of the Captivity of Clarissa Plummer, 1838.* New York: Garland
           Press.

Powell, John Wesley

   1888   From Barbarism to Civilization. *American Anthropologist,* 1st ser., 1:97–
           124.

Powers, William K.

   1980   Plains Indian Music and Dance. In *Anthropology on the Great Plains,* W. R.
           Wood and Margot Liberty, eds. Lincoln: University of Nebraska Press.

   1990   *War Dance: Plains Indian Music and Performance.* Tucson: University of
           Arizona Press.

Rawls, James J.

   1984   *Indians of California: The Changing Image.* Norman: University of
           Oklahoma Press.

Redfield, Robert, Ralph Linton, and Melville Herskovits

   1936   Outline for the Study of Acculturation. *American Anthropologist* 38:149–
           152.

Richardson, R. N.

   1933   *The Comanche Barrier to Southern Plains Settlement.* Glendale, Calif.:
           Arthur H. Clark Co.

   1963   *The Frontier of Northwest Texas, 1846 to 1876.* Glendale, Calif.: Arthur H.
           Clark Co.

Robinson, Lili Wistrand, and James Armagost

   1990   *Comanche Dictionary and Grammar.* Dallas: Summer Institute of Linguis-
           tics and the University of Texas at Arlington.

Roe, Frank G.

   1955   *The Indian and the Horse.* Norman: University of Oklahoma Press.

Ruíz, Jose Francisco

   1972   *Report on the Indian Tribes of Texas in 1823.* New Haven: Yale University
           Press.

Sapir, Edward

   1949   *Selected Writings of Edward Sapir in Language, Culture, and Personality.*

David G. Mandelbaum, ed. Berkeley: University of California Press.

Schilz, Jodye, and Thomas Schilz

1989   *Buffalo Hump and the Penetaka*. Southwestern Studies Series no. 88. El Paso: University of Texas at El Paso.

Scollon, Ron, and Suzanne Scollon

1979   *Linguistic Convergence: An Ethnography of Speaking at Ft. Chipewyan, Alberta*. New York: Academic Press.

1981   *Narrative, Literacy, and Face in Interethnic Communication*. Norwood, N.J.: Ablex.

Secoy, Frank R.

1951   The Identity of the "Padouca": An Ethnohistorical Analysis. *American Anthropologist* 53:525–542.

Shaul, David L.

1986   Linguistic Adaptation and the Great Basin. *American Antiquity* 51:415–416.

Shils, Edward

1981   *Tradition*. Chicago: University of Chicago Press.

Shimkin, Dmitri

1940   *Shoshone-Comanche Origins and Migrations*. Proceedings of the 6th Pacific Scientific Conference, vol. 4. Berkeley: University of California Press.

1986   Eastern Shoshone. In *Great Basin,* Warren L. D'Azevedo, ed. *Smithsonian Handbook of American Indians,* vol. 11. Washington, D.C.: Smithsonian Institution.

Sibley, John

1922   *A Report from Natchitotches in 1807*. Annie Heloise Abel, ed. New York: Museum of the American Indian, Heye Foundation.

Simmons, Marc

1977   *Border Comanches: Seven Spanish Colonial Documents, 1785–1819*. Santa Fe: Stagecoach Press.

Simmons, William S.

1986   *Spirit of the New England Tribes: Indian History and Folklore, 1620–1984*. Hanover, N.H.: University Press of New England.

1988   Culture Theory in Contemporary Ethnohistory. *Ethnohistory* 35:1–14.

Siskin, Edgar E.

1983   *Washo Shamans and Peyotists: Religious Conflict in an American Indian Tribe*. Salt Lake City: University of Utah Press.

Slotkin, J. Sydney

1956   *The Peyote Religion: A Study in Indian-White Relations*. Glencoe, Ill.: Free Press.

Smith, Ralph A., ed.

1951   Exploration of the Arkansas River by Bénard de la Harpe, 1721–1722. *Arkansas Historical Quarterly* 10:339–363.

1959   Account of the Journey of Bénard de la Harpe: Discovery Made by Him of Several Nations Situated in the West. *Southwestern Historical Quarterly* 62:246–259.

Smithwick, Noah

1983   *The Evolution of a State; or, Recollections of Old Texas Days.* Austin: University of Texas Press.

Spicer, Edward H.

1961   *Perspectives in American Indian Culture Change.* Chicago: University of Chicago Press.

1971   Persistent Cultural Systems: A Comparative Study of Identity Systems That Can Adapt to Contrasting Environments. *Science* 174:795–800.

1982   *The American Indians.* Cambridge, Mass.: Harvard University Press.

Stahl, Robert J.

1978   Farming Among the Kiowa, Comanche, Kiowa Apache, and Wichita. Ph.D. diss., University of Oklahoma, Norman.

Steward, Julian H.

1938   *Basin-Plateau Aboriginal Sociopolitical Groups.* Bureau of American Ethnology Bulletin 120. Washington, D.C.: U.S. Government Printing Office.

Stewart, Omer C.

1987   *Peyote Religion.* Norman: University of Oklahoma Press.

Stewart, Omer, and David Aberle, eds.

1984   *Peyotism in the West.* University of Utah Anthropological Papers, vol. 108.

Tate, Michael L.

1986   *The Indians of Texas: An Annotated Research Bibliography.* Metuchen, N.J.: Scarecrow Press.

Tefft, S. K.

1960   Sociopolitical Change in Two Migrant Tribes. *Proceedings of the Michigan Academy of Sciences* 28:103–111.

1964   From Band to Tribe on the Plains. *Plains Anthropologist* 10:166–170.

Thomas, A. B.

1932   *Forgotten Frontiers: A Study of the Spanish Indian Policy of Don Juan Bautista de Anza, 1777–1778.* Norman: University of Oklahoma Press.

1935   *After Coronado: Spanish Exploration Northeast of New Mexico, 1696–1727.* Norman: University of Oklahoma.

1940   *The Plains Indians and New Mexico, 1751–1778: A Collection of Documents Illustrative of the History of the Eastern Frontier of New Mexico.* Albuquerque: University of New Mexico Press.

1941   *Teodoro de Croix and the Northern Frontier of New Spain.* Norman: University of Oklahoma Press.

Thomas, Robert K.

1970   Pan-Indianism. In *The American Indian Today,* Stuart Levine and Nancy O. Lurie, eds. Baltimore: Penguin Books.

Thurman, Melburn D.

1980   Comanche. *Dictionary of Indian Tribes of the Americas,* 2:48–67. Newport Beach, Calif.: American Indian Publishers.

1982   A New Interpretation of Comanche Social Organization. *Current Anthropology* 23:578–579.

1987   Reply to Gelo. *Current Anthropology* 28:552–555.

Tribble, Joseph E.

1972   *An Index to the Social Indicators of the American Indian in Oklahoma.* Oklahoma City: State of Oklahoma.

Trigger, Bruce

1985   *Natives and Newcomers: Canada's "Heroic Age" Reconsidered.* Montreal: McGill-Queen's University Press.

1986   Ethnohistory: The Unfinished Edifice. *Ethnohistory* 33:253–267.

Trosper, Ronald

1981   American Indian Nationalism and Frontier Expansion. In *Ethnic Change,* C. F. Keyes, ed. Seattle: University of Washington Press.

Twitchell, Ralph E., comp.

1914   *The Spanish Archives of New Mexico.* 2 vols. Cedar Rapids, Ia.: Torch Press.

U.S. Bureau of Indian Affairs. Anadarko Area Office

1988   *Annual Report F.Y. 1988.* Anadarko, Okla.

U.S. Bureau of the Census

1986   *American Indians, Eskimos, and Aleuts on Identified Reservations and in the Historic Areas of Oklahoma (Excluding Urbanized Areas).* Washington, D.C.: U.S. Government Printing Office.

U.S. Commissioner of Indian Affairs

1841–   *Annual Report.* Washington, D.C.: U.S. Government Printing Office.
1945

U.S. Congress. Senate Committee on Indian Affairs

1937   *Survey of Conditions of Indians in the United States.* 75th Congress, First Session. Washington: U.S. Government Printing Office.

U.S. Department of the Interior

1978   *Annual Report of Indian Lands.* Washington, D.C.: U.S. Government Printing Office.

U.S. Indian Claims Commission

1978   *Final Report.* Washington, D.C.: U.S. Government Printing Office.

U.S. Public Health Service

1960   *Indians on Federal Reservations in the United States.* Washington, D.C.: U.S. Government Printing Office.

Vanderwerth, W. C.

1971   *Indian Oratory: Famous Speeches by Noted Indian Chieftains.* Norman: University of Oklahoma Press.

Vaughan, A. T.
   1982   From White Man to Red Skin: Changing Anglo-American Perceptions of the American Indian. *American Historical Review* 87:917–953.

Wagner, Roland Marshall
   1974   Western Navajo Peyotism: A Case Analysis. Ph.D. diss., University of Oregon, Eugene.

Wallace, Ernest, comp.
   1954   David G. Burnet's Letters Describing the Comanche Indians. *West Texas Historical Association Year Book* 30:115–140.

Wallace, Ernest, and E. Adamson Hoebel
   1952   *The Comanches: Lords of the Southern Plains*. Norman: University of Oklahoma Press.

White, Richard
   1983   *The Roots of Dependency*. Lincoln: University of Nebraska Press.

Wilmoth, Stanley
   1987   The Development of Blackfeet Politics and Multiethnic Categories: 1934–84. Ph.D. diss., University of California, Riverside.

Winfrey, Dorman H., and James M. Day, eds.
   1966   *The Indian Papers of Texas and the Southwest, 1825–1916*. 5 vols. Austin, Tex.: Pemberton Press.

Wissler, Clark
   1914   The Influence of the Horse in the Development of Plains Culture. *American Anthropologist* 16:1–32.
   1926   *The Relation of Man to Nature in Aboriginal America*. New York: Oxford University Press.

Wood, W. Raymond
   1980   Plains Trade in Prehistoric and Protohistoric Tribal Relations. In *Anthropology on the Great Plains,* W. R. Wood and M. Liberty, eds. Lincoln: University of Nebraska Press.

Index

ABOUT THE AUTHOR

Morris W. Foster was born and raised in Oklahoma. He attended the University of Oklahoma, receiving a B.A. with distinction in 1981. In the course of his graduate study in anthropology at Yale University, he began working with Comanche people in 1984, completing his dissertation in 1988. He has served as a consultant to the Comanche Nation on economic development projects and on other matters. Since 1987 he has taught in the anthropology department at the University of Oklahoma. Currently he is studying traditional Creek and Seminole conceptions of illness as part of a research project for the National Institutes of Health. He is also working on a second book, *The Unstained Grass: Social Organization on the Central and Southern Plains, 1803–1867,* which extends the reinterpretation of nineteenth-century Comanche social organization in the present book to other Plains communities.